FRACTURED
CONTINENT

FRACTURED CONTINENT

EUROPE'S CRISES AND THE FATE OF THE WEST

WILLIAM DROZDIAK

W. W. NORTON & COMPANY

Independent Publishers Since 1923

New York • London

For information about permission to reproduce selections from this book, write to
Permissions, W. W. Norton & Company, Inc., 500 Fifth Avenue, New York, NY 10110

For information about special discounts for bulk purchases, please contact W. W. Norton
Special Sales at specialsales@wwnorton.com or 800-233-4830

Manufacturing by LSC Communications, Harrisonburg
Book design by Chris Welch
Production manager: Lauren Abbate

ISBN: 978-0-393-60868-7

W. W. Norton & Company, Inc.
500 Fifth Avenue, New York, N.Y. 10110
www.wwnorton.com

W. W. Norton & Company Ltd.
15 Carlisle Street, London W1D 3BS

1 2 3 4 5 6 7 8 9 0

For Renilde

in love and friendship

Turning and turning in the widening gyre

The falcon cannot hear the falconer;

Things fall apart; the center cannot hold;

Mere anarchy is loosed upon the world,

The blood-dimmed tide is loosed, and everywhere

The ceremony of innocence is drowned;

The best lack all conviction, while the worst

Are full of passionate intensity.

The darkness drops again but now I know

That twenty centuries of stony sleep

Were vexed to nightmare by a rocking cradle,

And what rough beast, its hour come round at last,

Slouches toward Bethlehem to be born?

—WILLIAM BUTLER YEATS, "The Second Coming" (1919)

CONTENTS

INTRODUCTION

In capitals across Europe, the year 2016 earned its description as the continent's *annus horribilis* on many fronts. A surge of refugees from Syria's civil war threatened to overwhelm the continent. A succession of terrorist attacks by young Muslim militants pledging allegiance to the Islamic State raised security alerts to the highest levels. Russia pursued a spate of aggressive actions against the West by expanding its military presence in the Middle East and launching fierce bombing raids on behalf of the Assad government in Syria, escalating its preparations for potential conflict with the Baltic states, and waging a barrage of cyberattacks that disrupted the American presidential election.

An economic recession for much of Europe stretched into its sixth year of abysmal growth and fewer jobs. In June, Britain shocked its continental partners by deciding to leave the European Union after forty-three years. And in November, the election of Donald Trump as America's forty-fifth president alarmed European allies who feared he might renege on American security commitments and fan the flames of populist nationalism in their own countries.

The prospect of even greater instability looms on the horizon. Voters in the Netherlands braced for the possibility that Geert Wilders, the leader of the xenophobic far-right Freedom Party, might become the country's next prime minister. Italy could face early elections that might usher into power the anarchic Five Star Movement, which seeks to destroy the country's existing political and economic power structure. In France, the right-wing National Front, headed by Marine Le Pen, one of Europe's most prominent populist nationalists, moved closer to achieving its goal of winning the presidency and putting its radical legislative agenda of anti-immigrant and anti-European policies into effect.

Just a quarter century after the liberal international order of open markets, free speech, and democratic elections had triumphed over the forces of communism, the Western democracies now seem in danger of collapsing, as a backlash against globalization arouses angry opponents of immigration, free trade, and cultural tolerance. In an echo of the 1930s, the world economic flow of trade and investment is weakening and political demagoguery is growing. As income inequality divides rich and poor more than ever before, democracies are becoming susceptible to xenophobic and autocratic tendencies by leaders who are tempted to play the nationalist card.

The concept for this book grew out of my experiences as a journalist covering the exhilarating days when the forces of freedom had vanquished totalitarianism in what seemed like a climactic battle between good and evil. When thousands of East Germans, among them the future chancellor Angela Merkel, streamed across the crumbling Berlin Wall a generation ago to breathe the fresh air of freedom in the West for the first time, I was struck by their shell-shocked expressions of wonder as they moved past the glittering consumer showcases on the Kurfürstendamm promenade.

On that fateful day in November 1989, I had just arrived in Berlin after an exhausting flight from Thailand, where I had been touring

Asia as the foreign editor of the *Washington Post*. My boss, the legendary executive editor Ben Bradlee, was characteristically blunt when he woke me in my Bangkok hotel room with a phone call at three in the morning. "They're tearing down the Wall," Bradlee said in his raspy voice. "Get your ass to Berlin!" Once I finally arrived in Germany and saw the hordes of daytrippers walking across the Berlin divide from the Communist east, I knew from past encounters where their materialistic curiosity would lead them: to the KaDeWe (Kaufhaus des Westens, or Store of the West) shopping emporium.

As I watched them stroll through aisles where gourmet delicacies were stacked as high as the ceiling, their sense of amazement turned to rage and frustration. They railed against their Communist rulers as liars who kept them enslaved with a false narrative that Western affluence was a myth. As they trudged back to their drab apartments, past the mine-strewn buffer zone, tank traps, and concrete barriers that divided East and West Berlin, I became convinced it was a day that assured the collapse of Soviet-style communism as well as the victory of free market democracy. Within a month, Chancellor Helmut Kohl laid out a road map that would merge the two Germanys. Soon, other Communist regimes were toppled as democratic movements from Prague to Moscow swept them from power. Without a shot being fired, the Cold War had ended, and the Western model of democratic elections, free speech, and open markets was extolled as a model for the rest of the world that would usher in a new age of enlightenment.

At last, Europe seemed close to achieving its elusive goal of being "whole and free." The West's two key institutions, the North Atlantic Treaty Organization and the European Union, embarked on a phase of expansion to embrace the new democracies in Central and Eastern Europe. Besides merging former Communist states into Western institutions, Chancellor Kohl and France's president François Mitterrand insisted that the quest to build a United States of Europe would require other measures to deepen integration and bring Europeans closer together. They pushed through the Maastricht Treaty in 1992 that would culminate in the single European currency, the euro, so that people would not have to cash in their liras, francs, and deutschmarks when traveling to different countries. Three years later, European leaders agreed to abolish national frontiers by signing the Schengen Agreement so travelers would be able to move freely in a borderless continent.

These three initiatives—the expansion of NATO and the European Union toward Russia, the creation of the euro currency, and passport-free travel within Europe—were supposed to lay the foundations for a great leap forward toward the goal of a united, prosperous, and peaceful Europe that inspired Jean Monnet, Robert Schuman, and other visionaries amid the ruins left by World War II. In the heady days after German reunification and the collapse of communism a quarter century ago, there was almost universal support for such measures as the campaign for a united Europe seemed to acquire unstoppable momentum. Indeed, the basic tenets of Western democracy—including free elections, free speech, and free markets—seemed to have won the hearts and minds of people all over the world, so much so that Francis Fukuyama declared in his book *The End of History* that the great ideological struggles of the past were over now that Western values had captivated the world.

For Europe, the prospect of leaving behind centuries of nationalism, bloodshed, and destruction in favor of a cohesive continent whose postmodern ethos would forever banish thoughts of warfare between nation-states seemed to herald a new golden age. Europe would become in the eyes of the world the avatar of a noble experiment to pool national sovereignty and develop new and effective forms of supranational governance. Other continents, including Africa, South America, and parts of Asia, started to consider whether their states could band together into regional trade blocs and eventually follow Europe's example in striving for ever closer political and economic union. It seemed almost inevitable that a united Europe would evolve into the next global superpower, one that could capitalize on its influence as the world's biggest commercial bloc and most affluent market, and in the process become the envy of emerging powers such as China and India.

But along the way to this Kantian paradise, the European project seemed to fall off the rails. A grandiose scheme to draw up a constitution for Europe that would codify Western democratic values for the entire continent became bogged down in internecine squabbles and muddled bureaucracy. After years of arduous negotiations, the project was scrapped in 2006 after being rejected by voters in referendums held in France and the Netherlands. Soon thereafter, the three great initiatives that were designed to bring Europe closer together would start to unravel in ways that would cause deep fissures across the continent. Today the dream of European unity has begun to wither away and the future stability of the continent is clouded with uncertainty.

Some of Europe's greatest accomplishments now seem in jeopardy. The eastward expansion in 2004 that embedded former Communist nations inside NATO and the European Union has triggered hostility with a revanchist and aggressive Russia. Moscow fears the West is seeking to encircle their country and blunt its aspirations to regain superpower status. Russia's seizure of Crimea and its support for separatist rebels in eastern Ukraine has compelled the West to impose economic sanctions. It has also damaged Germany's strategic objective of energy and economic interdependence with Moscow that Berlin once viewed as a pillar of Europe's post–Cold War security.

The single European currency known as the euro has come under fire because of rigid austerity policies designed to reduce enormous debts of Greece, Spain, Portugal, and Italy, owed in large part to Germany and other northern creditors. Even though the financial crisis in early 2015 that nearly forced Greece to drop out of the nineteen-nation eurozone has eased, many experts fear it is only a matter of time before the North-South split in the eurozone leads to another existential crisis for the entire Union. In the absence of further steps toward integration such as common fiscal and banking policies, the agonizing complexity of orchestrating a single monetary policy with nineteen different national economies may turn out, in the long term, to be impossible to sustain.

The open borders assured by the Schengen Agreement, now linking twenty-six countries, are today disrupted by barbed-wire fences that have been erected in Hungary and elsewhere to block the flow of refugees streaming out of Syria and Libya. What was intended as a vivid demonstration of European ideals being integrated into the everyday lives of people across the continent has become a distressing symbol of nationalist rivalries fanned by fears about the impact of the refugee crisis. Nearly 1 million refugees—four times as many as the previous year—poured into Germany during 2015, fleeing wars and poverty in Africa and the Middle East.

Although Chancellor Merkel still defends her open-door policy as necessary to uphold European ideals about human rights, her political popularity at home has been hurt badly. Nonetheless, she remains Europe's most respected leader, and friends and allies, including President Barack Obama, persuaded her to run for a fourth term as chancellor in Germany's national elections in 2017. But the refugee crisis will continue to haunt Merkel, Germany, and Europe for years to come. When dozens of male asylum seekers were charged with molesting and robbing young women on New Year's Eve 2016 near the central train station in Cologne, popular sentiment swung so sharply against unchecked immigration that Merkel was compelled to accept some border controls. The once-popular agreement to establish passport-free travel across Europe seemed dead.

This perfect storm of troubles—Russia's new aggression, the Greek debt confrontation, a massive refugee crisis, and the prospect that Britain will withdraw from the European Union—has been compounded by a wave of terrorist attacks that has spread a pervasive mood of fear across the continent. A series of massacres carried out by sympathizers of the Islamic State killed well over a hundred people in France. An airport attack in Brussels using suitcase bombs cost more than two dozen lives. When a Tunisian immigrant plowed a truck through Berlin's Christmas markets in December 2016, Merkel and other European leaders appeared ineffectual in their efforts to protect their citizens.

The growing atmosphere of insecurity has sapped voter confidence in mainstream government leaders and fortified the xenophobic agenda of far-right populist parties in France, Hungary, the Netherlands, and Poland. It has also sowed deep distrust between Christians and Muslims, in particular the second and third generations of Arab immigrants from North Africa who migrated to Europe seeking temporary employment and then stayed far longer than anyone anticipated.

The waning appeal of a united Europe has much to do with a stagnant economy and the disillusionment of young people. Economic anxiety is magnified by fears about the impact of cheap migrant labor, even from fellow EU member states, as seen by Britain's determination to prevent Polish migrant workers from gaining their fair share of wages and benefits. The immigration threat mobilized a majority of British voters to abandon membership in the European Union and retreat into their island nation. Growing disaffection with Europe has become particularly acute among young people, who in the past embraced a borderless Europe. Continental millennials once fancied themselves as the "Easy Jet" generation that felt comfortable spending weekends crashing on sofas of friends in foreign cities, living abroad and studying in foreign universities, and learn-

ing to communicate in several languages. Now, the difficulty of finding sustainable jobs has caused many young Europeans to postpone
marriage and having children, losing faith in a Europe where they
risk becoming a "lost generation" with no career or family prospects
even as they approach middle age.

The 2008 financial crisis exacted a huge toll in public support for
Europe, as unemployment among young people soared as high as 50
percent in Spain and other parts of the Mediterranean periphery.
The appeal of Euroskepticism and anti-immigrant parties across
Europe grew as mainstream political leaders failed to find effective
remedies to the crisis of jobs and lack of economic growth. The failure to integrate alienated young Muslims, many of them second-and
third-generation European citizens living without hope in suburban
ghettoes, has impelled some of them to embrace radical jihadism,
like the perpetrators of deadly terrorist attacks in Madrid, London,
Brussels, Paris, Nice, and Berlin.

Today the dream of European unity has begun to wither and the
future stability of the continent is clouded with uncertainty. Given
the abiding clashes of culture, language, and history affecting EU
member states, perhaps it was always a fantasy to believe that such
a disparate continent could be unified. Yet many of the global challenges facing Europe today can be solved only with the pooling of
resources and surrender of national sovereignty that has helped the
continent deal with other crises in the modern era.

For the United States, a divided and weaker Europe poses a grave
risk to its global leadership. The Atlantic alliance has been adrift for
much of the post–Cold War era. Europe and the United States have
lacked the cohesion and common purpose that united them before
the disintegration of the Soviet empire. Many Europeans already
had grave misgivings about following America's lead in fighting wars
in Iraq and Afghanistan. When Barack Obama declared his desire to
pivot toward Asia early in his presidency, European governments felt

he was turning his back on seven decades of transatlantic partnership that left them feeling neglected if not abandoned. Even though Obama remained popular in Europe throughout his eight years in office, he could never dispel the belief among some allies that his frequent calls for Europe to assume greater responsibility for its own security was simply a coded message that America was seeking to cut its ties to the Old World. Obama's passivity toward the Syrian civil war compounded those anxieties when Europe was left alone to deal with threats of instability caused by the refugee surge out of the Middle East and North Africa.

Donald Trump's election has raised even more serious questions in Europe about the reliability of American commitments. In a sharp break with his twelve predecessors, Trump has declared that NATO may be obsolete and the European Union should be treated more as an economic rival. Despite much talk about the growing importance of Asia, the United States still depends on a vital partnership with Europe to maintain its dominant role in the world. Even with the rise of China, India, and other emerging powers, trade and investment between the United States and Europe still accounts for nearly half of all global economic activity. Shared democratic values and NATO military commitments still make the Atlantic alliance one of the most crucial foundations of global stability. The devastation caused by two world wars in the previous century should be sufficient warning to all concerned about the consequences of Europe falling apart.

Fractured Continent seeks to illustrate the myriad crises faced on many fronts by a divided Europe. In Germany, the most powerful and prosperous country in Europe, where job vacancies are still plentiful, there is growing concern that the country's vaunted stability may be at risk because of the influx of more than 1 million refugees, mostly from Syria. In France, the alienation of Europe's largest Muslim population has fueled the rise of radical jihadism, discredited the mainstream establishment parties, and tempted voters to turn to the far right National Front. In Britain, disenchantment with Europe is so strong that the country defied its own economic interests and voted to leave the European Union. In Brussels, the capital of Europe, where NATO and the European Union are head-quartered, the rapid expansion of both institutions to more than two dozen members has spread confusion and disarray about the direction of future policies and how these unwieldy supranational bureaucracies should execute decisions taken by Europe's lead-ers. In Spain, a protracted economic crisis has disillusioned young people and damaged public confidence in centrist political leaders. Spain's troubles are compounded by the rising challenge of regional independence movements in Catalonia and the Basque country. Italy now looms as Europe's next economic crisis, with its bank-ing system on the brink of collapse. In Poland, voters have turned toward the hard right, choosing to be governed by a populist nation-alist party that disdains Europe even though the country has greatly benefited from its EU membership over the past two decades. Den-mark, regarded as the world's happiest country, is now consumed with anxiety about the future of its generous welfare state and by the threat of inundation as sea levels rise with the melting of the gla-cial ice sheet in Greenland. In Latvia, where ethnic Russians now make up half of all residents in the capital, Vladimir Putin's vow to defend their interests has stirred worries about an invasion by Mos-cow. And in Greece, where years of austerity measures imposed by outside creditors have devastated the economy and spread immense hardship, tens of thousands of Syrian refugees with nowhere else to go have overwhelmed the country's ability to care for them.

Fractured Continent aims to provide insights into the painful and disturbing challenges facing Europe today and the root causes of political turmoil, economic insecurity, and social volatility across the continent. Europe's ability to deal with its multitude of current crises will have an enormous impact on the United States and the rest of the world. The Atlantic alliance remains the cornerstone of American security commitments. How we cope with Russia, Turkey, Iran, the broader Middle East, and other trouble spots around the world will depend to a large extent on cooperation and support from our European allies. Indeed, the fate of this fractured continent could determine the future survival of Western democracy in the face of ascendant authoritarian models around the world.

CHAPTER ONE

BERLIN

THE NEW EPICENTER OF POWER

O N THE MORNING OF SEPTEMBER 4, 2015, GERMAN CHANCELLOR Angela Merkel awoke to a human disaster unfolding at the Keleti train station in Budapest, Hungary. In her dreams, she was still haunted by pictures of a Syrian-Kurdish boy whose corpse had washed up on the shores of a Turkish beach resort just days earlier. Now, thousands of Syrian refugees were moving north from Greece and pouring into the Hungarian capital, with tens of thousands more on the way.

More than 3,000 refugees were already stranded at the station, where conditions were becoming rapidly intolerable. They would not be allowed to continue their sojourn until Hungarian authorities received assurances that Austria and Germany would accept them. Merkel contacted her Austrian counterpart Werner Faymann and insisted that they needed to make an urgent declaration saying their frontiers would remain open and that the refugees would be welcome. After receiving the green light from Merkel, Hungarian police finally allowed the vast horde of Syrian refugees fleeing civil

war to continue their northward journey to find safe haven in affluent Western countries like Germany and Sweden.

Merkel did not reach that fateful decision without grave misgivings. She is renowned for her habit of playing for time, postponing
critical decisions until she has carefully reviewed all potential consequences. Germans have even transformed her name into a verb;
"to merkel," meaning to procrastinate until the time is ripe for making a decision. But on this occasion, Merkel decided to move boldly,
even recklessly, to defuse what she viewed as a moral and humanitarian crisis that threatened to overwhelm Europe.

As she returned from her annual hiking holiday in the Alps, she
saw that the trickle of Syrian refugees in the spring had turned into
a late summer flood. By late August as many as 2,000 a day were tra-
versing the narrow isthmus between Turkey and the Greek island
of Lesbos. She feared this tsunami of migrants heading into Europe
could soon destabilize the entire continent. She also believed the
exodus had become a personal and not just political test of her character. A few days earlier, a van crossing into Austria was unlocked by
authorities only to find more than seventy corpses, mostly women
and children, who had been trying to reach Germany.

In July, Merkel became emotionally distraught during a poi-
gnant encounter with a young Palestinian girl named Reem. The
girl broke into tears as she pleaded with Merkel to grant her family
asylum before they would have to be deported. Merkel touched her
shoulder and tried to console her but to no avail. Merkel said nothing
further could be done and lamented that Germany could not afford
to care for everybody who left the Middle East. Then, during a visit
weeks later to a refugee hostel in the eastern town of Heidenau in
Saxony, Merkel was assaulted verbally by an angry crowd. As Merkel
returned to her car, a hysterical woman shouted: "You miserable
cunt, you stupid slut, you traitor!" as others voiced their fury with
her decision to allow in the refugees. Merkel would later recall that

she had never experienced such visceral hostility from fellow Germans. But the ugly confrontation only made her more determined to push ahead with her *Willkommenskultur* of welcoming those poor souls escaping the war in Syria.

Merkel did not bother consulting with other EU leaders before deciding to fling open Germany's doors. As hundreds, then thousands, of bedraggled Syrians, Afghans, and Iraqis began arriving daily at the Munich train station to an enthusiastic welcome from cheering Germans eager to offer generous hospitality, Merkel was besieged with warnings from her EU colleagues, who were surprised and exasperated by her action. They warned that her unilateral decision would backfire and exacerbate the refugee crisis in ways that could inflict political and economic damage on all of Europe. At a tense summit meeting convened at EU headquarters in Brussels, Hungary's prime minister, Viktor Orban, sharply lectured her about what he viewed as a foolhardy policy that he would not follow under any circumstances.

"I don't care what you may think, but I am going to protect my borders even if it becomes necessary to build fences all around my country," Orban said huffily. "I will not accept your moral imperialism. And believe me, Madame Chancellor, in the end you will be forced to do the same thing as I am doing on my borders." Merkel shoved her papers aside and stared icily across the vast conference table inside the Justus Lipsius Building, where EU leaders frequently gather in emergency session to ponder how to address their most pressing challenges, including the refugee influx, Russia's aggression in Ukraine, Greece's debt problems, and Britain's decision to leave the European Union.

"I grew up staring at a wall in my face," Merkel told Orban, with emotion rising in her voice. "And I am determined not to see any more barriers being erected in Europe during the remainder of my lifetime." The other heads of government sat back in stunned silence as they absorbed her message and realized how Merkel's fierce determination to maintain open borders for the refugees had become for her a personal test of humanitarian morality.

Raised in Communist East Germany in the shadow of the Berlin Wall—which she viewed every day on her way to school and on her way to work as a research chemist—Merkel was imbued with an abiding duty to assist those in need. Her father, Horst Kasner, was a Lutheran pastor who had moved his family from Hamburg to the town of Templin north of Berlin in East Germany in 1954, seven years before the infamous wall was built to prevent a hemorrhage of skilled workers from leaving for the west. After settling in his new community, he ran a center that cared for physically and mentally disabled people. He inculcated in his oldest daughter a strong obligation to assist those who could not care for themselves.

Merkel's decision to fling open Germany's doors to nearly 1 million refugees in 2015 is just one of several momentous challenges she has confronted as the pivotal figure now shaping the destiny of the continent, if not the West. Since being elected Germany's chancellor in 2005 at the head of a center-right ruling coalition, she has emerged, much against her own will, as Europe's indispensable leader. In the absence of a European partner with whom she could share the burdens, Merkel has been compelled to assume almost complete responsibility for coping with a succession of Europe's most vexing problems. She has seized the initiative in dealing with the continental refugee crisis, the risks of a financial meltdown resulting from a potential breakup of the euro currency, the resurgence of an aggressive Russia under President Vladimir Putin, and the impact of Britain's decision to leave the European Union.

When the fallout from the 2008 global financial crisis threatened to push Greece into insolvency, she and her flinty finance minister, Wolfgang Schäuble, orchestrated the arduous negotiations that led to three bailouts and eventually kept Greece from dropping out of the eurozone. At the same time, she served as the West's chief interlocutor in dealing with President Vladimir Putin and mobilized Europe's response to impose economic sanctions after Russia's annexation of Crimea and its support of breakaway rebels in eastern Ukraine. Now, in what may be her most difficult test, Merkel is striving to put the continent back on course toward a peaceful, secure, and prosperous future following Britain's decision to leave the European Union by 2019. Merkel did not seek a hegemonic role for Germany and says she would much prefer to share the burdens and responsibilities of leadership with others in order to guide Europe with a broad consensus. But in the power vacuum that has afflicted Europe since the 2008 financial crisis, Merkel has emerged by default as the most critical personality shaping Europe's fate.

Following Donald Trump's surprise election in November 2016, Merkel announced that, despite her personal misgivings about staying too long in office, she would run as her party's candidate for a fourth term as chancellor. Merkel was so shocked by Trump's election that she questioned whether she really wanted to continue in office given the prospect of such an incompatible American partner. She had been privately rooting for Hillary Clinton, with whom she has long maintained a close personal bond. A Merkel-Clinton duo might have become the most powerful partnership in world politics, given their strong mutual admiration and shared views on how to address many global issues.

During his farewell visit to Germany two weeks after the election, Merkel begged President Obama to explain what had happened and to offer his advice on what she should do. Obama urged her to pursue another term in office, arguing she was the only leader who could sustain faith in Western liberal democracy at such a perilous time. Obama also pleaded with her to keep an open mind in dealing with Trump, in the hope that the burdens and responsibilities of the Oval Office would moderate his views.

In her congratulatory message to Trump a day after his victory, Merkel said she would welcome continued close cooperation with the United States under his leadership. But she laid down some strict conditions. She insisted that such collaboration could only occur according to shared values between Germany and the United States that were based on "democracy, freedom and respect for the law and the dignity of man, independent of origin, skin color, religion, gender, sexual orientation or political views."

In spite of Obama's respect for her sagacity, Merkel denied she had any pretense of inheriting the mantle of Western leadership, saying "no single person, even with the most experience, can fix things around the world." But with Britain leaving the European Union, France facing an unpredictable future, and the United States entering uncharted waters with an inexperienced president espousing America First policies, Merkel has emerged as the chief defender of a Western liberal democratic order under siege from populist nationalists on both sides of the Atlantic.

Germany now ranks as the key strategic actor in Europe and has long displaced Britain as America's principal partner in managing the Atlantic alliance. American presidents since Ronald Reagan have recognized that all roads to cooperation in Europe lead to Berlin. Merkel's emphasis on common values as the basis of foreign policy cooperation between Washington and Berlin contrasts sharply with the transactional approach Trump proposed during his campaign. Yet any breakdown in German-American cooperation could destabilize Europe, weaken America's stature in the world, and give Russia an opportunity to expand its sphere of influence. Putin has demonstrated that one of the top strategic priorities for Moscow will be to sow further discord within NATO and the European Union in an effort to shatter the cohesion of these institutions. Trump has been warned by a long list of foreign policy experts to ensure that his desire for better relations with Russia does not undermine the Atlantic alliance.

Merkel has searched in vain for another worthy partner who could help share the burdens of guiding Europe through its current travails. Since World War II, Germany has shied away from exercising too much power and has traditionally sought to work closely with France in guiding the course of the European Union. But during her three terms as chancellor, Merkel has been deeply disappointed with the failed presidencies of Nicolas Sarkozy and François Hollande.

The lack of strong leadership in Paris has forced Germany into the role of a reluctant hegemon whose political clout has expanded to match its economic dominance over the continent. Merkel found Sarkozy too erratic, temperamental, and lacking in a strong vision of where Europe should go. His successor, the Socialist Party leader François Hollande, has been one of the least popular presidents of modern France and faced constant insurrections within his own party. Looking to the east, Merkel has been similarly discouraged by what has happened to Poland, which had blossomed as one of the success stories in post-Communist Europe but now has taken an illiberal and undemocratic turn under the Law and Justice party.

Despite her pro-American leanings, Merkel learned that she could not always depend on support from the White House. When Obama announced early in his presidency that it was time for the United States to pivot toward Asia, many Europeans feared the United States would abandon its role as Europe's military protector and shift its focus toward fast-growing markets in China, South Korea, and India. Obama's irritation with "free riders" among Euro-pean allies who refused to contribute sufficiently to their own defense seemed to encourage a "tough love" attitude. During their meetings, Obama would often remind Merkel that the United States believed it was time for Germany and its partners to take

care of their own backyard after seven decades of American tutelage after World War II. But over time, Merkel and Obama struck
up a close rapport and personal friendship that served the transatlantic partnership well. Obama awarded Merkel the presidential
medal of freedom and in his final weeks in office paid a farewell
visit to Berlin to show his respect for her leadership and urge her to
carry forward the torch of Western leadership in the world.

During her long tenure in power, Merkel has enjoyed remarkable
political stability domestically, which reinforced her political stature in Europe at a time when other leaders were enduring distract-
ing challenges at home. During two of her three terms in office, she
and her center-right Christian Democrats formed a grand ruling
coalition with the center-left Social Democrats, giving the country's two largest parties control of up to 80 percent of the seats in
the Bundestag.

One of Merkel's most formidable skills is her ability to co-opt the
positions of her rivals, as she has done frequently throughout her
time as chancellor. She disarmed the antinuclear Green Party by
declaring in the wake of the Fukushima nuclear disaster in Japan
that Germany would shut down all nuclear power plants by 2022.
Germany then embarked on an ambitious program, at enormous
cost but with strong public support, to fill the void by embracing
alternative energy sources such as wind and solar power. Today,
Germany leads the world in the transformative shift away from fossil fuels and now derives nearly one-third of its energy from alternative energy sources.

Merkel has also expanded the base of her center-right Christian
Democratic Union by adopting progressive policies in child care
support and women's rights that had once been the preserve of
the center-left Social Democrats. While some CDU stalwarts have
grumbled that she has muddled her party's identity and unsettled
its core constituency, Merkel's continuing popularity during her

three terms in office testifies to her skill in tacking with the political winds to stay in tune with the sentiments of German voters. In dealing with all of the crises that have marked her time in power, Merkel has managed to shift course whenever necessary in order to stay abreast of public opinion and ensure the country remains solidly behind her.

No crisis better illustrates Merkel's abilities to navigate shifts in public opinion than the massive influx of Syrian refugees that in 2015 threatened to destabilize the entire continent. At the apex of her power, Merkel decided to allow nearly 900,000 refugees into Germany at a time when Hungary, Poland, and other Eastern European neighbors adamantly refused to accept any more than a token number. At first, Germans took pride in their display of generous hospitality and setting an example to other European countries by welcoming mostly Syrian, Afghan, and Iraqi refugees into their country. Merkel's chant of *"Wir schaffen das!"* (We can do it!) echoed the Obama campaign refrain of "Yes, we can" that so captivated American voters in the 2008 campaign.

She exhorted the German public to view the arrival of Syrian refugees as a golden opportunity for her country to rejuvenate its population. She said the refugees might help unleash a burst of entrepreneurial energy in Germany after decades of low birth rates raised fears whether the country would be able to provide pensions and health care for its rapidly aging population. Indeed, the German Interior Ministry had concluded a study some years earlier showing that in order to sustain current living standards, Germany would require as many as 400,000 immigrants to fill job vacancies over the next two decades.

German civil servants began processing Syrian asylum seekers— the majority of whom were young males—and sought to channel them into locations and training programs that would help fill job vacancies. Once it was realized that many of the refugees would not

be returning anytime soon to the Middle East, the German Bundestag passed supplementary funding amounting to nearly $100 billion
over three years—a sum equivalent to $30,000 a year per refugee—to
cover the costs of language lessons, vocational assistance, and even
cultural sensitivity training to help the refugees adapt to their newly
adopted homeland.

But soon, some Germans started asking questions about the
potential impact of so many foreigners from the Middle East besieg-
ing their homeland and whether their own national identity was
coming under threat. In the wealthy state of Bavaria, where the
CDU's sister party the Christian Social Union has dominated politics for decades, the refugees dispatched to rural villages sometimes
outnumbered the local inhabitants. CSU leader Horst Seehofer complained that the populist, anti-immigrant Alternative for Germany
party—which was created in 2013—was starting to attract many CSU
voters disaffected by the generous asylum policy that they felt was
transforming their traditional Catholic culture in Bavaria.

Other regions across Germany, particularly in the formerly Communist east where xenophobic tendencies have always been strong,
reported rising attacks against refugee encampments. Then, on
New Year's Eve, dozens of women in Cologne and Hamburg went to
police accusing young Muslim immigrants of robbing and molesting
them during late-night celebrations in the city streets. The attacks
triggered a sharp backlash as many Germans demanded immediate changes in the asylum policy, insisting that the country could no
longer maintain the open-door policy that Merkel had supported.
To placate critics of her refugee policy within her Christian Democratic party, Merkel bowed to pressure to accept new laws that would
restrict the number of refugees allowed into Germany. Instead of
three years, asylum seekers would be allowed only one-year resi-
dency permits on a renewable basis and their family members would
not be allowed to join them.

Yet public anxiety about the impact of Merkel's policy continued to grow. How many of the refugees would be allowed to stay and for how long? How could young male asylum seekers from Syria be expected to integrate into local communities when their cultural attitudes were so much at odds with those of the West? Even though many Germans acknowledged the need for immigrants to fill job vacancies and generate the income taxes needed to cover pension and health care costs for an aging population, they also wondered aloud whether their society could absorb the shock of assimilating so many refugees—70 percent of whom are young Arab males unaccompanied by wives and children—from a Middle Eastern culture whose values clash with their own in so many ways.

In December 2016, disaster struck just when many Germans were preparing for year-end holidays. A twenty-four-year-old Tunisian immigrant drove a huge truck into the middle of Berlin's Christmas markets in the downtown Kurfürstendamm area, killing 12 people and injuring 50 in one of the worst terrorist attacks to strike Germany in recent years. The militant group Islamic State, which has been waging civil war in Syria and Iraq for the past five years, claimed responsibility for the attack. The method of using a large truck to mow down innocent civilians came straight from the Islamic State's terrorist playbook that had been disseminated over the group's website. In France five months earlier, another Tunisian immigrant had driven a truck down Nice's main promenade during a Bastille Day celebration and killed 84 people before he was shot dead by security forces. The perpetrator of the Berlin massacre was later tracked down in Milan, where he was killed by police in a shootout.

The attacks sparked more criticism of Merkel's policies from her party's conservative wing and increased support for the anti-immigrant, anti-Europe extremist party Alternative for Germany (AfD). Barely three years after being formed, the AfD surged in popularity and had gained seats in nine of Germany's sixteen regional assemblies. It captured 20 percent of the vote in Merkel's home state of Mecklenburg-Vorpommern and seemed on its way to becoming a significant force in the September 2017 national elections, when it hoped to become the country's third-strongest party.

Like other Western leaders, Merkel seemed at a loss about what to do to prevent a further spate of terrorist attacks. It was too late to close the doors to the huge waves of refugees that had come into Europe from Syria via Turkey. Hundreds of suspected Islamic State operatives were known to have entered Europe by hiding among the crowds of refugees to escape detection by security forces. Merkel had tightened restrictions on those refugees staying in Germany, such as banning the wearing of the burka in schools, and her government had taken other measures to clamp down on the abuses of German laws and culture. Negotiations were stepped up with African and Middle Eastern countries to take back many of the immigrants who had come to Germany, but many of those states were reluctant to cooperate. It was reported that, months earlier, German authorities had tried to deport Anis Amri, the Tunisian immigrant suspected of carrying out the deadly truck assault, but were unable to do so because Tunisia refused to recognize him as a citizen.

Merkel had long believed that the best way to defuse the refugee crisis would be to accelerate efforts to reach a peaceful settlement in Syria. In some ways, Germany was ideally suited to broker a deal that could put an end to Syria's bloody civil war, since the country maintained good relations with all key protagonists. Merkel was trusted and respected in Washington, where President Obama had often expressed his admiration for her steely patience in dealing with Vladimir Putin.

Obama recognized she was the only allied leader he could depend upon, given the weakness of London and Paris. He appreciated her help in maintaining Western unity in the protracted negotiations with Iran to thwart its development of nuclear weapons. Merkel had become, almost by default, the West's principal interlocutor with Putin. She spoke fluent Russian and they could also converse in German, which he perfected during his five years as KGB station chief in Dresden before the fall of the Berlin Wall. Despite their mutual disdain, Putin had developed a grudging respect for Merkel. She was also held in high esteem in Tehran, which had long enjoyed a healthy commercial relationship with Germany. During the reign of the Shah, many members of the Iranian clerical opposition who later gained power under the Islamic Republic took refuge in Germany.

But Merkel's efforts to push for a peaceful resolution in Syria proved fruitless. Russia and Iran, the leading allies of Syrian strongman Bashar Assad, would not pressure him into stepping down to allow an interim government to take power as a precursor to a lasting peace. The United States insisted that Assad's departure was the necessary first step to achieving a settlement, since none of the various anti-Assad factions would tolerate a deal with him staying in power. But Assad and his allies would later decide to double down on the military option, launching a brutal air and ground assault against Syria's second largest city, Aleppo, that by the end of 2016 had crushed much of the armed resistance to his rule.

Faced with a diplomatic stalemate on the war in Syria, Merkel turned to her old nemesis, Recep Tayyip Erdoğan, seeking to cut a deal that would stem the flow of refugees through Turkey and into Europe. The German initiative did not please her European partners, but Merkel pressed ahead anyway. She realized that other European countries, with the notable exception of Sweden, were unwilling to accept their fair share of refugees under a quota system she had proposed for the twenty-eight EU nations. She reluctantly concluded that Germany could not continue to absorb refugees at such an intensive pace without risking its own political stability. With elections approaching in 2017, Merkel was desperate to reach an arrangement with Erdoğan to curtail the flow of refugees coming into Europe even though she knew he was a volatile and untrust-worthy partner.

The deal struck between Turkey and Germany in March 2016 was roundly criticized, especially by human rights groups. The terms called for Turkey to accept the return of any further Syrian refugees crossing from Turkey into Greece. In return, for every Syrian returned to Turkey, a Syrian refugee would be resettled by the European Union. In addition, Turkey would receive from the European Union an extra $3 billion in aid—on top of an earlier $3 billion commitment—in order to feed and care for the 2.7 million Syrian refugees living on Turkish soil. The most controversial issue was Merkel's promise that Turkey's negotiations to become a member of the European Union would be accelerated and that all Turks would soon be granted the right of visa-free entry into Europe once Turkey complied with the necessary conditions.

The United Nations refugee agency and other human rights groups complained that such exchanges of refugees would violate international law. Several EU member states said they would not tolerate any special favors granted to Turkey and would not accept any more Syrian refugees as part of the transfer arrangements with Greece. But to the surprise of many experts, the flow of refugees out of Turkey slowed dramatically. Erdoğan ordered Turkish police and military forces to step up patrols of the coastline to prevent human traffickers from pursuing their lucrative trade. Many refugees, faced with the risk of losing their investment in being intercepted and returned to Turkey, abandoned plans to flee to Europe.

Within months, a sense of calm and relief spread through Germany and other European countries as the refugee crisis receded from the front pages. By July 2016, almost exactly one year after the first enormous wave of refugees began reaching Greece and making their way north toward Germany, the United Nations refugee agency reported that the closing of borders by Balkan countries and the

EU's agreement with Turkey had reduced the flow of migrants crossing the Aegean Sea into Greece to a trickle.

While large numbers of sub-Saharan refugees continued to cross
the Mediterranean Sea from Libya into Italy, the huge outflow of
Syrian refugees that sent more than 1.1 million people into Europe
in 2015—with the vast majority settling in Germany and Sweden—
had suddenly subsided. The specter that Germany might be overrun
by hordes of Muslim immigrants no longer seemed to grip the country, even though the financial costs and difficulties of absorbing so
many foreigners in such a short time still posed serious problems.
But Merkel survived what had appeared to be a lethal threat to her
grip on power.

The eurozone drama that played out over several years offered
a different kind of challenge. In contrast to her bold, even reckless
handling of the refugee crisis, Merkel acted in a slow, deliberate
manner by consistently kicking the can down the road during the
most fraught moments in the Greek debt crisis. When Greece first
acknowledged in 2010 that it could no longer repay its heavy debts,
Merkel insisted any bailout would be subject to a strict austerity regimen to ensure that Greece would break with its spendthrift ways.
Merkel also realized that unless Greece was forced to abide by draconian budget cuts, other countries facing debt problems exacerbated
by the 2008 global crisis, such as Portugal and Spain, would reject
similar discipline.

In the eyes of southern Europeans, Merkel was using her country's
economic and financial power to impose the German model on them.
A north-south split pitting rich creditors like Germany and the Nordic states against poorer debtors along the Mediterranean periphery
threatened to tear Europe apart. Christine Lagarde, the head of the
International Monetary Fund, repeatedly insisted that Germany
must recognize that the only logical course of action was to write off
a large share of the debts incurred by Greece, and perhaps Italy and

other southern European states as well. But Merkel knew German voters would be loath to accept that burden at a time when the country's aging population was struggling to save money for retirement. Many economists predict that Germany's refusal to acknowledge the need to cancel those debts is sowing seeds for another euro crisis in the near future.

Despite her pro-Europe convictions, Merkel refused all along to consider possible Europe-wide solutions that would have defused the debt crisis. The idea was raised early on by European Central Bank chief Mario Draghi that the pressures on Greece, Italy, and other southern European countries would greatly ease if the nineteen members could agree on a plan for debt mutualization—one in which the liability for all eurozone debts would be shared among the members. Draghi argued that such an agreement would convince the markets that the euro was irrevocable because it would be fully backed by the combined resources of all member states, particularly Europe's economic powerhouse, Germany.

Peer Steinbrück, a prominent Social Democrat and former finance minister who ran against Merkel for chancellor, was willing to embrace the idea. But the Social Democrats backed away when it became clear that they would pay a heavy price in elections if they endorsed such a dramatic measure. Italy's former prime minister, Mario Monti, pleaded with Merkel at the time to think about the historic importance of a quantum leap toward a more united continent, but he said she rejected his appeal because she did not want to get ahead of the thinking of German voters. "It was a great opportunity in terms of a larger vision for Europe and one that could have stopped the crisis in its tracks, but instead we ended up paying a price because of narrow political considerations in Germany," Monti told me.

But Merkel, ever conscious of how far the German public would go in helping their European neighbors, stuck to the hard line of her finance minister, Wolfgang Schäuble. They both feared that their

CDU party would lose large numbers of voters to the anti-euro populist party Alternative for Germany if they tried to impose an ambitious vision of a more united Europe. The rise of populism across Europe had made governments wary of ramming the idea of greater European integration down the throats of the voters—something that Merkel's mentor, Helmut Kohl, had not been afraid to do when it came to replacing the beloved deutschmark with the euro. So Merkel pulled back and went along with Schäuble's conviction that the German people were not prepared to assume shared responsibility for the debts of its European partners.

• Germany also rejected the idea of a Europe-wide deposit insurance system for eurozone banks, again because the government realized it would have to put German money at risk and that the German people did not want their own hard-earned money to provide insurance for any bank runs in other European states. Germany's refusal to consider such steps frustrated its other partners and hardened their belief that German support for European policies only extended to those that would benefit its own national interests. While Merkel and Schäuble proclaimed their support for greater European integration, including eventual political union and the creation of a United States of Europe, the obvious reality became clear to the Greeks and other Europeans that German voters were no longer willing to sacrifice their own interests for the benefit of the European project.

Opinion polls showed that Germans believed their government had been too indulgent with the Greeks and other European partners. They remain strongly opposed to providing any further bailout money. During the early stages of the Euro crisis, Germans felt they were being victimized by their own diligence in respecting EU rules and resented having to pay for what they viewed as the irresponsible behavior of their partners. Yet elsewhere across Europe, the opposite attitude has prevailed as strong majorities of Greeks, Italians,

French, and Spanish believed that Germans were far too selfish in refusing to offer more assistance to their EU partners in their hour of need.

On the streets of Athens, pictures of Merkel wearing swastikas and Hitler-style moustaches were plastered on walls throughout the capital. Merkel took such insults in stride and insisted Germany was not being cruel and heartless in its treatment of its southern neighbors. She argued that Germany merely wanted to ensure that any assistance offered to alleviate the debt burdens borne by Greece, Spain, and Portugal would be accompanied by budgetary reforms that would bolster the long-term health of their finances and help them compete more effectively in the global economy.

At home, Merkel faced intense pressures not to offer any financial help. German pensioners complained they did not want to see their precious resources lavished on their profligate neighbors to the south. The nation's most popular newspaper, *Bild Zeitung*, with 8 million daily readers, joined the campaign against the Greek bailouts. In one cover story depicting a plethora of yachts sailing in the Aegean Sea, the tabloid reported that while Germany had just raised its retirement age to sixty-seven, Greeks could still retire at fifty-five or even fifty if they worked in a "hazardous profession," which was defined so broadly that the list included being a hairdresser. For their part, Greek newspapers were equally scathing. They accused their German creditors of squeezing them dry in order to bail out French and German banks that had flocked to Greece following the creation of the euro to hand out dicey loans to customers who were not creditworthy.

The blame game continues to this day, with Germany accused by the southern EU states of being obsessed with an "eat your spinach" austerity regime. They insist the time has come for the European Union to focus on an investment splurge that would boost jobs and economic growth and provide a new sense of hope for Europe's growing population of unemployed young people. But the next European economic crisis could be one that directly affects Germany, which earns nearly half of its national income from exports. Since Germany sells most of its products to its European partners, the risk that Greece's troubles might spread to Italy or France through an EU-wide banking crisis or renewed recession would probably curtail German exports and drive up unemployment. While German voters may not wish to hear that their future prosperity may depend on their willingness to help their European neighbors stave off further economic decline, it is a message that Merkel and others may need to deliver.

Even while she was saddled with sorting out Europe's refugee and sovereign debt crises, Merkel was compelled to take the lead in juggling other challenges as well. In March 2014 she was confronted by one of the continent's biggest security threats since the fall of the Berlin Wall: Russia's blatant violation of international law through its annexation of Crimea and invasion of eastern Ukraine. Since becoming chancellor in 2005, Merkel has met and spoken often with Putin—far more than any other Western leader. She also has a strong understanding of his personal motivations. She says in their conversations he frequently refers to his determination to reverse what he describes as the greatest geopolitical catastrophe of the twentieth century—the dissolution of the Soviet Empire.

Putin is fully committed to resurrecting Russia's superpower role and has launched a seven-year, $700 billion military modernization program to carry out his ambitions. He operates with stealth and deceit, reflecting the habits and tendencies he developed as a career KGB officer. Having grown up in Communist East Germany in the suffocating Soviet-backed regime, Merkel well understands the psychological profile of Putin and his cohort of former KGB officers. She intuitively senses when he is lying to her, and he seems to know that she knows. In their talks about Ukraine, she often listened to him disavow any Russian interference until she confronted him with indisputable evidence of Russian involvement. At one meeting, she pulled out photographs and pointed out the Russian soldiers wearing uniforms without insignias, at which point Putin expressed feigned surprise and wondered how they could ever have found their way to Ukraine. These infamous "little green men" have operated with impunity in the Russian takeover of Crimea and on behalf of breakaway rebels in the Donbass and other parts of eastern Ukraine.

In the wake of the Crimea takeover, Merkel has met or spoken with Putin on more than seventy occasions. At Obama's behest, she has acted as the West's lead interlocutor in trying to persuade Putin that he cannot hope to restore a normal working relationship with the Western allies until he ceases his operations in Ukraine, withdraws from the Crimea, and accepts international law. Despite the heavy loss of revenue for German companies who reaped huge profits in trading with Moscow, she rallied the European Union behind economic sanctions against Russia. She has managed to maintain Western unity on sanctions by keeping the European partners on the same line as the United States, despite the misgivings of Italy, Hungary, and other EU states that believe that sanctions have outlived their purposes. But the Trump administration, which has promoted the idea of a closer relationship with Russia, could further aggravate divisions within Europe about what kind of approach to take with Moscow.

At home, Merkel has struggled against the growing band of "Putin Versteher," or apologists for the Russian leader, who yearn for a new era of East-West détente in spite of Putin's aggressive and mischievous actions. Former SPD chancellor Gerhard Schröder earned a fortune by becoming chairman of Russia's Gazprom after leaving office and celebrated his seventieth birthday party with Putin and other friends in Saint Petersburg. Schröder's former chief of staff Frank-Walter Steinmeier, who served as Germany's foreign minister before assuming the largely ceremonial role as the nation's president, has tried to put some distance between his party and Merkel's tough stand against Putin by speaking out on the need for the West to be more understanding of Russia's big power aspirations.

When NATO troops staged maneuvers in the Baltic states during the summer of 2016 to reassure those allies that they would be protected in the event of Russian aggression, Steinmeier lashed out against what he called needless "saber rattling and war cries" that would only antagonize Russia and escalate risks of military conflict. "Anybody who believes that symbolic tank parades on NATO's eastern borders will increase security is wrong," Steinmeier said. But German public opinion has remained steadfastly on Merkel's side in taking a tough line against Putin, as distrust has grown with his authoritarian ways and disregard for the truth.

At the outset of the Ukraine crisis, Germans were divided about what should be done in retaliation, but opinion swung sharply in favor of imposing sanctions against Russia following the shoot-down of a Malaysian civilian airliner that cost the lives of many Dutch and other European citizens. Putin's repeated denials that Russia was involved, even though it was clearly a Russian-made antiair missile that destroyed the plane, badly damaged his standing with the German public.

Germans were also outraged when the Russian media, at the government's instigation, tried to claim that a young Russian girl of fourteen named Anna had been brutally raped in a Berlin suburb by a gang of young men. When it transpired that the girl had simply gone to visit friends for a few days without telling her parents, Putin's propaganda machine continued to charge that Germany was covering up a horrible crime against an innocent Russia girl.

Nonetheless, Merkel believes very much in the need for the West to keep talking to Putin, emphasizing the need for dialogue as well as deterrence. She reprimanded Obama for disparaging Russia as a "regional power," saying such insults needlessly antagonized Putin, who is obsessed with restoring Russia to a prominent place on the world stage. She makes a point of staying in frequent touch with Putin because she believes that he needs to hear the unvarnished truth about why his behavior is so frightening to the West.

She often reaches the point of exasperation and says at times she is tempted to walk out while listening to his tirades. She shakes her head as she recalls how he drones on endlessly at their meetings about how the West is mistreating him and trying to encircle his country by expanding the forces of the North Atlantic Treaty Organization up to Russia's frontiers. Yet she believes it is important for Putin, who she realizes is surrounded by sycophants and kleptocrats, to learn directly from her about what she and other Western leaders think of him.

Merkel has led the effort to strike a peaceful resolution on Ukraine by implementing the terms of an agreement she struck with him in Minsk, the capital of Belarus. After listening to Putin's petulant complaints about mistreatment by the United States and its European allies for hours on end, Merkel was plunged into a dark mood. It was turning into another all-night bargaining session between Merkel and Putin. This time they were joined by French president François Hollande and Ukraine's president Petro Poroshenko. But they were only window dressing for the personal showdown between Merkel and Putin. For more than a year, she had been acting as the West's interlocutor with the Russian president, trying to use her fluent Russian language skills and her country's powerful business ties with Moscow to persuade him to work with her to reach a peace agreement in Ukraine. From their many phone calls and marathon meetings, she was by now well acquainted with his lying and obfuscation. Putin kept playing the aggrieved party, saying the West was out to get him and prevent Russia from regaining its rightful role as a world power. A black belt in judo, Putin prides himself on keeping his opponents off balance. At one of his first meetings with Merkel, Putin claimed to be unaware of her acute aversion toward dogs because of the traumatic experience she suffered after being bitten as a child, and summoned Koni, his black Labrador, into their breakfast meeting at his dacha. As the dog prowled around her, Putin seemed to relish her discomfort. Then, even more fiendishly, he offered the dog to her as a personal gift.

Around 6 A.M. at the Minsk summit, Merkel's patience snapped. She told Putin that she would no longer listen to his perpetual rants about Moscow's grievances. He must accept that the terms of a cease-fire or the West would ramp up sanctions. She got up to leave, expecting Putin not to cave in. To her surprise, he did. The Minsk accords, at least temporarily, were salvaged and hopes for an eventual peace settlement were kept alive.

But Merkel did not have much time to enjoy her success. From Minsk she flew to Brussels, where another marathon bargaining session awaited her. This time, she would play the tough cop in demanding that Greece's leftist prime minister, Alexis Tsipras, accept the need for drastic structural reforms of the Greek economy in return for further loans. After more late-night haggling, Tsipras walked out and called a surprise national referendum asking Greek voters whether to accept the latest offer from creditors. Merkel flew home angry and depressed, fearing that Tsipras's reckless decision would destabilize the eurozone. After Greek voters rejected the terms, Tsipras shut down the banks and imposed capital controls, but within weeks was forced to surrender and accept Merkel's austerity terms. He resigned but then was reelected with a mandate to carry out terms of the new deal. For now, at least, the euro was saved—on terms that were even more onerous for the Greek people.

Merkel's shuttle diplomacy during that hectic week was not finished. She flew home and barely had time to become reacquainted with her diffident spouse, Joachim Sauer, whose reluctance to be seen in public except at the annual Wagner festival in Bayreuth has earned him the nickname "Phantom of the Opera." After collapsing in bed for a few hours of sleep, she welcomed British prime minister David Cameron and his wife for an intimate weekend of pondering strategy about how to keep Britain inside the European Union.

Cameron had staked his leadership against the many Euroskeptics in his Conservative Party on a referendum to decide whether Britain should leave the EU. Merkel badly wanted to keep Britain in the EU, fearing that its departure could destabilize Europe and deprive her of a partner who shared her transatlantic perspective. She told the conservative British leader that she was prepared to do everything possible to help him, short of making any fundamental changes to the EU treaties. After several long discussions, she and Cameron reached a deal on a package of concessions for Britain about EU reforms that might mollify British voters and enable Cameron to carry the day in winning his bet. But the package failed to impress British voters, who rejected the referendum and opted to leave the European Union.

Merkel could never understand Cameron's rationale for taking such a foolish gamble on his political future and Britain's forty-three-year membership in the European Union. The outcome of a referendum often turns on those voters who may wish to vent their dismay, for any number of reasons, with the government. The Euroskeptic wing of the Conservative Party has long been a troublesome faction that roiled the work of the European Union, but after Cameron won an overwhelming victory in general elections in 2015, it was believed that his critics within his own party would finally be silenced.

Merkel thought it was absurd for Cameron to risk his strong mandate from the national election on an early referendum about Europe when many unknown factors could affect the outcome. She was mystified as to why Cameron would choose the date of June 23 for the referendum, during a week when British university students— perhaps the most enthusiastic cohort of supporters to remain in the EU—would be busy with final exams and the wildly popular Glaston- bury music festival. To her dismay, the impassioned views of British voters fearful of unchecked immigration and "little Englanders" who wanted to reclaim sovereignty from Brussels overwhelmed the sensible economic arguments of the Remain camp.

In the wake of the shocking referendum result, Merkel tried to restore a sense of calm to the European Union. While other European leaders insisted that Britain should leave the EU as soon as possible, she said there should be time for reflection in the hope that Cameron's successor—and the British people—might reconsider the damaging impact of the Leave vote on the British economy. She also insisted that once Britain invoked article 50 of the Lisbon treaty and the two-year countdown to its formal departure began, there could be no "cherry picking" and that London could not expect any favorable treatment in establishing a new relationship with Europe. Most of all, Merkel made it clear that Germany and other EU countries would insist that in return for remaining part of the single European market, Britain would have to accept the free movement of people within that market. That point may prove hardest to swallow for British Prime Minister Theresa May, who took over from Cameron with a promise to start Brexit negotiations in March 2017.

Britain's imminent departure from the European Union only strengthens Germany's dominant role on the continent—something that makes Merkel very uneasy. In dealing with Europe's various crises over the past decade, she said she would have been much more comfortable working closely with other leaders in Paris, London, Warsaw, and Rome in forging a broad consensus on the Euro crisis, the Russia-Ukraine conflict, the Syrian refugee problem, and the future vision of the European Union.

But in the absence of strong leadership in those capitals, Merkel has been compelled to take unilateral actions in ways she may not have liked. Inevitably, these decisions have drawn criticism in other parts of Europe about Germany throwing its weight around on behalf of its own interests. As Europe's most powerful nation, Germany must now decide virtually alone how to steer the continent toward an uncertain future at a time of economic dislocation and public disaffection with the European ideal.

Given public dismay toward greater European integration, Merkel has avoided any grandiose initiatives designed to invigorate the European project. She has developed a strong distrust of the European Union's executive commission and the European Parliament, both of which tend to favor federalist policies that would lead to a United States of Europe. Merkel says she prefers to respect the will of voters who have elected politicians to manage Europe on an "intergovernmental" basis rather than through the Brussels bureaucracy. At a time of profound political and economic insecurity, Europeans are seeking greater control over their lives within their own local communities and seem in no mood for "more Europe."

The European Union has long been regarded as an avatar of globalization by pooling the sovereignty of its nation states. In the view of many Europeans, the collapse of national frontiers has provoked recession and instability through the loss of manufacturing jobs that moved to low-wage countries in Asia and brought an influx of immigrants from Africa and the Middle East. It is a theme that echoes in Donald Trump's complaints about how working-class Americans have been victimized in seeing their jobs flee to Mexico and about how many foreigners are trying to illegally enter the United States.

Three generations after World War II, Germany is slowly shedding the burdens of its Nazi history that restrained its influence over the continent. With Britain and France wallowing in decline, Germany recognizes that the strategic and policy choices it chooses will shape Europe's destiny for much of the twenty-first century. Once again, the German question that haunted Europe for decades has surfaced in Europe. This time, it is no longer a matter of whether Germany is too strong or too weak. For the foreseeable future, the fate of Europe will be decided largely in Berlin.

CHAPTER TWO

LONDON

THE BREAKAWAY REALM

IT WAS BILLED AS THE LAST SUPPER. FOUR DAYS AFTER HE RESIGNED as prime minister in the wake of Britain's stunning vote on June 23, 2016, to leave the European Union, a chastened David Cameron flew to Brussels for a farewell gathering with his peers. As he sat down with the other twenty-seven heads of government for a final time, Cameron would later recall how he was struck by the sullen silence around the table and a pervasive mood of "sadness and regret."

He knew the other leaders were angry with his decision to hold the referendum. It was widely regarded as a historic blunder that destroyed his career and triggered Britain's gravest crisis since World War II. But there was no time for recriminations. He explained while he was deeply sorry about an outcome that would terminate Britain's forty-three years of EU membership, he felt he had no other choice but to call the vote in order to resolve a bitter power struggle in his party. In fact, he added, even if he could turn back the hands of time, he would still not do anything differently.

Several leaders rolled their eyes in bewilderment, still astonished by Cameron's reckless decision to roll the dice with a plebiscite that he never realized could have such damaging consequences for his own country and the rest of Europe. They tried to be polite and conciliatory. German Chancellor Angela Merkel was fatalistic and saw no possibility to reverse Britain's choice, saying "this was not a time for wishful thinking, but to see things as they are."

Taavi Rõivas, the youthful prime minister from Estonia who always sat next to Cameron at EU summits, expressed his gratitude to British soldiers for their help nearly a century ago in ensuring his country's independence. France's president François Hollande recalled how British and French soldiers fought side by side in the trenches of World War I. Ireland's prime minister, Enda Kenny, observed that, thanks to EU membership, Britain and Ireland were finally able to put an end to centuries of conflict and establish a durable peace. But their exasperation with Cameron could not be entirely concealed. When he inquired about the first course served for dinner, one of his peers replied: "It's quail salad. But perhaps it should be crow."

On the very same day, another British politician was also saying goodbye to his European colleagues in Brussels, but this time it was more like a victory dance than a wake. Nigel Farage, the irascible leader of the United Kingdom Independence Party which mobilized many of the Leave voters with scary warnings about rampant immigrants, was taking great pleasure in taunting his foes inside the European Parliament. "When I came here 17 years ago and said I wanted to lead a campaign to get Britain to leave the European Union you all laughed," he sneered. "Well, I have to say, you're not laughing now, are you?"

Farage mocked the legislators and their quixotic dream of a united Europe, telling them "virtually none of you have ever done a proper job in your lives." As other members of the European Parliament erupted in outrage, Belgium's former prime minister Guy Verhofstadt interjected: "OK, let's be positive. We are getting rid of the biggest waste of the EU budget: your salary!" EU Commission president Jean-Claude Juncker pleaded for calm and suggested it might be in the interests of everybody if Farage would depart the European Parliament—for the last time. "You were fighting for the exit and the British people voted in favor of the exit, so why are you still here?" Juncker asked. Farage then fired his parting shot at his erstwhile colleagues, insisting once again that he, and not they, stood on the right side of history. "The reason you're so upset has been perfectly clear from all the angry exchanges," he said. "You, as a political project, are in denial!"

Back in Britain, people were still reeling in shock over an outcome that neither side—Leave or Remain—really believed was possible. Polls had shown the Remain side comfortably ahead in the week before the June referendum by as much as ten points, yet Leave ended up winning by 52 percent to 48 percent. How did it happen? Scare tactics about unchecked immigration clearly worked. In many towns and depressed industrial areas, immigrants were blamed for stealing jobs from local citizens by accepting lower wages. They were also accused of putting pressure on public services like hospitals and schools, as well as driving up property prices. Farage and his supporters unveiled billboards showing a long line of dark-skinned refugees entering the country under the slogan "Breaking Point." The hatreds stirred up by the racist overtones and hostile confrontations during the campaign inevitably took a tragic turn. A week before the vote, Jo Cox, the mother of two young children and a popular Labour member of Parliament who was a strong Remain supporter, was shot and stabbed to death on the street in her constituency. The man accused of her murder, asked in court to give his name, would only say, "Death to traitors, freedom for Britain!"

As would occur in the American presidential election, postfactual journalism played a role in shaping the outcome. On the first day of

the vote, the anti-Europe *Daily Mail* newspaper published an inaccu-
rate story saying the European Union was preparing to admit Turkey as a member, which would give the right of free travel anywhere
in Britain and the twenty-seven other EU states to 76 million Turks.
Such misplaced fears clearly affected the decision of many voters. In
the northeast, where few immigrants live, local citizens were frightened that a new factory built by the Japanese automaker Nissan
would attract hordes of low-wage immigrants. Even those areas that
receive large-scale subsidies from the European Union, like Cornwall
and Wales, voted against their own financial interests and in favor of
Leave because of unfounded fears about a potential refugee surge.
Now the residents of those regions are asking the British government to
compensate them for their substantial loss of EU funds.

The biggest disappointment for the Remain camp turned out to
be young voters who were expected to be the decisive factor in keeping Britain in Europe. Many university students in Britain were
the most enthusiastic backers of staying in the European Union
and reveled in their ability to travel freely and live, work, or study
in any of twenty-eight member states. While 75 percent of eighteen-
to-twenty-five-year-olds who cast ballots voted Remain, only 39
percent of those over sixty-five years of age voted to stay in Europe.
The turnout among young people was 64 percent, higher than initial reports had indicated; but a remarkable 90 percent of those
over sixty-five voted and helped tilt the balance to the Leave camp.
Upon learning of the demographic patterns behind the British vote,
Martin Schulz, the president of the European Parliament, recalled
the famous words of George Bernard Shaw: "Old men are dangerous because it doesn't matter to them what is going to happen to the
world."

The government was counting on an overwhelming landslide
of ballots from young people in favor of Remain, but in the end fell
short. Some students, complacent in the belief that Remain would

win handily, later admitted they did not bother to vote either because they were preparing for their exams, celebrating the end of the school year, or heading off for a long weekend of music and entertainment. Within days after the referendum, many students showed their remorse by joining a petition campaign that drew more than 4 million signatures to hold a second vote, claiming they were not fully aware of the consequences.

Education was another clear divide: those who went to college voted to stay in Europe; those who left high school at age sixteen voted overwhelmingly to leave. The most visible dichotomy was between rich and poor, between prosperous cities and dilapidated towns. In London, where over 1 million immigrants from Europe now live and work, those who voted Remain comprised close to 60 percent, as was the case in the rejuvenated city of Manchester. Scotland, which has flourished with the help of a large influx of immigrants, also voted by 62 percent to Remain. Those in rural areas or small towns who were opposed to staying in Europe were not only those with little or no contact with immigrants and frightened by scare stories of foreign hordes about to invade Britain; they also included voters with a strong sense of nationalist nostalgia eager to see the island nation withdraw from the travails of continental Europe and retreat into the safe confines of smug Old England.

In that sense, the British referendum outcome neatly fit into the profile of the antiglobalization backlash that is driving populist insurgencies by voters against mainstream politicians in Europe and the United States. Just like jobless white males in industrial regions such as Michigan and Ohio who vented their frustration by voting for Donald Trump, many blue-collar Britons whose living standards suffered in recent years took their revenge on the pro-Remain establishment to express their dismay with the status quo. Cameron enlisted economists and business executives who argued that Britain would become much poorer by leaving the European

Union, but the Leave message of "Take Back Control!" resonated much more with older voters than the claim by Remain supporters that Britain would be "Stronger, Safer and Better Off" by staying in the European Union.

Yet in the end, Cameron's own political miscalculations led to his downfall. He had long disdained the Euroskeptics as a fringe group of "fruitcakes and loonies and closet racists." The voices of anti-Europe protagonists were effectively suppressed during New Labour's thirteen years in power under Tony Blair and Gordon Brown, followed by Cameron's first government in coalition with the pro-Europe Liberal Democrats. But in 2013, Cameron outraged his party's right wing by legalizing same-sex marriage in England and Wales just when the United Kingdom Independence Party was gaining support among right-wing conservatives.

In order to mollify far-right Euroskeptics in his own party, the prime minister announced plans to hold an in-or-out referendum by the end of 2017 about whether to remain in Europe. He said he was fed up with his fellow Conservatives who were always "banging on about Europe" and decided that he would put an end to the debate once and for all. In private, he said he never really believed that he would ever have to hold the referendum because he figured the coalition with Liberal Democrats would continue and they could be counted upon to veto any idea of holding the vote. Besides, in 1975, two years after first joining what was then called the European Economic Community, Britons had opted by a two-to-one margin under the Labour government of Prime Minister Harold Wilson to stay in Europe, so he figured he would be able to count on Labour's support—which turned out to be yet another mistake.

When Cameron defied the odds in the 2015 elections and surprised even himself to become the first Conservative leader in more than two decades to win a governing majority, his personal victory quickly became a liability. With his own party now fully in control of the government, he suddenly found himself backed into a corner on his earlier promise to hold a referendum about Europe. The UK Independence Party had won 4 million votes and continued to leach key Conservatives away from Cameron's party. So in February 2016, Cameron decided to roll the dice and announced that a plebiscite would be held four months later on June 23, when he thought warm weather and the imminent vacation season would put voters in a positive mood to vote Remain.

But Cameron's partners in Europe were dubious about holding the referendum. Europe nearly went off the rails when France and the Netherlands rejected the project of a European Constitution. German chancellor Merkel was particularly flabbergasted, telling visitors that she could not understand how "my good friend David" could be so foolish in taking such a reckless gamble. Merkel was prepared to do whatever she could to keep Britain in Europe, provided it would be consistent with EU treaties.

During a long weekend spent together with their spouses at the chancellor's medieval castle retreat in the Prussian woods about fifty miles north of Berlin, Merkel and Cameron held long discussions about how to craft a campaign strategy that would keep Europe's third-largest nation and biggest military power actively engaged on the continent. Merkel welcomed Britain's steadfast support of an open trading system that served Germany's interests because of its dependence on exports, which account for nearly half of the nation's economic output. But Merkel was not willing to grant Britain any further exemptions from EU rules; it had already been allowed to opt out of the European single currency zone, the Schengen Agreement on borderless travel, and Europe's social legislation. She insisted that if Britain were to remain part of Europe's single market, it would have to accept all of the "Four Freedoms" that are the core foundation of the European Union: free movement of goods, capital, services, and workers. Cameron reluctantly acceded to her wishes and managed to strike a deal calling for an "emergency brake" that would allow Britain to withhold access for benefits for new migrants for up to seven years. But the British press panned the arrangement as weak and ineffectual, particularly after the government reluctantly conceded that immigration in 2015 had soared to a record level of more than 330,000 people, well above the government's target of 100,000.

Cameron also felt personally betrayed by the decision of two prominent members of his inner circle of political allies to defect to the Leave campaign. Boris Johnson, the former mayor of London whose unkempt, iconoclastic style helped make him the country's most popular politician, cast his lot with the Leave campaign in a barely disguised challenge to Cameron's leadership. A former journalist who still writes a weekly column for the conservative *Telegraph* newspaper, Johnson acknowledged that he drafted two versions— one arguing in favor of Remain, the other for Leave—before deciding at the last minute to publish a column supporting the Leave campaign. At 10 Downing Street, Cameron could barely contain his rage about being knifed in the back by his ambitious friend. Johnson and Cameron had been classmates at Eton and Oxford, and they had enjoyed a warm and comradely relationship. After Johnson cast his lot with Leave, the two men stopped speaking to each other.

Cameron was equally incensed by the defection of another close friend, Michael Gove, the conservative justice minister who had been godfather to Cameron's late son, Ivan. Their wives were also good friends and they socialized together often, along with their children. Gove had agonized for months between his personal loyalty to Cameron and his fiercely Euroskeptic convictions before deciding to join the Leave campaign. He and Johnson were articulate, persuasive, and effective in communicating with mainstream voters in a way that those on the Euroskeptic fringe, led by Farage, were not. They kept the focus on the need to halt unfettered immigration and mocked the dire warnings of economic disaster from the Remain camp, known as "Project Fear," as a fantasy designed to intimidate voters. Meanwhile, Cameron and his team were pushed on the defensive by outlandish claims that Britain was being forced to contribute as much as 350 million pounds a week to the EU budget, a figure more than twice the true level of Britain's EU contribution. The Leave campaign suggested the same amount of money could be used instead to build a new hospital every week to relieve pressures on the National Health Service, a popular idea that Cameron could never quash even though it was clearly disingenuous.

Cameron's failure to connect with the voters during the referendum campaign caused him to plead for direct help from President Barack Obama. Although the White House had qualms about getting involved in British domestic politics, Obama recognized the stakes of Britain leaving Europe were too great for him to remain above the fray. Obama flew to London in April and made a direct appeal to British voters to stay in the European Union, saying it was in their own interests for Britain to preserve its global clout by remaining part of Europe.

Obama angered the Leave camp by warning that Britain would be "at the back of the queue" for a bilateral trade deal with the United States if it left the European Union. He thus undercut a key argument of the anti-Europe campaign that claimed the special partnership with the United States would be preserved by a new trade agreement. It was one of the strongest interventions by an American president in the political campaign of a friendly ally since the Cold War, yet it seemed to have little effect. A majority of British voters believed Obama's intervention was inappropriate; in any event, they said it would not affect their vote one way or the other.

Cameron realized that Obama's role would not be decisive. He believed the key to victory would be a strong Labour Party turnout in favor of staying in the European Union. He knew that the anti-Europe tabloid press—including mass circulation papers like the *Sun*, the

Express, and the *Daily Mail,* as well as the establishment *Telegraph* that castigates the EU "superstate" bureaucracy in Brussels—would inspire a majority of Conservative voters to opt for Leave. But he was confident that those votes would be offset by a substantial number of Labour Party members who would vote for Remain. It turned out to be one of his biggest political mistakes during his six years as prime minister.

Jeremy Corbyn, Labour's left-wing leader and an old-school socialist, had always distrusted the European Union as a capitalist club that served the interests of big business but not those of the working class. He was also disinclined to do any favors for Cameron. Corbyn believed that Labour's help in saving the cohesion of the United Kingdom during the Scottish independence campaign in 2014 had contributed to the party's electoral disaster in Scotland a year later in the general election.

Even though former Labour prime ministers Tony Blair and Gordon Brown were willing to campaign with the Tories, Corbyn refused to offer any help to his rival. He showed no desire to mobilize Labour voters and went on vacation just weeks before the vote was held. His derelict role caused an insurrection within Labour Party ranks after the referendum that Corbyn and his supporters quickly put down, but it showed yet again how mainstream parties in Western democracies these days have very little sway with voters. In the depressed regions of northern England, the Midlands and Wales, where Labour voters are dominant, the Leave turnout was surprisingly strong despite Labour's previous support for Europe.

Many of these lower- and middle-class citizens wanted to cast a protest vote against the European Union, which they saw as an avatar of the globalization forces they despise. They believed that Europe had evolved into a spiteful symbol of their discontent, in particular as a primary cause of their declining living standards due to factories shutting down, jobs going to foreign workers who gladly accept cheap wages, and state subsidies being cut off.

During the evening of June 23, as votes were being counted, the initial results looked positive for Cameron and his team. It seemed that the economic arguments in favor of Remain were convincing voters that staying in the European Union was a stable and secure choice. But as the evening wore on, the bad news started coming in. Cameron's communications director, Craig Oliver, and his American consultant, Jim Messina, who had served as Obama's campaign guru, noticed that Labour strongholds, like Sunderland in the depressed northeast, were defying predictions and voting in favor of Leave. In the final days, they had become extremely worried that all the energy and enthusiasm seemed to be channeled into protest votes against the government by poorer regions. The Remain camp had failed to make a convincing case that life for people in Britain was going to be better if they opted to remain in Europe. By midnight, Cameron realized the game was over. He started preparing his resignation speech to be given in the morning.

The referendum outcome roiled the markets and caused $2 trillion in value to be clipped from global stocks in a single day. The pound crashed to its lowest level in thirty years and would continue to decline against the dollar in the months to come. At first, the sharp drop in the pound would help to boost exports and attract tourists, but over time it would push up food prices since Britain imports about 40 percent of what it consumes.

With the leadership of both major parties now in question and Britain's future uncertain, Scotland's first minister, Nicola Sturgeon, announced that since Scottish voters wanted badly to remain inside the European Union, a redo of the 2014 vote over Scotland's independence would become "highly likely." The deputy first minister of Northern Ireland also hinted at a break from the United Kingdom in order to join the Republic of Ireland and thus remain inside the European Union. With Britain starting to look like it was coming apart at the seams, the Union's other twenty-seven members insisted they would do everything in their power to prevent the secessionist contagion from spreading to other countries where the EU was losing popularity, including Italy and France.

The departure of Britain—one of the "big three" pillars of the European Union—threatened to endanger nearly seven decades of European integration that had brought a remarkable degree of peace and prosperity to a continent ravaged for more than a millennium by bloody nationalist conflicts. Under Article 50 of the 2002 Lisbon Treaty, a member state that wishes to leave the European Union must announce its intentions and then engage in two years of negotiations to make a clean break.

Some EU leaders held out hope that Britain would reconsider once it began to comprehend the enormous costs and colossal administrative burdens in terminating a forty-three-year relationship with Europe. French President François Hollande said Britain must not be shown any special treatment and should be made to realize how bleak and uncomfortable life outside the EU will be, if only to show others that any path out of the European Union will be difficult to navigate. The target of Hollande's message was clearly the French and not the British voter: the right-wing National Front had already vowed to follow Cameron's example of holding a referendum on EU membership if party leader Marine Le Pen were to be elected president in May 2017 elections.

But other leaders said the will of the British people should be respected and that Europe should not act out of spite or vindictiveness. Merkel acknowledged that the British decision was irreversible and that Britain should be given some time to think over its options. But she also insisted that Britain would not receive favorable treatment and that any "cherry picking" by keeping benefits and ignoring costs was out of the question. Jean-Claude Juncker, the European Commission president, likened the situation to a romantic breakup. "When a girlfriend leaves you, you should not gaze after her forever," he told a top aide. "At some point, it's time to start looking around at other girls."

But the relationship between Britain and Europe was more like a decades-long marriage rather than like a summer fling. Juncker said he realized the divorce would be painful and complicated. But he insisted the onus of responsibility for Britain's plight laid squarely with the Cameron government because of its frequent carping about a so-called "European superstate" in Brussels harming British interests. "I do not consider David Cameron to be the enemy," Juncker told his aide. "But if you keep telling people for years that something is wrong with the European Union, you cannot be taken by surprise if the voters believe you."

Cameron's sudden resignation triggered a vicious leadership struggle within his party that many likened to the kind of treachery seen in the "House of Cards." Both Johnson and Gove, who together had spearheaded the Brexit campaign, seemed genuinely astonished by their victory. They vanished from public view in the aftermath of the vote and showed no signs of having prepared a strategy of what to do once they had convinced 17 million Britons to back their call to leave Europe. Johnson, as the country's most popular politician, was considered the natural heir to Cameron. Gove agreed early on to support his ally's campaign to become prime minister and head of the Conservative Party.

But within days, Gove seemed to develop second thoughts. He complained to friends about Johnson's chaotic behavior and questioned whether he had the temperament or the self-discipline required to run the country. He also feared that Johnson would renege on a commitment to leave the European Union and seek some kind of compromise deal that would outrage Brexit voters. Gove decided instead to make his own bid for the prime minister's job, informing Johnson in a late-night telephone call that he would be challenging him for the party leadership.

Johnson was dumbfounded. His staff had booked London's Saint Ermin's Hotel, where Johnson's hero, Winston Churchill, had established Britain's wartime special operations headquarters, to announce in the morning the formal launch of his campaign to become prime minister. Instead, just a few minutes before the noon deadline to enter the Conservative leadership race, Johnson raised the white flag and said that "in view of the circumstances in parliament" he had decided he could not become the country's next prime minister.

•The news of Gove's betrayal scandalized many prominent Tory members and doomed his hopes as well of winning the leadership battle. Johnson's departure after Gove stabbed him in the back left Theresa May, who had served as home secretary in charge of immigration matters for the past six years, as the only clear frontrunner. As one of four senior cabinet members under Cameron, May had remained loyal albeit as a lukewarm supporter of the Remain camp in the belief that Britain's security interests were best assured by staying in the European Union. But in the aftermath of the Leave camp's victory, she promised that the will of the people would be respected by her government and that "Brexit means Brexit."

May was viewed within the party as a tough, no-nonsense minister with an obsession for details who kept her head down and stuck to her brief. When Tory elder statesman Kenneth Clarke described her as "a bloody difficult woman" ahead of the leadership vote, she made a virtue out of his criticism and endeared herself to the Euroskeptics by saying "the next person to find that out will be [EU Commission President] Jean-Claude Juncker."

When Cameron resigned, he fully expected to stay on in a caretaker role as prime minister for several months while the party sorted out who would become his successor. But May, to the surprise of many of her colleagues, rallied enough support to take over the party leadership sooner than expected and moved into 10 Downing Street less than three weeks after the Brexit vote. She sought to unite the party and secure her own personal authority by appointing several anti-Europe politicians to key cabinet posts in a bid to gain their loyalty: David Davis was named to head up a special ministry as the chief negotiator to take Britain out of Europe; former defense minister Liam Fox became the new trade minister with a mission to build a network of new commercial agreements once Britain leaves the EU; and, to the amazement of pundits, including himself, Johnson was appointed foreign minister to serve as the face of May's government to the outside world.

Upon taking office as prime minister, May quickly showed that she would run the country much differently than Cameron. She fired several ministers close to him, including his heir apparent George Osborne, the chancellor of the exchequer. In her inaugural speech, she vowed to address the social injustices and class divisions that had grown more acute under Cameron's austerity policies and insisted that she had no intention of governing "on behalf of the privileged few." May attributes her desire to create a fairer society to the moral values she learned from her father, an Anglican vicar, whose death in a car crash when she was twenty-five left her devastated, but determined to make a difference through politics. She once told a party gathering that Conservatives needed to change their public image as "the nasty party" with a cruel and heartless attitude toward the downtrodden. The referendum vote, she declared upon becoming prime minister, was not just a mandate to leave the European Union but also a demand for serious social change from people "who had lost control of their day-to-day lives." She emphasized that her government was determined "to build a country that works for everyone."

May's social conscience is tempered by a deeply pragmatic streak, according to close aides who say that when confronted by a perplexing problem she focuses on the most practical solution she can find. That aspect of her character will be sorely tested by the challenge of taking Britain out of the European Union. In her address to the Tory party conference three months after taking power, May vowed she would invoke Article 50 of the Lisbon Treaty by the end of March 2017 (which she did). The clock then started ticking on a two-year negotiating process to achieve the approval of a deal in 2019, a year before Britain's next national elections are scheduled to be held. The biggest challenge she will face during these complex negotiations will be holding firm to her promise that Britain will take back control of its borders in order to curtail immigration while at the same time persuading her European partners to allow Britain to remain part of the EU customs union and single market.

All EU member states have made it clear that if Britain stays in the EU single market it will have to accept free movement of labor—which May's government has insisted is unacceptable. May faces tough bargaining over the Brexit bill, which some experts believe could run as high as $60 billion over the next decade to pay off EU-funded projects and its contributions to EU pension funds. The impact on Britain's service economy could mean the loss of as many as 75,000 jobs, $50 billion in lost annual revenues, and $12 billion in lost taxes.

May's first contacts with other European leaders have left them perplexed about how she will conduct the negotiations. She strikes many of her peers as phlegmatic and reluctant to reveal many of her inner feelings. She has come across to them as all business, without much in the way of a sense of humor. One aspect of her professional profile that is readily apparent is her feminism. In contrast to Britain's first female prime minister, Margaret Thatcher, May has taken an active interest in bolstering the political fortunes of other women. She founded a group called Women2Win which actively campaigns to elect more Conservative women to Parliament. While Thatcher preferred the company of other male politicians and did little or nothing to help other women seeking elected office, May has built a powerful network of devoted women supporters who operate below the radar of the male-dominated political establishment.

Since she first entered Parliament in 1997, May has helped increase the number of female Conservative members in the body from thirteen to sixty-eight. Besides her feminist politics on behalf of other women, she is also different from Thatcher in having a keen flair for fashion that is avidly followed by the British press, who document her unusual choices such as leopard-print heeled shoes. She says her only luxury is a lifetime subscription to *Vogue* magazine. "You can be clever and like clothes," she once said. "One of the challenges for women in politics is to be ourselves."

In making her first trip abroad as prime minister, May decided to travel to Berlin to call on another female politician: Germany's chancellor Angela Merkel. May says she has long admired Merkel for her low-key, head-down diligence in the way she governs, which led many of her male rivals to misjudge her tenacity. Both women share much in common—they are daughters of Protestant clergymen who imbued them with a strong sense of moral duty to help those in need. They are both without children, rather aloof and disdainful of socializing with other politicians, preferring to spend their private time with their taciturn husbands, who stay scrupulously in the background. During a long discussion about Europe followed by dinner, Merkel and May struck up a cordial relationship—but there was little or no warmth.

After consulting in advance with other EU leaders, Merkel delivered a blunt message to May: there would be no special treatment. If

Britain wanted to remain in Europe's single market, like other outside countries such as Norway and Switzerland, it would have to accept the European Union's core rules allowing the free movement of goods, capital, services, and workers. Since the main goal of those who voted for Brexit was to stop the unfettered flow of European workers into Britain and take back control of immigration policy, May seemed to face an impossible quest even before negotiations started.

After her first round of meetings with her European peers, May recognized the acute difficulty of Britain's dilemma: If Britain stays in the single market to protect its trade relationship, it will have to accept free movement of labor. Yet by remaining part of the customs union, it will lose the opportunity to negotiate bilateral trade deals with third countries. But stepping out of these arrangements would also take Britain out of many multinational supply chains, with huge costs in terms of trade, investment, and most of all, employment. The forces of globalization are such an established fact of life that virtually every line of international business is now defined by intricate cross-border supply chains in which a finished product has multiple origins. Any disruption of that chain would force a country to drop out of the large-scale manufacturing process, in particular for automobiles, which for Britain would mean a huge loss of jobs.

From the start, Merkel and other EU leaders wanted to signal a hardline approach toward Britain in order to discourage secessionist movements in France and the Netherlands and show there would be a steep cost for any populist attempt to leave the Union. After considering all options, Merkel believed that offering any softer choice to May's government could ultimately lead to the unraveling of the European Union. While Merkel sees Britain's departure as a foregone conclusion, others still hold out hope that the economic costs will make Britons change their mind. Former British prime ministers Tony Blair and John Major have started a campaign to convince their compatriots to reconsider the costs of leaving Europe, which is already being called the most expensive divorce in history.

But EU leaders say they have no time to entertain such a fantasy. When Boris Johnson met with other EU foreign ministers for the first time and later said he believed that the British "might be able to have their cake and eat it too," he was rudely slapped down by Donald Tusk, the president of the Union's Council of Ministers. Speaking on behalf of the EU's twenty-seven government leaders, Tusk said in very blunt language that Johnson was being completely delusional. "The brutal truth is that Brexit will be a loss for all of us," Tusk said. "There will be no cakes on the table for anyone. There will be only salt and vinegar."

Tusk said the May government should brace for very painful consequences that will ensue if Britain follows through with its vow to leave Europe. In his warning, Tusk held out a small ray of hope that the financial burdens involved in departing the European Union would bring May and her government to their senses. He wished she might consider holding a new referendum to reverse the decision to leave Europe, but admitted such an option was a long shot. "The only real alternative to a hard Brexit is no Brexit at all," Tusk said. "Even if, today, hardly anyone believes in such a possibility."

As May delved more deeply during her first months in office into the details of the administrative and economic burdens involved in pulling out of Europe, she acknowledged to close friends that she was astonished by the magnitude of the task. Taking the country out of the European Union would soon become the biggest peacetime project ever undertaken by a British government. She was pleased, if only out of spite, that she had appointed to her cabinet several prominent anti-Europe ministers—principally Davis, Fox, and Johnson—and saddled them with the onerous mission of finding a way out of Europe. But she also realized that ultimately she would be held accountable.The plunge in the value of the pound that followed the Brexit vote soon started pushing up food prices, triggering a consumer uproar when grocery stores felt compelled to briefly remove local specialties such as Marmite spread from supermarket shelves.

Every week seemed to bring news of additional costs that Britain would have to bear: the government did not realize that Britain, for example, is responsible for an 8 percent share in funding the European Union's 60-billion-euro pension fund. May's decision to trigger the two-year negotiating process by March 2017 deprived her government of some leverage, but she felt she had no choice because of pressure from the Brexiteers. How will she compensate for the loss of EU funds to Britain's elite universities and top medical and scientific research centers? She also realized that Britain would have to revise more than fifty free trade agreements that until now had been covered by the European Union within the World Trade Organization. When Davis informed the government that up to nine hundred accountants, lawyers, and other negotiators would be required for the tasks of managing Brexit, a recruiting campaign was launched in Australia, New Zealand, and Canada to find suitable personnel to help prepare for the negotiations with the EU.

Most of all, the United Kingdom now will face renewed pressure to maintain the cohesion of its own union. Scotland is likely to reexamine its options and may again pursue independence through a second referendum. Northern Ireland will be tempted to explore how to remain within the European Union by integrating with the Republic of Ireland. These secessionist movements could inflict a heavy blow to Britain and result in the loss of more than 5 million citizens and one-third of its land mass. Britain's departure will also be expensive for Europe. The loss of the EU's second-biggest contributor in terms of financial payments will require a net shrinkage in the European Union budget by about 10 billion euros. That will increase the economic load carried by the remaining member states. The German finance ministry estimates that Germany alone will have to pay an extra 5 billion euros a year starting in 2019.

Many Europeans, however, have become resigned to seeing Britain leave. Ever since the end of World War II, Britain has maintained an ambivalent connection to continental Europe. Once Britain's colonial empire began to dissipate and the United States and the Soviet Union emerged as the new rival superpowers, Prime Minister Harold Macmillan felt he had no choice but to join the European integration process. His bids were rejected twice by French president Charles De Gaulle, who never believed Britain could ever be part of the continent. When Britain was finally allowed under Tory prime minister Edward Heath to join the European Economic Community in 1973, as it was known at the time, there was no great display of enthusiasm.

Even after an initial referendum held two years later succeeded by a two-to-one margin under the Labour government of Harold Wilson, Britain always seemed to have one foot in Europe and one foot out. For more than a decade, Margaret Thatcher disrupted European summit meetings with her constant demands for a British rebate, insisting her country got a raw deal and should not have to be such a large net contributor to the EU budget. Later, following the fall of the Berlin Wall and Germany's reunification, Britain refused to join Europe's plans for a single currency in 1992 and insisted it would not be part of EU social legislation.

Britain has long cherished its proud identity as "the sceptered isle" that maintained a safe distance from the continent. When bad weather halts shipping across the English Channel, British tabloids still like to report that "fog has cut off Europe from Britain." Such parochial sentiments, combined with growing anxiety about the immigration crisis afflicting Europe, eventually pushed many British voters to disregard their own economic interests and "take back control" of their nation. But as a former colonial empire whose global clout continues to diminish, Britain may find that its presence on the world stage will shrink even more dramatically in the years to come. That, in turn, will cause Europe as a whole to lose clout in the world. It is an outcome that both Britain and Europe will regret.

CHAPTER THREE

PARIS

IN SEARCH OF LOST GLORY

THE ÉLYSÉE PALACE WHERE FRENCH PRESIDENTS HAVE LIVED and worked for nearly 150 years resonates with majestic grandeur. You enter through an imposing black iron gate at 55 rue du Faubourg Saint-Honoré where Republican Guard members adorned in feather plumes and bayonets guide you across a gravel courtyard before entering the famed Hall of Honor, where the president greets visiting foreign leaders. There, a sculpture honoring the French Revolution, composed of 200 white marble flags, is framed by two stunning crystal and bronze candelabras.

You climb the Murat Staircase, with its handrail adorned in gilded palm leaves, to reach the first floor. There you are greeted by a bronze statue by Auguste Rodin, which stands before an 1811 painting by Dubois called *Europe*. Then you walk through two antechambers filled with portraits of former presidents of the republic before entering the vaunted seat of power. The Golden Room, which serves as the president's office, is decorated with Gobelin tapestries and a Napoleon III crystal chandelier. As you sit down across from France's paramount

leader, the most striking effect is the soft warmth and serenity con-
veyed by the masterpiece in the room: an uncluttered Louis XV walnut
desk, now occupied by Emmanuel Macron. In May 2017, thirty-nine-
year-old Macron achieved a remarkable ascendancy to France's most
powerful office by capturing 66 percent of the vote in the presidential
run-off as an independent centrist candidate, despite having never
held elective office nor received the backing of a major political party.

The ministers who run the day-to-day affairs of the French government also enjoy the plush trappings of imperial luxury. The prime
minister is ensconced in the grandiose Hôtel Matignon on the Rue
de Varenne, where Talleyrand once wined and dined Europe's aris-
tocratic elite. The culture minister defends the virtues of arts, film,
and letters in the stunning Palais Royal, once the personal residence
of Cardinal Richelieu. The justice minister oversees courts and prisons from the Hôtel de Bourvallais on the Place Vendome, next door
to the ornate Hôtel Ritz. In another elaborate palace on the banks of
the Seine along the Quai d'Orsay, France's chief diplomat ponders the
state of the world, negotiates treaties, and supervises 163 embassies
just as his predecessors have done ever since Henri III appointed
Louis de Revol as the world's first foreign minister in 1589.

These sumptuous privileges have traditionally steered France's
best and brightest students into lifelong careers in government,
where they are assured of comfortable perquisites and insulated
against the laws of the jungle competition in the private sector.
While France has its share of successful engineers, business executives, or internet entrepreneurs, the first choice of many graduates is
to seek the cushy security of government jobs. Macron followed that
path to power by studying at the elite schools of Sciences Po and the
École Nationale d'Administration (ENA) before becoming an investment banker with Rothschild. He later served as economy minister
in the Socialist government but resigned when his reform plans
were rejected. He then launched his own political movement En

Marche (On the Move!) to promote a radical reform agenda designed to unleash France's entrepreneurial energies and curtail the role of government in people's lives.

More than one in five French people are employed by the state. The public sector controls about 57 percent of the French economy, a higher proportion than in any Western nation except Finland. The cosseted life of senior civil servants may explain why France's ruling elite seems so far removed from the quotidian travails of the people. Their privileged existence is stirring greater controversy than ever before about whether the state is more of a problem than the solution to what ails the country. Macron has promised to eliminate 120,000 government jobs and shrink the heavy footprint of the French state. He also wants to relax French labor laws to make it easier for businesses to hire and fire people.

The 2017 presidential race was one of the most tumultuous campaigns in French political history. One by one, the favored candidates were spurned by voters yearning for dramatic change. Among the traditional conservatives, former president Nicolas Sarkozy and former prime minister Alain Juppe were spurned in the primary vote in favor of François Fillon, also a former prime minister, who promised a Thatcherite revolution that would prune the state sector and encourage the growth of private business. He also promised to instill greater integrity in the political class.But he became embroiled in a scandal for having put his wife and children on his parliamentary payroll for doing little or no work. The fact that Fillon's nepotism was legal and that other members of the National Assembly routinely followed the same practice of employing their family members only heightened public outrage over the special privileges enjoyed by the ruling elite.

On the left, Socialist president Francois Hollande's performance was so dismal that he decided not to run for reelection. His prime minister, Manuel Valls, a tough, probusiness politician, expected to win the party's nomination handily but was upset by a more progressive candidate, Benoît Hamon. He was so obscure during the campaign that he barely won 6 percent of the vote in the first presidential round. Hamon was overshadowed on the left by the quasi-Communist candidate Jean-Luc Mélenchon, who ran on an anti-Europe, soak-the-rich platform that included a 100 percent tax on incomes over 400,000 euros. Voter disaffection with the ruling class, encompassing the center-left Socialists and center-right Républicains who have taken turns running the country in the postwar era, was so great that the mainstream parties failed for the first time in sixty years to make it into the presidential run-off. That left Macron and his start-up movement pitted against the far-right candidate Marine Le Pen. It was seen as a battle between open markets and internationalism versus populism and protectionism. When Macron emerged as the victor, virtually all of Europe breathed a sigh of relief that Le Pen and xenophobic, anti-European campaign had been decisively rejected by French voters.

Although Le Pen and her National Front party were defeated, they still won almost 11 million votes—more than double the number her father won in the 2002 presidential election. She vowed to lead the opposition to Macron's presidency and predicted she would expand support for her message of populist nationalism ahead of the next election in five years. France remains deeply divided over whether to embrace Le Pen's call to retreat into a nationalistic, protected cocoon or to accept Macron's difficult mission to transform itself into a modern, dynamic presence in Europe and in the world. The young president chose to deliver his victory speech by walking somberly to a stage in front of the Louvre's glass pyramid heralded by the European anthem of Beethoven's "Ode to Joy" rather than France's traditional "Marseillaise." As he spoke to the nation after his election, Macron sensed the enormity of the challenge ahead of him, acknowledging that he is well aware of "the anger, the anxiety, the doubts" of a fragmented society divided between those who have suffered and those who have profited from the forces of globalization.

More than two centuries after its violent overthrow of the monarchy shook Europe to its core, France at times appears on the brink of renewed revolutionary fervor. Strikes, protests, and wanton acts of destruction have become more frequent throughout the country since the global financial crisis of 2008. Resistance to France's governing class has grown so entrenched that even the most basic proposals to improve schools, labor markets, and the welfare state can trigger street marches and work stoppages that routinely paralyze the country. Even more than in the United States and other Western countries where populist movements are flourishing, much of France seethes with disgust and resentment about what the sociologist Michel Crozier first diagnosed four decades ago as a "stalled society" (la société bloquée). A prime reason for this protracted stasis is considered to be the self-serving governing caste, which has lost the trust of the French people to carry out the kinds of reforms needed to revitalize the country.

To an outsider, the exalted role of the state and France's illustrious history give the impression that the country still has an abiding destiny to play a leading role in the world. Yet behind the façade of fading glory, France faces a daunting array of crises that is testing its fundamental identity in ways that some experts believe could eventually lead to the collapse of the Fifth Republic. Blinded by the nation's past grandeur, France's ruling elite seems more remote from the problems of common citizens than ever before. Public support for the mainstream parties has plummeted because of years of financial scandals and ineffectual governing.

Opinion polls show more than three-quarters of the population believes France's political leadership is corrupt. Public disgust with the ruling aristocracy has fueled the growth in popular support for the National Front. Under Marine Le Pen, who inherited the leadership of the far-right movement from her father, Jean-Marie, the National Front has softened its rough extremist edges and now focuses its message on disillusionment with the elite, the antiglobalization backlash against the European Union, and the dilution of France's Catholic identity by the influx of Muslim immigrants. During the campaign, Le Pen hammered away at Macron's elitist background as a graduate of posh schools and as a wealthy investment banker. She will no doubt continue playing the class conflict card as a prominent voice in the political opposition.

Le Pen projects a much more polished image than did her bullying father, who was expelled from the party for crude anti-Semitic remarks, such as dismissing the Holocaust as "a detail of history." Twice divorced, and with a current partner who is the Front's vice president, Marine Le Pen believes that time and momentum is on her side. Throughout her political career, she has often predicted that she would be ensconced in the Élysée Palace no later than 2022 and still hopes to achieve that goal if Macron should fail. She derides the governing elites for living in Bourbon royal luxury while ignoring the deteriorating plight of common French citizens. She has cleverly expanded the Front's appeal and recruited many young professionals into the party. At the same time, Le Pen has remained faithful to its core message about the need to restore respect for law and order, curtail Muslim immigration, and revive French national identity.

Like Donald Trump in the United States, Le Pen's populist themes have found a receptive audience among many French voters who have grown dismayed by what they perceive as the decline and decay of their country. She has attracted some of her strongest backers from industrial workers, many of whom were once devotees of the Communist Party but now feel greater political kinship with the xenophobic far right. These sentiments have hardened since the 2008 global financial crisis badly damaged France's competitive position in the world.

More than 1,000 factories have been shut down in the last five years, and France's industrial sector, in terms of value added, is now only half as large as that of Germany. What was once a thriving industrial region in northern France, based on coal and steel, now looks abandoned and desolate. The economy is languishing to such a degree that youth unemployment hovers around 25 percent, spawning a brain drain that is driving ambitious young men and women to leave the country and seek their fortunes in London, New York, or Silicon Valley.

Most worrisome of all, the core security of the state has come under threat from radical Islamist terrorists who have staged a string of brutal attacks that have killed hundreds of French civilians. Many of those involved in the jihadist violence have turned out to be second and third generation Muslims born and raised in France but who feel alienated from its secular society. Some of them were among an estimated 1,500 French Muslims who have traveled to Syria to fight on behalf of the Islamic State.

As home to Europe's largest population of Muslims, France now faces the prospect of living in a permanent state of emergency, anxiously awaiting what many fear will be the next wave of attacks. Meanwhile, the government's repeated efforts to reconcile disparate communities divided by racial and religious tensions are perceived as increasingly futile, further eroding public confidence in political leadership.

How did France reach such a dire condition? For much of the postwar era, France was considered the paragon of the good life and the envy of much of the world, blending elegance with erudition, along with a keen appreciation for fine wines, excellent food, and the arts. While its famed "joie de vivre" has assumed a lower profile in an age of terrorism, France still possesses many assets and virtues. Despite the primacy of the state, there are many world-class private business corporations, such as the luxury brand group LVMH, the tire manufacturer Michelin, and the aircraft maker Airbus.

Thanks to the thirty-five-hour work week, French workers spend

far less time than their American counterparts at the office. Many can
retire at age sixty; if and when they are laid off, French workers enjoy
unemployment benefits as high as $8,000 a month. France offers
excellent health care for its entire population at much less cost than in
the United States. It enjoys the highest birth rate in all of Europe, with
much healthier demographics than Germany, Japan, or China, in part
because of hefty tax incentives for large families. Working mothers
are encouraged to remain in the labor force more than in other societies thanks to full-day child care that is subsidized by the government.
French schoolchildren earn some of the highest rankings in the world
for their knowledge of mathematics, literature, and philosophy.

But France also suffers from bloated government, a stubborn
reluctance to embrace stricter economic discipline in order to adapt
to fierce global competition, and a lack of social mobility that discour-
ages the rise of a meritocracy. While the French constitution offers
more powers to the presidency than is granted to any other leader
in a Western democracy, a succession of French heads of state from
both the right and the left have failed to enact an aggressive reform
agenda to deal with the country's structural problems because they
fear an eruption of hostile protests in the streets.

As a result, the glory and grandeur of France that is so often evoked
by presidents and prime ministers sounds ever more hollow. Indeed,
French leadership in Europe and the world risks becoming a relic of
the past. More than at any time in the postwar era, France's stature
in Europe has been overshadowed by a powerful Germany, whose
growing domination of the continent carries haunting echoes for a
neighbor with whom it shares a bloody history of conflicts going back
more than five centuries. The dysfunctional relationship between a
dynamic Germany and a feeble France has become a major factor in
the distorted balance of power within the European Union.

The French-German axis has served as the driving force of the
European Union for more than six decades, dating back to the early

days of recovery after World War II. After the humiliation of Germany's four-year occupation during the war, President Charles de Gaulle embarked with obsessive zeal on restoring France to what he saw as its rightful place in the pantheon of global leadership. France became a nuclear power and one of the five permanent members of the United Nations Security Council. As the economy rebounded from the devastation of the war, France thrived during an unprecedented era of success celebrated today as *les trente glorieuses,* or three decades of glorious peace and prosperity.

Meanwhile, two French statesmen, Jean Monnet and Robert Schuman, promoted the idea that France could best advance its strategic interests through a Europe that merged its coal and steel industries in order to make future wars with Germany impossible. De Gaulle sought to fortify the French-German partnership as the nucleus of a revitalized Western Europe by striking a close personal bond with Germany's first postwar chancellor, Konrad Adenauer. De Gaulle's script for Europe's triumphant return to the global stage envisioned France providing political guidance while Germany supplied economic clout. He likened the relationship to that of a horse and carriage, "with Germany being the horse and France the coachman."

In the wake of the 1956 Suez crisis, de Gaulle felt betrayed "by perfidious Albion" when Britain decided to cast its lot with the United States rather than build a new partnership with continental Europe. De Gaulle never forgave Britain's decision to pivot toward a special relationship with Washington. He later vetoed on two occasions Britain's attempt to join the Common Market, the precursor of the European Union, and it was only after he left power that Britain succeeded in becoming a member of the "country club" in 1973.

As France and Britain, under pressure from the United States, beat a hasty retreat from their colonial zones of influence in the Middle East after Suez, Adenauer consoled de Gaulle by telling his prime minister, Guy Mollet, that "Europe shall be your revenge." He and de Gaulle then moved ahead in forging the partnership that would steer European integration in its early years, with Germany deploying its growing economic might in tandem with France's political clout as a nuclear power and permanent member of the United Nations Security Council. Later, Helmut Schmidt and Valéry Giscard d'Estaing would build on that cooperation in laying the foundations together, first as finance ministers and later as heads of government, for Europe's economic and monetary union.

Then, in return for French acceptance of German unification after the fall of the Berlin Wall, Chancellor Helmut Kohl decided to abandon Germany's cherished deutschmark in favor of a single European currency, the euro. His closest advisors had warned Kohl that the euro would not survive without being backed by a fiscal union, but Kohl believed that moving full speed ahead with the euro was a price that must be paid to assuage French anxieties. French president François Mitterrand insisted that Germany's expansion in terms of territory and population into a Central European powerhouse with 82 million citizens required an irrevocable embrace of European unity through the single currency.

Despite their opposite political leanings, Kohl struck up a close personal bond with Mitterrand. A devout European federalist, Kohl told me that one of his most moving experiences was clasping hands with Mitterrand as they commemorated the seventieth anniversary of the killing fields at Verdun, where so many French and German soldiers lost their lives. In sacrificing Germany's vaunted symbol of postwar economic recovery in favor of the euro, Kohl believed that his gamble was worth the price of assuring France that Germany would channel its growing might in the interests of a more united Europe.

But Mitterrand's fears would prove prescient. As the European Union expanded in size to embrace former Communist states in Eastern Europe, the continent's center of gravity abruptly shifted toward Germany's newly restored capital in Berlin. The French-German connection began to unravel after the Social Democratic chancellor Gerhard Schröder undertook a series of painful labor market reforms that would set the stage for a remarkable economic recovery. Germany would soon emerge from its status as "the sick man of Europe," while France lapsed into a state of decline.

Schröder's reforms outraged his working-class constituents who form a large bloc of Social Democratic voters, costing him the 2005 election that brought Angela Merkel and the Christian Democrats to power. Merkel and her center-right government would benefit from the bold and courageous reforms adopted by Schröder, whose political career was ruined by the pain associated with the recovery plan. Germany moved ahead in restructuring its economy and adapted to the harsh winds of global competition at a time when France would continue to stagnate. By repeatedly postponing a similar economic overhaul, the French leaders, by their neglect, created a disequilibrium between the two European partners that has damaged the partnership. As Merkel told close aides on several occasions, "France's weakness has become one of Europe's—and Germany's—biggest problems."

The imbalance has been aggravated by Merkel's difficult personal relations with two French presidents, the center-right Républicain Nicolas Sarkozy and the center-left Socialist François Hollande. Merkel hoped to pursue the postwar tradition of a French-German leadership duo with Sarkozy, but she found it difficult to deal with his impetuous, insecure personality. For his part, Sarkozy complained about Merkel's lack of imagination and her slow, ponderous style, comparing her to an old diesel truck that chugs along so slowly it often takes months to reach its destination.

He would make catty asides about her to colleagues at European summits, telling his peers that "she tells me she is on a diet and then takes a second helping of cheese." Such remarks would invariably find their way back to the German delegation, displeasing Merkel all the more. Once Sarkozy tried to make amends for his intemperate outbursts. "Angela, we are made to get along. We are the head and legs of the European Union," he told her. But Merkel was not amused nor impressed. "No, Nicolas, you are the head and legs. I am the bank."

Merkel hoped for a fresh start when Hollande defeated Sarkozy in the 2012 election to become France's first Socialist president since Mitterrand. But she was sorely disappointed by his reluctance to embark on the labor and educational reforms that France desperately required to catch up with Germany and become once again an equal partner. Hollande's lackluster record and ineffectual leadership was not helped by his strange behavior, such as when he was caught on camera leaving his mistress's apartment on the back of a motor scooter driven by his bodyguard. He privately mocked the poor, insulting them for their bad teeth and poor hygiene. As a Socialist leader whose party's principles were based on improving the plight of the disadvantaged, Hollande's remarks only served to illustrate how aloof and cynical he and his party had become during their years in power.

Late into his five-year presidential term, Hollande's standing with voters had sunk so low that opinion polls showed he had only a 4 percent approval rating. No other French president since World War II had ever dropped to such depths in public esteem. Bruno Cautres, one of the architects of the survey, described the findings as one of the most devastating results in the history of French postwar political leadership. "For the French," he said, "it was confirmation that Hollande doesn't know how to behave like a president." Faced with such miserable poll numbers, Hollande announced six months before the end of his term that he would not run for reelection.

Hollande's decision not to run for a second term transformed the presidential campaign into a wide-open race that was viewed as critical not just for France but for all of Europe. In recent years, the absence of strong French leadership had not just undermined the partnership between Paris and Berlin but had impeded progress toward a more functional and cohesive European Union. Hollande's pitiful reputation with the voters and other European leaders had demoralized his cabinet colleagues, who believed he was inflicting serious harm on the country's image that would prove difficult to alleviate. During the Greek debt crisis, in which France eventually persuaded Merkel to keep Greece within the eurozone, French ministers involved in the heated EU debate complained about the dismissive attitude their European colleagues had adopted toward them.

At one meeting in Brussels, Pierre Moscovici, a former Socialist finance minister who had left the French government to become vice president for economic affairs at the EU Commission, spotted his old friend and successor, finance minister Michel Sapin. Both had been Socialist whiz kids whose political careers flourished under the mentorship of France's president François Mitterrand. After serving as finance minister, Moscovici passed the baton to Sapin and moved to Brussels to become the European Union's vice president for economic affairs.

At the meeting, Moscovici pulled Sapin aside and made an impassioned plea on behalf of poor southern European countries suffering under crushing debts and tough austerity measures imposed by Germany. "You must stand up to the Germans now, or we could face an economic disaster for all of Europe," Moscovici said. With a wistful sigh, Sapin responded in a way that illustrated the new power realities of Europe. "You don't understand, cher ami," Sapin said. "La France is not what it used to be."

France's diminished influence with Germany and the rest of Europe is not based solely on the personal shortcomings of its leaders. There are many social and economic factors that have contributed to its decline, including high taxes that have steadily eroded economic growth, an expansive state sector, and a failure to encourage entrepreneurial dynamism that has spawned a brain drain. The quest for better jobs has driven more than 300,000 French people to live in London, making it France's sixth-largest population center. Some 80,000 young French people have flocked to Silicon Valley, where their math skills are in high demand among start-up technology companies. Many others have moved from Paris to Brussels, opting for a seventy-minute commute by high-speed train to take advantage of cheaper housing and lower taxes.

France's domestic troubles have distracted its leaders from playing a more assertive role in Europe's various crises, particularly during the first surge of refugees. While Merkel earned praise for her humanitarian response in opening Germany's doors to Syrians fleeing civil war, Hollande at first resisted her idea of establishing compulsory quotas for all European Union countries to take in a fair share of refugees. When barbed-wire fences started going up on several frontiers and undermining the policy of a borderless Europe, Hollande stood by helplessly as Merkel was forced to shoulder full responsibility for the crisis.

Eventually, France agreed to take in just 24,000 asylum seekers, a fraction of the nearly 1 million refugees who flocked to Germany in 2015. Lurking behind the French government's reticence on the refugee issue was a deep-seated fear that accepting a large number of foreign immigrants would alienate many voters and serve the political purposes of Marine Le Pen and the National Front. France had struggled for years to cope with 6,000 desperate refugees holed up in Calais, who were trying to cross the English Channel into Britain. When the government finally dismantled what had become known as "the Jungle" and dispersed its inhabitants around the country, there was a massive outpouring of anger directed against Hollande and Valls from various French towns and suburbs that were compelled to receive the unwelcome guests. As their popularity levels fell in advance of the 2017 elections, the two French leaders nursed deep grudges against Merkel for prodding them to adopt European policies anathema to many voters.

More than anything else, the reputation of France's leaders was damaged by a series of terrorist attacks that occurred over the course of eighteen months that generated a wave of anxiety across Europe. French people believed their leaders seemed feckless in their efforts to protect the population. The deadly assaults overwhelmed concerns about the state of the economy and made personal security one of the most dominant priorities of contemporary French life. First came the murder in January 2015 of more than a dozen *Charlie Hebdo* journalists, ostensibly because the satirical French weekly had published insulting cartoons of the prophet Mohammed, including one depicting a bomb in his turban.

Ten months later, a coordinated assault by Islamic State militants on the Bataclan theater, an outdoor café, and a soccer stadium killed 130 people and wounded nearly 500 others in the most deadly onslaught suffered by France since World War II. The following July, a deranged immigrant from Tunisia plowed his rented truck through crowds assembled on Nice's main promenade to watch Bastille Day fireworks, killing another 84 people. The fact that all of the perpetrators claimed their heinous acts were inspired by Islamic extremist propaganda sowed further suspicions against France's large Muslim community and fortified support for the xenophobic message of the far-right National Front.

As prime minister, Valls responded by declaring a state of emergency that dispatched more than 10,000 heavily armed police into the streets of Paris. Security forces were granted sweeping powers to order house arrests, stage raids without judicial warrants, and impose bans on public assemblies, including the closure of mosques. In the year following the attacks, the police carried out more than 4,000 raids on homes, yet the Interior Ministry said police interventions led to only a single prosecution. The vast majority of the raids

and house arrests were conducted against French Muslims, typi-
cally of North African descent.

Many of France's estimated 5 million Muslims have long complained about systematic discrimination at the hands of police.
They have also endured much greater difficulty than France's white
population in finding jobs, housing, and educational opportunities.
While French Muslims represent about 9 percent of the country's
population, they comprise about 60 percent of the nation's prison
population—a proportion higher than African-Americans and Lati-
nos incarcerated in American jails. Yet France's prolonged state of
emergency has failed to address the root causes of anger and alienation among third-generation Muslims.

A study by the Paris-based Montaigne Institute that surveyed
more than 1,000 French Muslims in the wake of the terrorist attacks
across France found a gaping disparity in the attitudes of different generations. The first generation, many of whom came from
Morocco, Tunisia, or Algeria to take jobs involving menial labor
four or five decades ago, said they felt relatively well assimilated into
France's secular society. While some said they eat only halal meat
and believed women should wear a hijab, a strong majority of close
to 70 percent said they respected the secularism of French society
and the republic's model of ethnic integration. But a separate group
known as the "ultras," who represented 28 percent of those polled,
said they adamantly rejected the French way of life and believed
that Islamic law, or sharia, should take precedence over the laws of
the French republic. They approved of polygamy and believed in a
rigorous form of Islam. Of this group, half were between fifteen and
twenty-four years old, reflecting a sharp generational cleavage that
showed many young Muslims leaning toward extremist views.

Hakim el Karoui, a former advisor to the French government on
Muslim affairs who conducted the study, said for many disaffected
Muslim youths, the retrograde version of Islam has become a new

identity. "Islam is the mainstay of their revolt," he said. "This revolt is embodied in an Islam of rupture, conspiracy theories and anti-Semitism." He said many young French Muslims believe the French model of assimilation simply does not work for them and that local schools seem incapable of inculcating secular values in them.

They often become further alienated because ready access to events in the Middle East through the Internet has made them believe they are experiencing multiple crises, including the Syrian Civil War, the transformation of Arab societies where women are becoming better educated, and de-industrialization which has greatly reduced the number of jobs available to them. The study, which is the first detailed survey of French Muslims, found that a majority of the terrorists involved in recent attacks were young Muslims born in France or Belgium who did not have a job or professional skills, had spent time in prison for petty crimes, and who believed the state had turned its back on them.

The Interior Ministry believes that terrorist networks have radicalized as many as 10,000 young people and has identified about 1,800 members of jihadist networks. In searching for more effective policies in coping with the threat of alienated young Muslims, the French government has looked for guidance from the country's leading scholars of radical Islam. Yet opinions diverge widely over the causes of terrorism. In studying the cases of terrorists who staged the assaults, nobody seems sure whether those youths who embraced violent jihadism were driven by religious conversion to Islamic extremism, or whether they were criminals who exploited Islam as a way to channel their hatreds.

The debate has grown so heated that it has taken an ugly personal turn. Two of France's most distinguished academics in the field, Gilles Kepel and Olivier Roy, have published many respected books on the Middle East and French Muslims and collaborated in the past. Now they no longer speak to each other. They were close friends for more than two decades before their opposing interpretations of the reasons behind the rise of jihadism in France dissolved into a bitter quarrel that destroyed their personal relationship.

Kepel, a professor at the Paris Institute for Political Studies, or Sciences Po, believes that the murderous attacks in France grew out of the radicalization of Islam that occurred when France failed to integrate its Muslim population. He traces the hinge moment to 2005 when suburban ghettoes outside Paris erupted in an orgy of street riots and car burnings as the frustrations of young French Muslims boiled over into violence. Kepel believes this outpouring of rage reflected the ascendancy of a third generation of Islam in France, following a first generation of postcolonial immigrants who came seeking work and a second generation that struggled to find their social and political place in the country.

At the same time as the 2005 riots were taking place, an Islamist radical named Abu Musab al-Suri published a lengthy online text called "Appeal to Global Islamic Resistance" on "jihadosphere" websites urging disaffected Muslim youths to wage a civil war in Europe. Kepel says this militant appeal became the playbook for atrocities committed a decade later by the Islamic State terrorists who have staged devastating attacks in France and Belgium. Kepel draws a straight trajectory from the recent attacks to the 2005 riots when Muslim youths came to believe in "the need to dissociate from France, and leave it."

But Roy, who has spent much of his professional career doing firsthand research in the Middle East as well as in the French suburbs, insists that what we are witnessing is the Islamicization of radicalism. He believes that the alienated youths and petty criminals who turn to jihadist violence are seeking to disrupt society just as terrorists like the Red Brigades and Baader-Meinhof group tried to do four decades ago. He said many of those involved in terrorist acts in Europe today do not have religious or militant convictions but are seeking to use Islam as a cover to pursue acts of extreme violence. Roy believes that most French Muslims, contrary to common belief, are reasonably well integrated and that those who are perpetrating acts of violence are doing so because they are marginalized delinquents.

Regardless of what provoked the wave of terrorist attacks, the prospect of a prolonged phase of ethnic warfare has deeply affected France's popular imagination. In 2015, Michel Houellebecq published—by a bizarre coincidence on the same day as the *Charlie Hebdo* attacks— what soon became a best-selling novel called *Soumission* (*Submission*). The novel is set in the year 2022 and describes the election of a French Muslim president who restores order and legitimacy by abolishing France's secular traditions and installing a form of Islamic law. The same year, Jean Rolin produced another popular novel called *Les Événements* (*The Events*) that paints an even bleaker portrait of a France descending into chaotic civil war, with regional militias of various political and religious allegiances engaged in violent conflict that requires the deployment of United Nations peacekeeping forces.

While Rolin's fictional work may seem like a far-fetched if not preposterous vision of the future, some security experts take it seriously. Patrick Calvar, director of France's domestic intelligence agency, the DGSI, believes the possibility of armed conflict in France is distinctly real. He warned a French parliamentary panel investigating the terrorist attacks of November 2015 that "we are at the brink of a civil war . . . I think it will happen. One or two more terrorist attacks and it will come." Calvar singled out violent factions of French ultraright-wing groups that have undertaken armed guerrilla training lessons and appear poised to instigate violent confrontations with French Muslims and foreign immigrants.

With anxiety running so high in the wake of the terrorist attacks, the 2017 French presidential campaign took place in an atmosphere of fear and suspicion that divided racial and ethnic communities to a degree never before seen in the nation that aspires to live by a code of

Liberty, Fraternity, and Equality. During the conservative primary race, Sarkozy's bid to recapture the presidency focused on a strategy of moving sharply toward the hard right, adopting positions against Islamist radicals that even Marine Le Pen found rather extreme. He vowed to lock up under administrative retention all suspects on a terrorist watch list known as the "S file" and suspend their rights as citizens until they were proven innocent. Sarkozy's rival, former prime minister Alain Juppé, denounced the proposal as "Guantanamo a la Française" and even Le Pen said such camps would be "contrary to our Constitution."

Sarkozy was accused by the media of pandering to neofascist instincts by "fishing in brown waters," and many voters in his party clearly felt that he was exploiting the climate of insecurity in the wake of the terrorist attacks. Sarkozy vowed that he would be "pitiless" in restoring the state's authority over every part of France. He promised to halt immigration for five years to focus on assimilating those who had recently arrived and help them adopt French values. He also rejected the code of political correctness that "in the Anglo Saxon world allowed communities to live side by side while ignoring each other." To those who preached on behalf of tolerance for cultural diversity, he said "it was time to stop being quiet and excuse ourselves for being French."

Sarkozy, whose father is of Hungarian origin, rejects a vision of multicultural diversity and insists all immigrants should embrace France's national identity, including its original history and values. "If you want to become French, you speak French, you live like the French and you don't try and change a way of life that has been ours for so many years. Once you are French, your ancestors are the Gauls." But Education Minister Najat Vallaud-Belkacem, who was born in Morocco, sharply rebuked him in public for inflaming ethnic resentment and ignoring the diverse background of many French citizens. "Yes, there are Gauls among our ancestors," she said. "But there are also Romans, Normans, Celts, Corsicans, Arabs, Italians, Spanish. That's France."

In contrast to Sarkozy's febrile appeal to security fears, Juppé sought to project the calm aura of a wise elder statesman who promised to heal France's divided communities. Long known for his acute intelligence and arrogant manner, Juppé shrewdly held himself up as a serene alternative to Sarkozy and his aggressive pit-bull manner. Instead of the dystopian vision expressed by his rival, Juppé chose as the slogan for his presidential campaign "The Happy Identity." He believes that France should capitalize on its ethnic diversity, national culture, and strong republican values. Juppé said he wanted to achieve a more unified, successful, and egalitarian society by encouraging compromise rather than confrontation; instead of forcing Muslims to adopt French cuisine, he says, there is no reason why schools could not offer halal meals in their cafeterias.

But it was clear to many conservative voters that Sarkozy and Juppé were too stuck in the past. Neither of them could overcome the fact that they were perceived as retread politicians promoting visions that failed in the past. Instead, conservative voters chose Fillon as the center-right candidate, who, despite having served as prime minister under Sarkozy, managed to present himself as a fresh face. Fillon's ascendancy as the Republicain candidate was also due to his emphasis on traditional values. A practicing Catholic, he capitalized on public outrage among French conservatives in the rural heartland known as *"la France profonde"* over the recent passage of a law approving gay marriage. But when he became trapped in the pay scandal involving his wife and children, Fillon's standing plummeted with voters who viewed him as a hypocrite. That allowed Macron to fill the centrist vacuum as a probusiness reformer who might restore France to its former glory.

As president, Macron's biggest political nemesis remains the National Front, which stands out as the most prominent and most enduring of Europe's far-right populist parties. After lingering for years on the edges of French political life, the National Front moved to the forefront of French politics during the 2017 presidential election campaign as Le Pen expanded her appeal and protest candidates across Europe gained popularity. Like many voters in major Western democracies, the French had grown deeply disenchanted with the failure of their traditional ruling elites to address what they saw as fundamental issues affecting their lives, such as threats from crime and terrorism, growing income inequality, and confusion over cultural identity. Despite their intense rivalry, the Républicains and the Socialists have traditionally worked together to block the National Front from gaining power by uniting behind whoever emerges as the centrist candidate after the first round of presidential elections. The mainstream parties previously managed to thwart the Front's aspirations for power when Jean-Marie Le Pen surpassed the Socialist candidate in 2002 to reach the final round against incumbent president Jacques Chirac. In the 2017 election, despite doubts about Macron's lack of experience, the same parties urged voters across the political spectrum to cast their ballots for the only remaining candidate who could hold back the National Front's ambitions for power.

As in other parts of Europe where populist nationalists have proliferated, the question of identity politics has become critical in France's efforts to grapple with its many problems. The terrorist attacks, the failure to integrate millions of Muslims, and the loss of control over borders have revived basic issues about what it means to be French. Those issues are not going to disappear. The identity war has become a central debate in the schools, where some teachers and parents are demanding that courses be taught with a nationalistic narrative that emphasizes French culture and values as an antidote to a more global perspective. "So many people have a French identity card, but the question of what is France and how to transmit the knowledge or the love of France has been overlooked. That question is now being asked with much greater urgency in the wake of the terrorist attacks," says Alain Finkielkraut, a conservative social philosopher who has written extensively about the contradictions caused by multicultural identity and how these strains have eroded French educational standards.

Ever since a 1905 law established the principle of *laïcité* to keep religion out of public life, a crucial foundation of France's modern identity has emphasized the importance of a secular society. But the rising tensions over Islam and security have brought the culture and religious wars back to the forefront of daily life. During the summer of 2016, France was consumed with what seemed at times a ludicrous debate over the "burkini"—a swimsuit that covers a woman's entire body—that was banned by fifteen towns on the French Riviera. Valls insisted the burkini should be forbidden because it was an Islamist uniform that reflected "the enslavement of women" and could be construed as a means to impose Islamist rule. France banned the headscarf and other "conspicuous" religious symbols from all state schools in 2004, as well as the facial veil known as the burqa from public places in 2010. But images of police forces patrolling the beaches and evicting women who were fully clothed held the government up to ridicule, particularly after Valls suggested the proper role model should be Marianne, the female figure symbolizing the French nation, who is classically depicted as bare-breasted. It was almost as if the prime minister was insisting women who want to be loyal to French values should go topless.

The battle over the burkini shows how identity politics and cultural issues have moved to the forefront of political life, in France as well as in the United States. In this age of rising populism, voters on both sides of the Atlantic tend to look at sensitive political topics like immigration as a fundamental challenge to their nation's identity as well as their security and sovereignty. As in the United States, French commentators warn that the plethora of crises they are facing is calling into question the survivability of their democracy. But in a land where existentialism has thrived as a philosophy, the French people are proud of their ability to cope with adversity even when it seems the very foundations of their society are in jeopardy.

One year after the Bataclan was transformed into a charnel house when terrorists shot and killed 89 music lovers attending a concert, the theater was again packed to the rafters for a special anniversary performance by the British rock star Sting, who dedicated his show to the memory of the victims. Ever since becoming a great power in the thirteenth century, France has shown a remarkable ability to recover from the depths of despair and rise to new levels of achievement, such as during the Age of Enlightenment and following the humiliating Nazi occupation in World War II. Perhaps the city motto of Paris best sums up the resiliency of the nation: "She may be tossed by the waves, but she does not sink."

CHAPTER FOUR

BRUSSELS

CAPITAL OF EUROPE, TOWER OF BABEL?

THE ARCHITECTS WHO DESIGNED THE GARGANTUAN DOME THAT houses the European Parliament in Strasbourg, France, say they were thinking in terms of a classical Roman amphitheater. But the modernistic structure actually bears an eerie resemblance to the Tower of Babel in the famous 1563 painting by the Flemish master Pieter Brueghel. In many respects, the symbolism is uncanny. Like Brueghel's tower, the Parliament structure seems only half finished, a state of limbo that could describe the uncertain struggle to build a united Europe. With twenty-four official languages and a veritable army of linguists and interpreters deployed to translate all speeches and documents, the European Parliament and its 751 members manage to convey a Babylonian kind of confusion about where they want to take Europe, aptly implied by the legislature's slogan: "Many Tongues in Search of One Voice."

The European Parliament's main base is located in the European Quarter of Brussels, adjacent to other key institutions, including the

European Union's Executive Commission and its Council of Ministers, which represents the twenty-eight national governments. Yet once a month, at the insistence of France, the entire EU apparatus—legislators, support staff, lobbyists, journalists, and translators, or about 10,000 people in all—must pack up and make the five-hour train trip from Brussels to Strasbourg to attend plenary sessions. It would be as though the members of the U.S. Congress could only pass laws one week a month and were required to do so during special sessions held in Pittsburgh. The annual cost of maintaining this traveling circus between two homes is estimated at about $200 million, footed by the hapless European taxpayers.

One of the biggest criticisms of the European Union is that it lacks democratic accountability—a complaint often voiced during the referendum campaign leading up to Britain's vote in June 2016 to leave the Union. Of the EU's seven institutions, only the European Parliament is directly elected by the voters, and yet this voice of the people is so feckless that it cannot initiate legislation of its own.

The most powerful EU body is the Council of Ministers, headed by former Polish prime minister Donald Tusk, whose job is to chair the frequent summit meetings of leaders from the twenty-eight member governments and try to thrash out compromises that will steer the course of European policies. As president of the Council, Tusk is appointed by the general consent of the national leaders who want to keep power over EU decisions firmly in the hands of their governments.

Then there is the European Commission, the EU's executive body, which negotiates trade agreements, enforces antitrust rules, and proposes legislation. The president of the commission is selected by the European Parliament, usually from the largest political faction, while the other twenty-seven members of the Commission are chosen by their governments subject to approval by the president. Traditionally, a Brussels posting has been seen as a way to reward political allies with a cushy sinecure or to send annoying rivals into gilded exile.

Jean-Claude Juncker, who has served as the EU Commission president since November 2014, rose to that position as the candidate of the center-right European People's Party, which holds the largest number of seats in the European Parliament. Widely regarded as one of the most experienced and savvy politicians in Europe, Juncker held office as Luxembourg's prime minister and finance minister for nearly two decades. A committed federalist who has long believed in the concept of a United States of Europe, Juncker embodies what is good and what is bad about the management of Europe's institutions.

His long tenure in running the tiny duchy of Luxembourg—where he ensured the prosperity of its 400,000 citizens by bolstering its reputation as an international tax haven—positioned him on the front lines of the protracted crusade to achieve his dream of a unified Europe. But his ascendancy to the Commission presidency stirred cries of outrage from many critics who said he was too much of a creature of Europe's opaque institutions that are considered too unresponsive to the public will. These critics claim that what Europe needs to emerge from its state of morose decline is a fresh pair of eyes and ears, not a consummate insider who will pursue the elusive quest for a United States of Europe that is so out of step with many voters.

Juncker's arrogant manner rubs many of his colleagues the wrong way. Even though they come from the same political family, German chancellor Angela Merkel harbors an intense dislike for him and was incensed when he slyly circumvented her opposition to become commission president. During the height of the euro crisis, he coined a phrase known as "Juncker's curse" that sums up the difficulty faced by politicians trying to reconcile European and national interests. "We all know what to do," he said in his capacity as prime minister. "What we don't know is how to be re-elected when we've done it."

Upon taking over the EU Commission presidency, Juncker enlisted as personal allies several key members of the European Parliament, notably those who share his conviction that Europe needs to shift more sovereignty from nation states to European institutions in order to achieve greater impact on the international stage. One of Juncker's closest friends is Martin Schulz, a German Social Democrat who served for two terms as president of the European Parliament before returning home to run for chancellor. When the assembly was in session, Juncker says Schulz would call him nearly every morning at seven o'clock, especially in moments of crisis. "It is a habit I sometimes wish he would drop," Juncker sighs.

Both men have been ardent defenders of the European dream for decades and even acknowledge that they know how to finish each other's sentences. Like all true believers, they are convinced their path is righteous and vindicated by the European Union's historic success in maintaining peace and prosperity on the continent for seven decades since World War II. In their view, they are carrying forward the idealistic legacy of Europe's founding fathers, led by Jean Monnet and Robert Schuman.

They believe Europe can only achieve superpower status by combining forces; its cumulative weight as the world's biggest commercial bloc—with more than 500 million affluent consumers—now commands enormous influence over world trade. They also insist that such twenty-first-century challenges as coping with climate change and huge refugee flows can best be tackled at a European level rather than by scattered responses from national governments.

But Juncker and Schulz fear the tide is turning against them. The grand federalist dream of building a United States of Europe that inspired Monnet and his fellow visionaries no longer seems to resonate with the voters or their elected leaders. A powerful backlash against globalization has fueled the rise of populist forces on the left and the right, which in turn has weakened mainstream governing parties to such an extent that they are afraid or incapable of defending the cause of Europe.

Despite these adverse trends, Juncker and Schulz decided in the wake of the Brexit vote that they had no choice but to stand up and speak out against such parochial thinking across the continent. They have long subscribed to the "bicycle theory," first enunciated by former EU commission president Jacques Delors, that Europe must always keep moving forward toward the goal of a unified continent or risk falling down.

On the morning after the Brexit referendum, as Europe reeled in shock over an outcome deemed unthinkable by many public opinion polls, the two presidents agreed that the Commission and the Parliament needed to assert their leadership to fulfill their duties as "guardians of the treaties" that established the postwar European order. They talked about embarking on sweeping reforms that would transform the Commission into a proper European government, with legislative oversight by the European Parliament and a federal council of member states that could serve as a second chamber, like a European Senate. They decided the European renewal project would be unveiled at a grand summit conference in March 2017 marking the sixtieth anniversary of the Treaty of Rome, which is considered the Magna Carta of the European Union.

Juncker and Schulz agreed that more powers should be invested in the European Parliament as a way of showing a greater willingness to connect with voters. While the Parliament can veto trade deals and decide who will get top EU positions, it still lacks the ability to raise taxes and revenue or even propose European legislation, which remains the Commission's job. Without any power of the purse, nearly all EU budgets remain under tight control of the national governments. Even though direct elections to the European Parliament were launched in 1979 as a way to allow voters to choose their own representatives, the process has failed to generate much support or popular legitimacy.

Voter turnout across Europe in the 2014 elections was a dismal 42 percent. The worst showing came in the former Communist states of the east; only 18 percent of the Czechs, 13 percent of Slovaks, and 24 percent of the Poles bothered to vote. Many of those elected members of the European Parliament (MEPs) have turned out to be hostile to the European dream and generally favor returning more powers to the national level. Indeed, as many as one-third of the 751 MEPs who were elected for five-year terms in 2014 are considered to be Euroskeptics, including Le Pen and Farage.

But diehard opponents aside, Juncker and Schulz found the greatest resistance to reviving momentum toward a more united Europe has come from EU leaders themselves. The constant uphill battle and the frustrations of losing virtually every power struggle to the national governments finally took its toll on Schulz. After more than two decades of fighting for greater powers to be invested in the European Parliament as the direct voice of the people, Schulz decided to abandon Brussels to return to domestic politics. As one of Germany's most prominent Social Democrats, Schulz realized that the best way to achieve his ambition to build a stronger Europe was for him to seize the leadership of his party and make a bold challenge for the leadership of Germany.

With his party seeking a fresh face to lead them into the September 2017 elections, Schulz was chosen by the Social Democrats as their standard-bearer to challenge Angela Merkel in her quest for a fourth term as chancellor. After being out of national politics for so long, Schulz faced a difficult road in convincing German voters that he is closely attuned to their concerns. But at this stage in his career and with Europe on the brink of disaster, he felt there was no other choice but to pursue the path of political power through national government channels in the hope that he would bring a more European perspective to Berlin. Schulz says he is appalled by the alarming spread of anti-Europe sentiment in Germany, where the anti-immigrant and anti-EU agenda of the Alternative for Germany fringe movement is gaining ground as the party threatens to make a dramatic entry into the German federal parliament after the 2017 elections.

The Brexit vote has emboldened populists of every stripe in every part of Europe, including Germany. Rather than fight the anti-EU message, many European leaders are tailoring their political views to the populist tune and have recoiled from any suggestion of surrendering more power to European institutions. With his principal Brussels ally now out of the picture, Juncker's chief rival in Europe's institutional struggle has turned out to be none other than Tusk, who sees his role as president of the Council of Ministers to enforce the priorities dictated by the national governments. Tusk is strongly backed by Chancellor Merkel, who as the EU's dominant figure maintains that Europe should be run on the basis of decisions reached between EU governments that effectively relegate the Commission and the European Parliament to second-tier status.

Merkel believes above all in the power and legitimacy of those elected at the national level, not in the further transfer of more authority to Brussels. She says decisions taken by EU government leaders by mutual cooperation or compromise should remain paramount in guiding the course of Europe. Tusk echoes that view, insisting that EU governments are the true "masters of the treaty" and should provide the political leadership for the legislative agenda enacted by the Commission and the Parliament. Both Merkel and Tusk say they have become even more entrenched in their thinking by the rise of populism and voter distrust toward Europe. In their view, a faltering Europe in a protracted phase of crisis is not capable of enduring a thorough overhaul that would involve dramatic new initiatives imposed from above by supranational institutions with little basis of democratic support.

That conviction is particularly strong among new members in Central and Eastern Europe, where former Communist states have been reluctant to cede further sovereignty to Brussels after being compelled by them to embrace the tangled web of EU rules and regulations—encompassed in 140,000 pages known as the *acquis communautaire*, or its body of established laws. While acknowledging that their nations have become more prosperous since joining the EU, leaders in the eastern half of the continent say they did not struggle to regain their long-lost national sovereignty following the collapse of the Soviet empire only to surrender it anew to a faceless bureaucracy in Brussels. Indeed, in the aftermath of the Brexit vote the governments of Poland, Hungary, Slovakia, and the Czech Republic have formally disavowed Juncker's proposals for moving ahead toward a more integrated union and called for a "cultural counter-revolution" in Europe that would strip the Commission of some prerogatives and restore more powers to the national capitals.

The emotional debate over whether to pursue "more Europe or less Europe" reached its climax in the months after the British referendum when Juncker entered the Tower of Babel legislative chamber in Strasbourg to deliver his annual "state of the union" address before members of the European Parliament. This political ritual, held every September when Europeans have returned from their summer holidays, was inaugurated some years ago to emulate the January address given by American presidents before Congress. The American version usually sticks to a predictable script designed to foster a symbolic display of patriotic unity, with the president invariably claiming the state of America is strong and the legislators roaring their approval. But Juncker realized any kind of "rally the troops" speech would be disingenuous following the turmoil Europe endured in 2016. The future also looked pitifully bleak, given the clashing visions about Europe's future, the fierce rivalry among EU institutions, and the staggering array of crises over how to deal with refugees, a belligerent Russia, rising sovereign debt, failing banks, and the tortuous negotiations looming over Britain's departure from the European Union.

Juncker decided he would not mince any words and laid the blame for Europe's malaise squarely on the selfish attitude of national governments. He warned that Europe faced "an existential crisis" driven in large part by incessant criticism of EU institutions by the national capitals that has eroded public confidence in Europe. "Never before have I seen so much fragmentation. There is almost no intersection between the EU and its national capitals anymore," he told the assembly. "Never before have I seen such little common ground between our member states, so few areas where they agree to work together. And never before have I seen national governments so weakened by the forces of populism and paralyzed by the risk of defeat in the next elections."

Juncker angered legislators and EU governments by emphasizing that the ascendancy of national interests over common European goals has fueled political extremism in many countries. He lamented the "petty envy between various institutions" in running Europe but insisted that the EU Commission was determined to regain the upper hand in the tug-of-war over policy with the Council of Ministers and the national governments it represents. He proposed several initiatives to galvanize public opinion in support of the European cause, offering to set up free Wi-Fi systems for all population centers by 2020 and to establish a youth volunteer army to perform public services across the continent as part of a European "solidarity corps." To cope with high youth unemployment across Europe, he laid out plans for a $700 billion investment fund to create new jobs. And to encourage migrants to stay home, he said Europe needed to finance initiatives that bolster economic growth in Africa.

But Juncker's modest proposals fell flat with his many critics in the Parliament and in national capitals. The lingering shock of Britain's decision to leave the EU deflated any desire among most EU politicians to launch new programs to revive Europe. Government leaders were in no mood to lavish funds on what was derided as a "Christmas tree" full of ornamental ideas deemed unlikely to rekindle enthusiasm for a European cause that was clearly in retreat. Indeed, the lukewarm response to Juncker's plans reflected the considerable loss of authority suffered by the EU Commission in recent years as European governments have sought to regain control over their treasuries and their territories.

Once regarded as the driving force of European unity, the EU Commission no longer attracts the best and brightest idealists from across the continent, individuals of the type who flocked to Brussels in the early 1960s when the European Coal and Steel Community's "high authority" was merged with the Common Market's executive to form Europe's largest institution. Many of the early Eurocrats were inspired by the challenge of inventing new ways to break down barriers dividing Europe's nations and building a supranational form of government that would serve as a model for regional cooperation in Asia, Africa, and Latin America.

As the Commission grew in size along with the EU's expansion from six to twelve and eventually twenty-eight member states, the expanding body of European laws transformed the Commission's image. Instead of being seen as pursuing the noble goal of binding together a continent with a history of bloody wars, the EU Commission became viewed as a monstrous bureaucracy that spent its time deciding on frivolous matters such as the shape of cucumbers or bananas, which according to one infamous decree must be "free from malformation or abnormal curvature."

Even though the current number of 23,000 civil servants in the EU Commission is actually smaller than that found in many national government ministries, it is much larger than the combined number of officials who work in the European Parliament and the Council of Ministers. The generous salaries and low taxes enjoyed by these European mandarins make them prime targets of public envy. During the referendum campaign in Britain, Leave voters were incensed to learn that many EU civil servants take home more pay than the British prime minister.

Juncker's predicament illustrates many of the reasons behind Europe's troubled plight. He and other custodians of Europe's institutions are too weak and divided to take remedial action on their own. If they push too hard for necessary reforms, they find themselves slapped down by the leaders of EU governments who believe that they, as the elected representatives of their people, are the only legitimate voices in deciding the course of Europe.

EU government leaders struggle to defend the cause of Europe to dissatisfied voters who are too easily swayed by anti-Brussels diatribes from populist movements on the left, such as Syriza in Greece or Podemos in Spain, or from those protest parties on the far right, such as France's National Front or the Alternative for Germany. Many leaders are reluctant to face up to the stark choice posed by Juncker in his Strasbourg speech: that it is time for an urgent leap forward toward greater unification or else witness the inevitable disintegration of the European Union. As a result, they have generally opted to kick the can down the road in dealing with their problems because they feel that further steps toward European integration in the face of populist antagonism would be politically foolhardy. Yet when pressed, almost every European leader today will admit that the status quo is unsustainable.

With his own power too diffuse, Juncker has been forced to navigate battle lines among the EU member states. In Europe's fractured condition, he must deal with a deep north-south split over how to enforce fiscal discipline and how best to revive the continent's sluggish economy. He also faces a growing East-West cleavage over how to deal with the influx of refugees from Africa and the Middle East, as well as coping with a Russia that seeks to expand its influence and control over its neighbors that were once part of the Soviet Empire.

The tricky question of how to deal with Russia's ambitions and its authoritarian president, Vladimir Putin, looms as one of Europe's biggest long-term strategic challenges. Juncker aligned himself with Greece's prime minister Alexis Tsipras in seeking to encourage dialogue with Moscow to explore ways to end the confrontation over Russian aggression in eastern Ukraine and what could be done to ease sanctions against the Russian economy. Juncker's decision to meet with Putin over the heads of EU leaders infuriated Chancellor Angela Merkel and others who felt he was acting beyond his mandate and risking the fragile European unity against Russia's violation of international law in seizing Crimea and arming eastern Ukrainian separatists.

Despite their differences over Russia, Juncker backed Merkel's controversial decision to open Germany's frontiers during the 2015 surge of refugees out of Turkey and argued in favor of her idea for a resettlement quota system that would involve the EU countries sharing the burden of hosting immigrants. He also sought to preserve the EU's open-border policy against those leaders, such as Hungary's prime minister Viktor Orban, who wanted to erect razor-wire fences to block the procession of those refugees fleeing Syria's civil war who were looking for safe haven in Europe. While Germany and Sweden magnanimously opened their frontiers during the initial surge to hundreds of thousands of migrants, eastern European states have insisted they do not want to participate in any plan to resettle Muslim refugees in their countries. Juncker's efforts to implement a quota system for 165,000 refugees—with each member state allotted a certain number based on their population—collapsed soon after it was proposed in the face of angry opposition from those member states who claimed their national and cultural identity would be damaged by an influx of Muslims.

Juncker and his fellow EU Commission members have also tried to walk a fine line on the sovereign debt crisis between northern creditors and southern debtors. Germany, backed by Finland and the Netherlands, demanded major structural reforms involving deep pension cuts and job losses in return for approving any further financial bailouts, notably more than 300 billion euros for Greece.

But as Europe's economic stagnation since the 2008 global financial crisis has persisted through nearly a decade of austerity, southern states rallied around urgent calls by Italy's prime minister Matteo Renzi and France's president François Hollande for Europe to shift the policy emphasis toward more jobs and growth, particularly for young people whose protracted phase of joblessness has evoked fears of a "lost generation." After backing Germany's "eat your spinach" attitude for years, Juncker now acknowledges the policy failure and supports arguments in favor of a fresh boost for jobs and growth. He caved in to demands to flout the EU's rules on curbing budget deficits and exempt France and other transgressors from having to pay penalties. While careful not to antagonize Germany as the EU's dominant power, Juncker shrewdly enlisted greater cooperation in changing the course of EU economic policy from Mario Draghi, the president of the European Central Bank, whose quantitative easing measures were designed to keep interest rates low and channel funding to small businesses so they could hire more young people.

The negotiations over Britain's departure from the European Union threaten to be highly divisive among EU member states. There are sharp disagreements over how accommodating Europe should be toward Britain, which wants to maintain access to the single European market and allow banks based in London's City to offer their financial services across the European Union, known as "passporting." The government of Prime Minister Theresa May wants above all to be able to restrict immigration flows into Britain, arguing that the flow of immigrants mainly from other EU member states has overwhelmed public services in many communities. May's predecessor, David Cameron, had vowed to impose a ceiling that would restrict immigration to no more than 100,000 a year, but by the time of the referendum it was revealed that more than 330,000 immigrants—many from eastern EU countries—had entered Britain within the previous twelve months.

The immigration issue was the principal grievance of many British voters who decided they wanted to leave the European Union. But Juncker and other EU leaders insist that if Britain hopes to maintain continued access to the European market, May's government will need to abide by the "four freedoms" that guarantee the unfettered flow of goods, services, capital, and people in the European Union. For many EU leaders, this is an absolute red line that must be accepted by Britain.

The discussion over a future relationship with breakaway Britain will be complicated not just by the need to untangle more than four decades of shared rules and regulations. Negotiators will also need to determine how the EU will cope with financial and security issues posed by the loss of the second-biggest contributor to the EU budget and the loss of Europe's most powerful army. The talks are supposed to conclude within two years from their launch in March 2017. But the complexity of the negotiations suggests that it will take up to a decade for Britain to shape its future relationship with Europe. Who really speaks on behalf of Europe will also be a troublesome issue, not least because the EU Commission, the Council, and the European Parliament have each appointed their own representative to conduct the divorce negotiations with London. Once again, the Tower of Babel syndrome that characterizes the European Union and its institutions threatens to disrupt highly sensitive discussions about the future ties between Britain and its erstwhile partners.

Despite the EU's confusing lines of authority, the United States and the rest of the world have learned to their chagrin that their own national interests can be powerfully affected by the Brussels-based bureaucrats. Juncker's commission possesses clearly defined powers in two areas that have made the outside world sit up and take notice: the ability to negotiate comprehensive trade agreements on behalf of all EU members and the power to enforce antitrust rules against global corporations.

The United States and the European Union had hoped to achieve an ambitious new deal, called the Transatlantic Trade and Investment Partnership (or TTIP) by the end of the Obama administration, a deadline that will now have to be extended. TTIP was supposed to abolish not just tariffs but also many regulations that inhibit greater trade and investment across the Atlantic in a bid to spur growth and jobs. Despite the rise of China, India, and other emerging powers, about half of global trade and investment is still conducted between Europe and the United States.

TTIP was designed to reaffirm Western leadership of the global economy and allow the West to set future standards for the rest of the world. The EU Commission says that TTIP would bolster the economies by an extra 120 billion euros for Europe and 90 billion euros for the United States. But those optimistic predictions have met fierce skepticism on both sides of the Atlantic where antiglobalization protests have imperiled the fate of the trade agreement. Those protestors who disdain TTIP claim it would dilute food safety and environment protections, as well as undermine banking regulations and the authority of local governments. What was once heralded as a farsighted initiative to bring Europe and the United States closer together and create millions of new jobs has been victimized by the gathering backlash against globalization.

Europe has also shown that it can use its regulatory powers to foil the grand ambitions of America's corporate titans. The European Union's status as the world's biggest commercial bloc endows it with the clout to dictate the terms of competition to companies on a global basis. As perhaps the most powerful antitrust authority in the world, the EU's competition directorate can act as judge, jury, and prosecutor when scrutinizing the international impact of corporate mergers, abuse of dominant positions, and tax strategies.

When General Electric tried to acquire Honeywell nearly two decades ago, its powerful chief executive, Jack Welch, thought winning EU approval would be a mere formality after the U.S. Justice Department approved the deal. But Mario Monti, the commissioner in charge of competition issues, decided to block the merger, saying it would damage the interests of European consumers by leading to substantial price increases. When Welch failed in a personal bid to persuade Monti to accept the deal, he slammed his fist on Monti's desk in frustration. He told Monti he was fed up with the EU and was returning home to write his memoirs. "Very well, Mr. Welch," Monti told him. "You can make this trip to Brussels your last chapter."

More recently, EU authorities have pursued U.S. technology giants like Google, which has been accused on three counts of abusing its virtual global monopoly in digital search markets. The Commission has also demanded that Apple pay as much as $14 billion in back taxes and penalties that were avoided because of a sweetheart tax deal it worked out with the government of Ireland. Such cases have caused growing dismay within the U.S. government, which believes the EU Commission is going too far in breaching its mandate with decisions that have an impact far beyond European markets.

Chief executives of U.S. technology companies complain they are being unjustly penalized for their excellence at innovation and that Commission antitrust officials are seeking to tilt the playing field in favor of homegrown European firms. While the Commission denies a pro-European bias, international antitrust cases are emerging as an important new arena of conflict in the Atlantic relationship. Under the America First ethos of a Trump presidency, it is easy to imagine how antitrust and other regulatory conflicts could become linked with American demands that Europe must assume a greater share of future costs in providing for its own defense.

Europe's refugee crisis, its feckless efforts to defuse conflicts in the Middle East, and its failure to halt Russia's invasion in Ukraine have underscored the continent's abiding weakness in defending against military and security challenges in the twenty-first century. The terrorist attacks in Paris and Brussels finally drove home to many European leaders how helpless they now appear to their constituents in failing to cope with new threats to their nations. Aware of their political vulnerability, they have recently awakened to one of the most glaring shortcomings in the Atlantic partnership: the lack of cooperation between the European Union and the North Atlantic Treaty Organization.

For anybody who spends time in Brussels, one of the more baffling mysteries has been the striking absence of policy coordination between two of the West's most critical institutions. Even though there is a greater overlap in membership than ever before—twenty-two out of twenty-nine NATO countries also belong to the European Union—and despite the fact that their headquarters are located just a few miles away from each other, the leaders of the two institutions have rarely communicated with each other. "Sometimes it seems as if the EU and NATO are living on two different planets and not in the same city," said Donald Tusk, the president of the EU Council of Ministers. "Today we face the same threats, whether they come from the East, the South or from within. Our citizens are demanding greater security, no matter whether they live in countries that belong to the EU, to NATO, or both. It is our democratic responsibility as leaders to deliver."

During the heated debate in 2003 over whether to go to war in

Iraq, France and Germany tried to launch a new security initiative that would create a European Union military headquarters distinct from NATO so that Europe could avoid being drawn into future conflicts by their shared military commitments with the United States. But the conflict in Syria, the upsurge in terrorist attacks in Europe, and the refugee crisis have convinced many governments that it would be a foolish waste of resources to duplicate NATO's structure on a European level.

Britain's imminent departure from the European Union has also spurred EU capitals to consider how to keep Britain, as well as the United States, engaged in defending the continent. Europe's continuing economic crisis means that nobody can afford to see the EU and NATO go separate ways in dealing with the multitude of security challenges, including the protection of energy pipelines, cyberattacks, a newly aggressive Russia, and homegrown terrorism by Islamic State sympathizers.

Most of all, Donald Trump's election has reinforced fears across Europe that America will no longer live up to its commitments. A generation after the end of the Cold War, Trump's observation that NATO is "obsolete" has caused European leaders to tremble at their complacency in remaining so dependent on the United States rather than taking bold steps toward becoming more responsible for their own defense. As a businessman, Trump seems intent on transforming the NATO alliance into a transactional set of arrangements with European nations. This new doctrine, if that is what it becomes, could soon threaten to destroy the Atlantic partnership as we have known it.

At the Warsaw summit in July 2016, NATO and EU leaders finally decided the time had come to enhance security cooperation between two of the West's most important institutions. The accord calls for closer military planning and sharing of intelligence on new threats, such as potential terrorist attacks in Europe and the Middle East. It also expands the practice of joint exercises and naval patrol support in the Mediterranean Sea to thwart the human trafficking in refugees seeking to enter Europe.

The deal is also supposed to encourage a more rational sharing of costs on defense, training, and capabilities in dealing with modern forms of hybrid warfare. By fortifying ties between NATO and the EU, European leaders hope to see a reinvigorated commitment by the United States and Britain to their security.

But much will depend on the Europeans themselves. Europe's defense capabilities will also require more investment, since most NATO countries fall well short of the alliance goal of spending 2 percent of GDP on defense. Europe has structural military problems as well: one indication is that while European countries have 2 million men and women in uniform, only about 40,000 are thought to be capable of engaging in combat. Instead of the 1-in-25 "teeth to tail" ratio that prevails in Europe, American combat forces represent about 1 in 6 people in uniform.

Future security threats will demand more pluralistic responses that can best be accomplished by combining resources. In the fight against terrorism, for example, NATO could work with the European Union to connect national criminal databases and deploy the EU's special powers to seize financial assets of suspected criminals. In the Arctic region, another difficult challenge looms in preserving peaceful control over energy resources and global shipping lanes that are opening up with the melting polar icecap.

These new transport routes will shave thousands of nautical miles and up to seven days of travel time off current passages through the Suez and Panama canals. And Europe's most recent trauma in dealing with the Syrian refugee crisis may only be the start of something much bigger. The United Nations predicts that the world will need 70 percent more food to feed a global population that will grow to 9.6 billion by 2050. Wars, famine, and drought will accelerate the exodus of refugees from Africa toward sanctuaries in Europe. Indeed, climate change experts say at least three dozen countries could become desperately short of crops or fresh water within the next ten years by spreading desertification across the continent that may affect up to 250 million Africans.

The West needs to prepare now for these potential catastrophes. A holistic approach linking NATO's hard-power capabilities with the EU's soft-power assets in dealing with new security challenges could help reinforce public support in America and Europe for a revitalized Atlantic alliance. A joint policy-planning council should be created to harness the brainpower of the two institutions in ways that could inspire greater ingenuity, innovative thinking, and smarter use of resources among Western governments.

Jens Stoltenberg, NATO's secretary-general, says one of his main objectives is to bring an opaque institution like NATO into closer contact with everyday citizens and persuade them that their security concerns are being properly addressed. During his time as Norway's prime minister, Stoltenberg says he would often spend his weekends masquerading as a taxi driver in order to engage his customers in candid conversation about the performance of his government. But the biggest challenge he faces as chief executive of the Atlantic alliance is not so much finding ways to engage in dialogue with voters. The real test will be to impress upon a new American president and his European counterparts that Western leadership in world affairs can only be sustained by restoring faith in effective security cooperation on both sides of the Atlantic Ocean.

CHAPTER FIVE

MADRID

WILL THE CENTER HOLD?

"THE SECOND REVOLUTION HAS ARRIVED!" WITH THAT CHANT, Spaniards greeted the stunning results of national elections in December 2015 as the most momentous political development since the toppling of the dictator Francisco Franco forty years earlier. The poor showing by the mainstream parties—the ruling Popular Party of prime minister Mariano Rajoy and the opposition Spanish Socialist Workers' Party headed by Pedro Sánchez—reflected voter disgust with an epidemic of corruption scandals that plagued both parties during their time in and out of power.

The meteoric rise of two new parties—the far left Podemos movement led by Pablo Iglesias and a liberal, probusiness group known as Ciudadanos (Citizens)—reflected a strong desire by many Spaniards to depose a bipolar governing order that dominated the country for four decades. The outcome illustrated the powerful impact caused by years of economic suffering, banking failures, real estate busts, and despair felt among 24 million unemployed young people in Europe that has taken a serious toll on political stability, a trend reflected not just in Spain but across the continent.

Post-Franco Spain has been one of the great success stories of the European Union. The peaceful transition from dictatorship to democracy and the rapid improvement in living standards since Spain and Portugal joined the EU served as a proud template for the Union's wave of expansion to embrace the post-Communist nations in Eastern Europe. Spain grew into one of the most dynamic manufacturing bases in Europe, second only to Germany in car production.

But in the wake of Europe's worst economic downturn since the Great Depression, the Iberian economic model has been sorely tested. A real estate boom turned to bust, undermining the banking system, causing debt to spin out of control and personal bankruptcies to soar. With one in four people unemployed and more than 150,000 families evicted from their homes since the start of the crisis, Spain has at times appeared close to the breaking point as one crisis magnifies another. Spain's Great Recession damaged confidence in the ruling establishment, disrupting the political order to such a degree that the country was left rudderless for nearly a year through two inconclusive elections until Rajoy could patch together a minority government.

The power vacuum coincided with another revolution—the resurgence of a secessionist movement in Catalonia. The eruption of separatist sentiment in one of Spain's wealthiest regions was yet another manifestation of the new nationalism flourishing in much of Europe. Other countries also confront regional demands for independence: populist nationalists in the affluent regions of Flanders in Belgium and in northern Italy are seeking to break away from central rule. But in Spain, the challenge to Madrid's rule has become nothing less than an existential threat, with Basques, Galicians, and even the people of the Canary Islands demanding autonomous control over their lives. During the ten months in 2016 when they were stranded without any federal government, many Spaniards asked themselves if the time had come when the fragile cohesion of their nation was about to shatter into regional enclaves that could foreshadow the fragmentation of the entire continent.

Catalonia has always believed it was a different country than Spain. It has a distinct culture that can be traced back more than a millennium. Iberian tribes along the Mediterranean coast traded with Greeks and Carthaginians, and the region's separate political identity took root during the Middle Ages. Catalans never accepted the loss of national sovereignty following their defeat at the hands of the Spanish monarchy in 1714. For the past three centuries, Catalonia has struggled to regain its independence despite the brutal suppression of its local government, language, and cultural values.

The "Catalan question" was an important factor in the Spanish Civil War from 1936 to 1939 and Catalan fighters battled courageously to defend the Second Republic. When democracy and autonomy were eventually crushed by the forces of Generalissimo Francisco Franco, the dictatorship imposed harsh measures on the region, seeking to stamp out any vestiges of an independence movement. The Catalan language was ruled illegal, and Franco's security forces went to extreme lengths to suppress any displays of the Catalan flag or other cultural symbols in schools, churches, and local councils.

Following Franco's death in 1975, the remarkable transformation of Spain into a multi-party democracy led to the restoration of Catalonia's proud and historic identity. The 1978 Constitution ruled out any right to secession among Spain's seventeen disparate regions but nonetheless raised hopes that local cultures would be respected and the country would evolve into "a nation of nations." The new bill of rights recognized Catalonia's limited authority to establish its own presidency and parliament, and schools were once again allowed to teach in the Catalan language.

Unlike the ethnic nationalism that has inspired other separatist movements, Catalonia's quest for independence has been largely driven by issues related mainly to politics, economics, language, and culture. It has also been a remarkably peaceful movement, in contrast to the violent terrorism campaign waged by Basque separatists in the past. When Spain joined the European Union, many Catalans believed it was only a matter of time before the nation-state would suffer an erosion of power in favor of greater local control under a "Europe of regions."

But over the years, the major political parties and the federal judiciary took steps to shore up the central government and strengthen the cause of Spanish nationalism, supported by other regions that feared the impact of Catalonia's quest for independence and the potential loss of its wealth transfers. The 2008 financial crisis and the bursting of Spain's real estate bubble hit Catalans particularly hard, and the forced redistribution of their income to poorer regions in Spain inflamed resentment over what they perceived as fiscal looting by the Madrid government.

Catalonia, which represents 7.5 million people located in the northeast corner of Spain, is one of Europe's most affluent regions and on its own would be the eighth-largest economy in the European Union. Catalonia accounts for about one-fourth of all Spanish exports, yet for every euro that its residents pay in federal taxes, only 57 cents get spent in their region. Unable to draw on its own tax base, Catalonia was further outraged during the financial crisis by having to ask the central government for a bailout. Catalonia's then-president Artur Mas, whose Convergence party has governed the region for decades, sought financial concessions similar to those received by the Basque region but his demands were rejected.

Facing growing pressures among his restive Catalan voters, Mas sought repeatedly to stave off the simmering independence revolt by drawing up an expanded autonomy statute, but his efforts were rebuffed by the Madrid government and the Spanish Constitutional Court. Having exhausted every alternative, Mas bowed to the separatists and agreed to a binding referendum that would determine whether Catalonia should become independent in spite of the Spanish constitution's ban on secession.

On September 11, 2012, more than 1 million people poured into the streets of Barcelona demanding that Catalonia should be allowed to vote on becoming Europe's next independent state. Mas reacted by dissolving the regional parliament to strengthen his hand in negotiations with the central government headed by Rajoy. As a pragmatic politician in the mold of his mentor Jordi Pujol, who had managed for much of the post-Franco era to keep Catalan nationalism in check, Mas insisted that he needed to achieve some measure of progress toward a compromise with the central government if he was to maintain control of the region's growing band of separatists.

But his repeated appeals for more favorable autonomy measures fell on deaf ears as Rajoy refused to engage in any negotiations involving greater self-rule. During his first four-year term as prime minister, when he enjoyed an absolute majority, Rajoy became convinced that any concessions to Catalonia would open a Pandora's box of fresh independence demands from the Basque country, followed by other regions such as Galicia, Valencia, and Andalucia that expressed the desire for greater latitude in running their own affairs. He feared any hint of weakness in dealing with potential breakaway regions would exacerbate growing public distrust of the central government, not least because of the unpopular austerity measures he had imposed on his people at the behest of Germany and other EU partners. Rajoy pushed through new measures that fortified the powers of the Constitutional Court in order to repel any possible unilateral moves by Catalonia toward secession.

In the absence of any compromise with Madrid, the separatist movement in Catalonia continued to flourish. "Catalan Day" is now observed every year on September 11 with a protest march by hundreds of thousands of separatists demonstrating peacefully in the streets of Barcelona to show their support for an independent state. Meanwhile, the financial pressures in favor of separatism have been growing. Even though Spain is starting to show signs of an economic recovery, the Catalan government complains that the substantial tax payments they are forced to pay to Madrid are holding back the region's return to economic health. They argue that the gap between their tax payments and returned investments had grown as large as $15 billion a year, or about half of the region's annual budget. Rancor is growing on both sides. The governor of the Bank of Spain has warned that further moves toward independence could result in capital controls on Catalan bank accounts.

In turn, Catalonia, which accounts for about one-fifth of Spain's economy, has threatened to stop paying its share of the national debt. Opinion polls showed that support for independence has grown from 20 percent at the start of the financial crisis in 2009 to nearly 50 percent. When Scotland was allowed by the British government to proceed with a referendum in 2014 that resulted in a 55 percent majority to remain within the United Kingdom, Mas decided that Catalonia would stage a referendum of its own regardless of Madrid's opposition. The nonbinding Catalan referendum produced an 80 percent vote in favor of separating from Spain, though only about 37 percent of all voters turned out because Spain's Supreme Court had invalidated the results in advance on the grounds the vote would violate the constitution, which declares Spain to be indivisible.

Ever since Spain became a constitutional democracy in 1978, the mainstream parties have managed to govern on their own. The desire to avoid messy ruling coalitions can be attributed in part to the painful memories of the Second Republic, a volatile democratic regime that collapsed during the civil war. In the post-Franco era, the conservatives and the Socialists have managed to carry out smooth transitions which have preserved the country's political stability under the genial reign of King Juan Carlos and, since 2014, his son Felipe VI. Spain's first postauthoritarian government brought together fourteen center-right parties known as the Union of the Democratic Center under the leadership of prime minister Adolfo Suárez.

Besides managing the peaceful emergence from the Franco era, Suárez pushed through political reforms that established free elections, enacted the first democratic constitution since 1931, and brought Spain into the North Atlantic Treaty Organization. Suárez's minority government also survived a military coup while battling ETA, the armed Basque nationalist group that killed more than 200 people in terrorist attacks during his tenure in power. But the UDC was devastated in an electoral landslide that brought the Socialists to power in 1982. Spain's conservatives later regrouped during a long stint in opposition, deploying help from other European parties, notably German chancellor Helmut Kohl's Christian Democrats, to modernize their movement and overcome the historical association with Franco. It was renamed the Popular Party, which first came to power under former prime minister José María Aznar's leadership from 1996 to 2004.

The Spanish Socialist Workers' Party, which was originally founded in 1879, was brought back to life after Franco's death and transformed from a radical Marxist group into a pragmatic social democratic movement along the lines of the German Social Democratic Party. The SPD even printed and paid for the Spanish Socialist party's election campaign posters and pamphlets. Former German chancellor Willy Brandt became a personal mentor for Felipe González, who ruled Spain as prime minister from 1982 to 1996. During that period, known as the golden years of Spain's post-Franco era, the country joined the European Union, expanded the welfare state, and modernized the economy.

Later, under the leadership of José Luis Rodríguez Zapatero, the

Socialists carried out a second social transformation that relaxed abortion and divorce laws and made Spain the first Roman Catholic country to authorize same-sex marriage. Under German tutelage, Spain also took the first steps toward coming to terms with the human rights abuses of Franco's dictatorship and the Spanish Civil War by passing the 2007 Law of Historical Memory, which offered monetary compensation to Franco's victims.

But one-party rule, even if it alternates between rival political groups, often carries the risk that power may be abused. In Spain's case, the stench of corruption has become closely associated with the traditional ruling class. When the Socialists were in power, prominent ministers became embroiled in bribery scandals related to construction projects for the Seville World's Fair and the Barcelona Olympics. During its most recent turn in government, the Popular Party under Rajoy's leadership has been encumbered by numerous indictments on charges of embezzlement, bribery, influence peddling, and money laundering involving several leading officials, including cabinet ministers and prominent mayors in cities throughout Spain.

The Popular Party's treasurer was accused of siphoning secret donations from construction companies and other business groups to set up a slush fund that was used to make cash payments in envelopes to senior party leaders, including Rajoy. The party leaders vehemently denied the allegations and pinned the blame on the party treasurer, Luis Bárcenas, who became the target of a criminal probe after it was learned he had amassed more than $50 million in secret bank accounts in Switzerland and elsewhere.

The persistent accounts of corruption among the ruling establishment have also ensnared a former chief justice of Spain's supreme court and King Juan Carlos's son-in-law, who was charged with embezzling funds from charitable organizations. But much of the public disenchantment has focused on the country's two leading political parties and exacted a heavy toll on their electoral support.

Indeed, the share of votes in national elections for the Popular Party and the Socialists plummeted from 80 percent in the 2011 elections to less than 50 percent four years later. The main beneficiaries have been the new upstart parties, Podemos and Ciudadanos, who have made transparency and clean government the main planks in their political platforms since they emerged on the political scene in 2014.

With memories of fascism still strong in Spain, Greece, and Portugal, it is the radical left that has surged in voter support across the southern European periphery. Podemos, which translates as "We Can," was founded in 2014 as a far-left protest party by a group of university professors in Madrid who were angry with abuses of power by the mainstream parties. Podemos grew out of the Los Indignados uprising that followed the 2008 financial crisis and spawned massive street protests against political corruption and social inequality. The movement gained further momentum during Spain's painful housing crisis and the harsh austerity measures imposed under Rajoy that caused rampant unemployment, particularly among young people.

Podemos hoped to emulate the Greek far-left party Syriza, which gained power in 2015 by exploiting the failures of mainstream socialist and conservative parties that drove the country into economic depression. Syriza gained notoriety for standing up to Germany and other creditors over Greece's bailout terms, even though it eventually complied with EU demands in order to keep Greece in the euro zone. Podemos has backed Syriza in its confrontation with its creditors by staging massive rallies in support of its radical leader, Prime Minister Alexis Tsipras.

The leadership of Podemos has also drawn inspiration from the left-wing populist movement of the late Venezuelan strongman Hugo Chávez. One of the party's founders served as an advisor to Chávez and its media campaign strategies are similar to those employed by Chávez. Led by the charismatic, pony-tailed Pablo Iglesias (named after a founding father of Spanish socialism in the nineteenth century), Podemos waged frequent attacks against Spain's "caste system" and mobilized grass-roots support in their demands for greater accountability to prevent abuses by the leading political parties, the business community, and the Spanish royal family.

Iglesias disdains the radical leftist label and says his party is "post ideology." He says the main causes driving his party are the income and social inequality growing out of the European debt crisis as well as the series of corruption scandals afflicting Spain's rich and powerful. He and his party have clearly resonated with young voters and emerged as a potential kingmaker of Spanish politics by capturing 20 percent of the vote in December 2015 national elections.

Like Podemos, the center-right movement Ciudadanos became a national force in the 2015 elections by winning 13 percent of the vote to become Spain's fourth party. The party appeals to conservative voters who like its liberal, probusiness philosophy and focus on individual freedoms, but who are fed up with the arrogance and corruption that has soiled the reputation of the Popular Party during its time in power. Ciudadanos is based in Catalonia but is staunchly opposed to the secessionist movement in the region. Led by Albert Rivera, who like Iglesias is still in his thirties, the party wants to reform Spain by rooting out corruption and shifting power to a new generation of reformers who are eager to cleanse the system.

But unlike Iglesias, Rivera says his political program advocates "sensible change" through market reforms designed to bolster investment and promote job growth by cutting taxes and regulatory hurdles for business. Despite their ideological differences, both new parties want to do more than get rid of the current generation of ruling politicians; they want to overhaul what they believe are ineffective institutions and introduce greater transparency to halt the endemic corruption afflicting the political establishment.

Even more than the lingering economic crisis, the separatist threat posed by Catalonia may be the biggest challenge confronting the nation. Of Spain's four national parties, Podemos is the only one that insists on allowing Catalans the right to decide their status in a referendum. All of the other parties have rejected the notion of a plebiscite on the basis that it would violate the Spanish constitution. But the longer Spain waits to allow Catalans a voice in determining their own future, the stronger the secessionist movement seems to grow.

The 2015 election resulted in a political stalemate. Both Rajoy and Sánchez failed in their attempts to form a stable coalition government, and King Felipe VI was forced to call for a new round of elections. Six months later, Spanish voters went again to the polls to break the deadlock. The vote was scheduled just three days after the historic referendum in Britain in favor of leaving the European Union. The shock of Brexit clearly had an impact on a Spanish electorate worried about a prolonged phase of political instability. The day after the British referendum, Spain's stock market index plunged more than 12 percent. Rajoy also warned about past links between Podemos and the Venezuelan regime of Hugo Chávez. Rather than take a leap into the unknown, he urged voters to opt in favor of a safe pair of hands over upstart populists.

The strategy of stirring voter fears worked. The Popular Party performed much better than pollsters predicted, emerging as the clear winner even though it fell well short of an overall majority. Podemos, which had come out of nowhere to capture 20 percent of the vote in the previous round, lost ground while the mainstream center-left Socialists recovered some support. It seemed, at least for a while, that the old two-party system might still show some resilience.

Nonetheless, Spain's political stalemate persisted as Rajoy failed to come up with a stable ruling coalition after the second national election in less than a year. The precarious economic plight in Spain and Portugal was about to become worse—both countries had run up excessive budget deficits that broke the rules governing the European single currency and faced the prospect of having to pay millions of euros in sanctions. A fragile left-wing government was barely holding together in Lisbon, and the prospect of a prolonged deadlock in Spain threatened to transform the Iberian Peninsula into a new zone of instability at a time when European leaders were confronting troubles on many other fronts.

Crisis upon crisis was piling up across Europe in the summer of 2016. A wave of terror attacks in Belgium, France, and Germany had alarmed their populations. Italy was facing a major banking meltdown and a constitutional referendum that would soon topple its government. Hungary and Poland were taking legislative measures that called into question their commitment to democracy. Greece was still mired in enormous debts and the prospect of another eurozone crisis loomed on the horizon with Europe's anemic economic recovery, slow growth, and continuing hemorrhage of jobs. The British vote to bolt the EU had taken everybody by surprise, leaving European leaders with no clear idea how such a withdrawal was going to proceed. But it soon became clear that complex negotiations over a British exit would further snarl their efforts to regain voter confidence and repulse the populist challenge.

Once again, Germany's chancellor Angela Merkel felt compelled to take action. Finance minister Wolfgang Schauble, her most trusted political ally and the second most powerful person in the German government, decided that everything must be done to save Spain and Portugal. During a meeting of the G20 ministers in China, Schäuble told colleagues that if the EU Commission imposed the hefty sanctions as prescribed by euro rules it could trigger more political and economic turbulence at a time when Europe could scarcely afford any further turmoil. There was more than a touch of irony in his intervention, since Schäuble is often characterized as the scourge of spendthrift southern Europeans for his fiscal hawkishness. But he realized that inflicting political damage on his friend Rajoy was a greater risk to Europe's stability than undermining the credibility of the euro.

After Schäuble went around his back and persuaded a majority of EU commissioners to cancel the financial penalties against Spain and Portugal, Jean-Claude Juncker was not amused. The chief executive of the EU Commission told his colleagues that Europe would suffer in the long run from such blatant political interference, but he acknowledged that neither he nor anybody else was in a position to challenge Germany's power and influence. "We must not be more Catholic than the Pope, but please make it known that the Pope wanted to impose a fine of zero," Juncker sarcastically told his colleagues, reflecting his frustration over the impotence of EU institutions in a confrontation with the dominant power of Germany.

But in the minds of many Spaniards, Germany remains more closely associated with oppressive austerity measures that Rajoy felt obliged to follow, as prescribed by the European Union in the wake of the collapse in property prices that nearly wrecked the Spanish economy. While a close political ally of Rajoy, Chancellor Merkel is also regarded as the primary cause of much pain and suffering across Spain and the rest of southern Europe. For the past decade, Germany has insisted that Spain and other countries that lived beyond their means must curtail spending and increase taxes to restore economic credibility. The magnitude of the economic recession, particularly in terms of lost jobs, has made such measures extremely unpalatable.

Spain, along with Greece and Italy, has suffered through perhaps the worst crisis of youth unemployment in the postwar history of Europe. In some regions, as many as 50 percent of young people under age thirty cannot find sustainable jobs. The lack of labor reforms that would open up the economy is often cited as a debilitating factor harming job prospects for young people in Spain as well as elsewhere in the southern periphery. Whether the economy recovers and whether the government can find the courage to undertake bold reforms will determine whether Spain can regain the energy and dynamism that quadrupled its living standards within thirty years after joining the European Union.

Europe's worst economic downturn since the Great Depression has caused voters across much of the continent to become alienated from the centrist ruling parties. In their anger and frustration, they have turned toward the radical fringes on the right and the left. In Germany, Austria, the Netherlands, and the United Kingdom, formerly loyal supporters of the Tory or Christian Democrats on the right or Social Democrats on the left have become attracted to the anti-European, anti-immigrant message of far-right populist parties.

In some ways, the diminished appeal of the mainstream parties is rooted in the fact that the large ideological debates between the left and the right have been resolved. Most countries in Europe now take it for granted, regardless of who is in power, that universal health care and generous unemployment payments will be covered by a large state sector funded by hefty income taxes. What was once regarded as a progressive policy agenda by Social Democrats has been embraced by every part of the political spectrum. In the absence of any debate about sustaining Europe's generous social welfare programs, the mainstream political parties in Spain, France, Italy, and Britain have struggled to find their political voice. In the process, they have lost about two-thirds of their supporters over the past two decades.

The economic crisis has generated not only new populist political forces and spurred the cause of regional separatism. It has also fomented an antiglobalization backlash and deep resentment toward the concept of supranational governance as represented by EU institutions in Brussels. While unhappiness with the idea of a united

Europe has fueled the rise of far-right parties in France, the Netherlands, and Denmark, the southern states of Spain, Greece, and Portugal still nurture hostile memories of previous fascist dictatorships.

Thus, voters in southern Europe have turned instead toward radical leftist insurgents to show their displeasure with mainstream
parties. In the view of many political experts, the prolonged social
and economic turmoil caused by crises over the euro, austerity measures, and the influx of refugees could lead to further political disintegration across Europe. As the ruling establishment falls apart,
voters may be tempted by the extremist message of regional separatists and populist nationalists. In that regard, Spain may be the
canary in the coal mine.

With the country reluctant to go to the polls for the third time in
a year, Rajoy managed to secure another term in office in late 2016
when the Socialists decided to allow him to become prime minister of a minority government rather than face an even bigger defeat
in another election. Despite his tenuous grip on power, Rajoy was
determined to promote Spain's economic recovery in order to keep
the nation from coming apart. But he acknowledged that the fragmented state of Spanish politics would make it difficult to manage a
country that had moved from deadlock to gridlock.

"Having a government that cannot govern is just as bad as not having a government," he told the new parliament. "I take it for granted
that every day we will have to build a majority to govern the country."
A dogged administrator who shuns the limelight, Rajoy cast himself
as the custodian of Spanish unity in the face of the secessionist challenges in Catalonia and the Basque region. He also wants to subdue
the electoral appeal of the two new upstart parties—Ciudadanos
and Podemos—and return his country to a more stable equilibrium
between centrist parties on the right and the left.

After steering Spain through a turbulent debt crisis and property crash that required a banking bailout in 2012, Rajoy has man-

aged to slow the country's economic deterioration and reduce its high unemployment levels. He spent much of his first term in office strengthening the powers of Spain's Constitutional Court to fine or suspend public officials and to thwart the separatist program. "Catalonia is not going anywhere, nothing is going to break," Rajoy said in a nationally televised address after the Catalan regional parliament first voted in favor of a plan to establish an independent state.

In his first test after securing a second mandate, Rajoy won a major victory when the Constitutional Court ruled against holding a referendum in September 2017 that the prosecession Catalan government saw as a definitive turning point on the road to independence. Leaders of the movement vowed to press ahead with the plebiscite on secession, saying the court's decision should be declared null and void because it blocked the democratic will of the voters. "The institutions of the Spanish state should know that they cannot silence the will of a majority of our people," declared Jordi Sànchez, the president of the Catalan National Assembly.

Rajoy is fiercely determined to prevent any moves toward secession and does not want to go down in history as the prime minister who presided over the breakup of his country. He is prepared to invoke Article 155 of Spain's constitution that allows the national government to compel an autonomous regional authority to meet its obligations under national law. Not only is secession already illegal under the constitution, even if Catalonia were about to break free it would be unlikely to gain membership in the European Union.

Rajoy has promised to veto any attempt by Scotland to become an EU member if it were to separate from the United Kingdom because he insists it would be political suicide for EU member states. Other EU governments who confront similar secessionist challenges, such as Italy, Belgium, and Germany, say they will never approve EU membership for Catalonia because it could set a dangerous precedent.

Nonetheless, many politicians in Europe say the appeal of regional separatism in Spain and other countries does not appear to be dissipating. They say that regardless of constitutional law, national governments must find more effective ways of defusing the drive for independence among breakaway regions. Indeed, the multitude of crises afflicting the European Union and member governments could accelerate the rise of populist and separatist forces across the continent.

Within Spain, the Catalan movement has inspired a coalition of separatist parties in the Basque region to submit legislation to their local parliament asking for a referendum to allow Basque citizens the right to decide their own future, which could include independence. Elsewhere across Europe, Scotland is not the only region where the quest for independence is running strong. Separatist movements are gaining influence because of what are seen as unfair fiscal burdens among the Flemish majority in Belgium and in wealthy northern Italy, where the Northern League is picking up voters under new leadership. Even Bavaria in rock-solid Germany has stepped up its occasional calls to establish a separate state, reflecting a proud regional identity, which is why it is often called the "Texas" of Germany.

Indeed, the possible splintering of nation states across Europe represents a real danger to the European integration project, largely because these separatist movements stem from the same kind of backlash by social and economic forces opposed to globalization. Just as EU institutions in Brussels have become unpopular because they are viewed as too remote from the daily preoccupations of the people, there is a strong desire on the part of many voters to see more governing powers restored to local and regional levels, where they can better address the concerns of individual communities. In this sense, what happens in Catalonia could have a substantial impact on the success or failure of the European idea.

The independence drive gained renewed momentum in 2012 when

Rajoy battled Catalonia's then-leader Artur Mas over his demands to reduce his region's tax contributions to the federal government in Madrid, which then redistributes wealth to poorer regions of Spain. Rajoy's refusal to negotiate triggered outrage among many Catalans, sparking renewed calls for independence. "We are sitting at the table, saying we want to negotiate with the Spanish government, but first they refuse to talk and now there is nobody on the other side of the table," Catalonia's foreign minister, Raül Romeva, told me. "We are being squeezed dry financially by Madrid. Our people and our society are pushing us to move toward independence." In the meantime, pressures from Spain's economic crisis have ratcheted up tax increases on the wealthy Catalan region, further inflaming separatist sentiment.

Two proindependence parties formed the Together for Yes coalition in Catalonia and won a clear majority in the regional parliament in 2012. They quickly pushed through a motion to kick-start the process toward independence. Elsewhere in Spain, the Catalan movement has inspired a coalition of separatist parties in the Basque region to submit legislation to their local parliament asking for a referendum to allow Basque citizens the right to decide their own future, which could include independence.

Carles Puigdemont took over from Mas in January 2016 as Catalonia's president after it became clear that Mas was not radical enough to secure a majority of independence-minded legislators in the regional parliament. Unlike his moderate predecessor, Puigdemont has always been a strong advocate for Catalonian independence. Upon taking the oath of office, he immediately promised to put in place a fast-track plan to establish, within eighteen months, the structure for an independent Catalan republic that would include a separate constitution, treasury, social security system, and diplomatic service.

He said the region had no choice but to press ahead with the infrastructure of a new state so that it would be able to function as soon as a binding referendum on Catalonia's future would be held, possibly by late 2017. Catalans already enjoy extensive autonomy in education, health, and policing. But their leaders are still eager to acquire the other trappings of an independent state. Now they want to hold a legitimate referendum that will determine their own future, just as Scotland did. But a key part of the problem they face is that Catalonia is worth much more in terms of economic value to Spain than Scotland is to the United Kingdom.

Madrid has always faced difficulty in imposing central rule on the country's seventeen regions. Devolution of power was accepted in the post-Franco era as a crucial foundation of Spain's newly fledged democracy. By giving some degree of autonomy in fields like education and police forces to all regions, Madrid's central government was able to disguise the restoration of historic rights to the Catalans and the Basques, whose stubborn belief in their own nationhood, culture, and language could never be eradicated under Franco's dictatorship.

In the four decades since Franco's death, Spain has struggled to uphold the constitution's insistence on the indissoluble unity of the nation against the powerful centrifugal forces of regional separatism. These tendencies are deeply entrenched in local history and acquired heroic status in the resistance against Franco. In order to quell the violent separatist war led by the Basque guerilla force ETA, the Spanish government offered enormous concessions that now enable the Basque region to collect their own taxes and pay much less back to Madrid than Catalonia. Now the Catalans say if they cannot set up an independent state, they want, at the very least, the same kind of generous deal as was given to the Basques. As the wealthiest region in Spain, Catalans now pay to Madrid about ten times what Basques do on a per capita basis. With the Spanish government still recovering from the economic crisis, Madrid cannot afford to offer such concessions at a time when it desperately needs Catalonia's contributions to cover the health and pension liabilities of an aging population.

The forces of populist nationalism that are disrupting the Western democratic order are not just directed against a European superstate bureaucracy in Brussels. The revolution in travel and digital communications that has brought the impact of an entire planet and its 7 billion inhabitants into our living rooms is also spurring calls to manage political affairs closer to home. Even as Catalans enjoy high living standards thanks in large part to their sophisticated connections with the rest of the world, they also insist on the right to assert as much local control as possible over their own culture, education, and politics. One of the great ironies of this age of globalization is that while our prosperity and well-being may depend more than ever on finding global solutions to disease, famine, commerce, and climate change, there are growing demands in Europe, the United States, and other parts of the world for government to be brought down as closely as possible to the daily lives of the people.

CHAPTER SIX

ROME

THE ETERNAL CITY, FOREVER IN DECLINE?

TALIANS ARE RENOWNED FOR THEIR WORLD-WEARY CYNICISM about politics, crime, and the pathetic deterioration of their ancient capital. They love to disparage their political leadership, whether it be for the endemic culture of bribes that brought down the once-dominant Christian Democrats or the bunga-bunga antics of the media entrepreneur turned prime minister, Silvio Berlusconi. They savor the picaresque tales of brave prosecutors pursuing evil godfathers of famous crime syndicates, including the Cosa Nostra of Sicily, the Camorra of Naples, and the 'Ndrangheta of Calabria.

In particular, they relish mocking Rome as a fading beauty whose best days are long past. Popular social media sites like "Roma fa schifo" (Rome is disgusting) display countless pictures of huge potholes, burnt-out cars, and overflowing trash bins lining the capital's streets. When ISIS terrorists once threatened to plant the caliphate flag on the dome of St. Peter's Basilica, thousands of Italians went online to ridicule the jihadi threats because they claimed ISIS would never be able to penetrate the morass of urban garbage.

Those phenomena have collided in a scandal of enormous proportions that has shocked even the most jaded Italians and demonstrated how Rome's plight is even worse than they imagined. The
"Mafia Capitale" indictments were first unveiled in a 1,200-page
arrest warrant released in December 2014 following a two-year
inquiry by Rome's chief prosecutor, Giuseppe Pignatone. More than
one hundred politicians, senior administrators, and civil servants
were accused of taking bribes for years in exchange for providing
favors to organized crime.

The scandal illustrates how the long tentacles of the Mafia have
infiltrated all levels of Rome's municipal services, including the processing and treatment of more than 300,000 desperate refugees who
have poured into Italy in recent years. The ringleader of the Rome
crime syndicate was a former neofascist terrorist, Massimo Carminati, whose far-right Armed Revolutionary Group was previously
involved in the bombing of the Bologna train station that killed more
than eighty people. His main associate, Salvatore Buzzi, came from
the left side of the political spectrum. Buzzi was a former convict
who operated a huge cooperative dedicated to social services.

The Rome mafiosi managed to corrupt successive city governments from the right and the left by paying monthly bribes to key
politicians of the major parties in exchange for gaining a monopoly
over public tenders that included bus and subway transport, garbage
collection, and refugee camps. For decades, the mobsters drained
city coffers while providing little in the way of reliable maintenance
or public services.

A safety review in 2016 showed that 40 percent of Rome's streets
are riddled with potholes. Bus drivers routinely walk off the job
whenever important soccer matches are being played. Parents are
forced to buy toilet paper for their children's schools. But the callous
exploitation of the refugee situation by the mob is what has really
incensed public opinion. In one wiretap intercept released by the

police, Buzzi boasted to Carminati, also known as the Blind Pirate for having lost an eye in a gunfight, about how he had pocketed $50 million by seizing control of the main reception centers around Rome that were housing the influx of migrants, asylum seekers, and refugees who had washed up on the shores of Sicily. "Do you have any idea how much money we are making on the immigrants?" Buzzi said. "Even drug trafficking is not as profitable."

The Mafia Capitale scandal will evolve for years through a cavalcade of corruption trials that is likely to follow multiple investigations of the former mayor Gianni Alemanno, who ruled the city from 2008 to 2013 when the mob's activities reached their peak. The initial probes have ensnared the capital's own anticorruption czar, Italo Walter Politano, as well as many other prominent politicians and civil servants.

In some ways, the scandal enveloping the city of Rome came as no surprise. Rampant corruption in the form of bribes, kickbacks, and extortion has long been taken for granted as part of daily life by many Italians, especially in the south, where various mafias are entrenched in every part of society. But the discovery of a previously unknown crime syndicate that acquired nearly total control over the shoddy municipal services in the nation's capital shocked many Italians. It also awakened them to the sad fact that they remain the principal victims of the criminal activity and political malfeasance that permeates much of the country.

Besides explaining the decay in public infrastructure and the multibillion-dollar hole in Rome's finances, the revelations have led to much soul-searching across Italy. Many people from every social class in every corner of the nation are asking whether a dynamic country of 57 million that is Europe's fourth-largest economy has become so impervious to the idea of reform that the entire nation, and not just Rome, may simply have become ungovernable.

In some ways, the situation in Rome represents in microcosm

many of the problems plaguing the entire country. Italy has been try-ing to bolster the integrity and efficiency of its political and economic systems for more than two decades. In the early 1990s, a nationwide corruption scandal erupted that became known as Tangentopoli, or "Bribesville." Italy's investigating magistrates uncovered how the two leading parties at the time, the Christian Democrats and the Socialists, had been moving in and out of power for decades while receiving bribes in exchange for political favors as a way of funding their operations. Both parties were soon swept away in a wave of public revulsion that ushered in a new political order, led by the bil-lionaire media entrepreneur Silvio Berlusconi, who claimed he was too wealthy to be corrupt.

Berlusconi is now seen as an early version of Donald Trump, who was elected to the presidency on a similar platform of populist nationalism built around his own personality as a media and prop-erty mogul. For over two decades, Berlusconi dominated Italian politics and served three terms as prime minister. He failed to carry out his promised reform agenda and spent much of his time in office fending off prosecution for his own scandals involving sex parties and illicit business practices.

Under pressure from other European leaders, Berlusconi was forced to resign and was replaced in November 2011 by a govern-ment of technocrats led by Mario Monti, an economics professor and former EU commissioner. Now eighty years of age and in failing health, Berlusconi still complains that he was the victim of a quasi–coup d'état led by German Chancellor Angela Merkel. But at the time, there were palpable fears that Europe could suffer a financial meltdown and the eurozone might collapse if he did not leave office because bond buyers had lost confidence in Italy's ability to meet its debt payments.

Monti was seen as a potential savior for Italy and Europe because he was held in high esteem by Merkel and the other EU leaders.

While known for his steely integrity and intelligence, Monti lacked charisma and political wiles. He tried to use the looming financial crisis over Greece and Italy as a way to pressure Merkel into accepting the notion that responsibility for all debts should be shared among the eurozone's nineteen members. Monti argued that debt mutualization would have solidified the euro and defused the financial crisis once and for all. "This was an opportunity to deal with the crisis at an early stage and use it as an opportunity to move Europe forward, but it became impossible because of political resistance in Germany," Monti told me. Conscious of how German voters would loathe sharing the debt burdens of profligate partners, Merkel refused to consider any change in the rules. She also realized that even entertaining the idea would cut short her political career.

As a result, the EU has been forced to follow Merkel's habit of "kicking the can down the road" when dealing with Europe's periodic financial crises. Monti lasted as prime minister little more than a year. In the spring of 2013, his government of centrist technocrats was dissolved following fresh elections that brought to power the center-left Democrats, who evolved from their Communist roots during the Cold War era into a moderate social democratic party.

Looking back on his time in office, Monti says the most disappointing aspect of governing during a crisis was the lack of political courage he encountered among EU leaders who knew the right thing to do was to push ahead with bold policy responses in the face of public anxiety and skepticism. Jean Monnet, one of the founding fathers of European integration, had always said that Europe would be forged through a succession of crises that would elevate public understanding of the need to build a United States of Europe.

Monti believes the severity of so many difficult challenges at once overwhelmed European leaders and paralyzed their ability to respond effectively. At the time, they were dealing with protracted financial turmoil, surging refugee flows, a newly aggressive Russia,

and jihadist terrorism on a daily basis. As a result, many governments shunned moves toward greater European unity in favor of a
retreat into nationalism, as seen in Britain's vote to leave the European Union. Monti fears the urge to retreat into the womb of the
nation-state will accelerate the momentum of populist extremism
and could lead to the complete disintegration of the European Union.

The anti-Europe trend is particularly striking in Italy, one of the
founding members of the European Union. Since the Treaty of Rome
was signed in March 1957 establishing the main institutions of the
European Union, Italy has received many benefits from EU membership and has traditionally viewed Brussels as a symbol of economic opportunity and the guardian of continental peace. Most of
all, Italians came to believe that Brussels served as a *vincolo esterno,*
or external constraint, which protected their country from its most
debilitating afflictions, such as corruption, budgetary laxity, and a
fragmented economy split between the wealthy north and the poor
south.

Yet today, Italians of all ages and social classes have lost faith in
the European Union. They tend to blame it for the country's feeble
economic performance, which has suffered a triple-dip recession
since 2008. Much of their criticism is focused on the euro, which
when it was first put into effect shocked many Italians because it
caused prices of their beloved espresso coffee to double overnight.
"Italians have always been some of the strongest supporters of European unity, but now we are paying the price for years of irresponsible political leadership which sought to lay the blame for all of our
problems on Brussels," former prime minister Giuliano Amato, one
of the architects of Europe's ill-fated constitution, told me. "Europe
is not the source of our problems but, on the contrary, should be recognized as the only realistic way for us to resolve them."

Italians are convinced that one of their biggest blunders was to
abandon the national currency, the lira, in favor of the single EU cur-

rency, the euro. In the past, they could devalue the lira and inflate their way out of economic difficulty. Now they are tethered to euro-zone rules designed to appease Germany's anti-inflation obsession. As a result, Italy has suffered through an agonizing recession for the better part of a decade and recorded the worst economic performance of any EU member country outside of Greece.

Ever since the euro was introduced in 1999, Italy has failed to achieve any growth at all in productivity. Income levels have actually declined and unemployment is now higher than in any EU country except Greece. Public debt has soared to 2.3 trillion euros, or 133 percent of the Italian gross national product. Italy's banks are in deep trouble, burdened by nearly $400 billion in bad loans, or about one-fifth of the country's national income. In the decade since the 2008 financial crisis, Italy has lost at least one-quarter of its industrial production as factories close and jobs move to China.

The EU's Schengen treaty that established borderless travel within much of Europe is reviled as the root cause of the refugee crisis that has overwhelmed social services in many parts of the country. As politicians have sought to shift the blame for Italy's troubles to Brussels, it is no surprise that a recent poll showed that public support of the European Union has plummeted from 73 percent in 2010 to less than 40 percent in 2016. After Britain voted to leave the EU, polls showed that 48 percent of Italians were willing to do the same.

When Matteo Renzi, head of the center-left Democratic Party, became Italy's youngest-ever prime minister in 2014 at age thirty-nine, he vowed to clean up the country and carry out much-needed reforms with an urgency that was lacking among his predecessors. Renzi had been a popular and energetic mayor of Florence, breathing new life into a city that lived off tourism, Renaissance art, and not much else. He brought the same kind of can-do enthusiasm to the capital when he took over control of the Democratic Party and elbowed aside Enrico Letta, a prominent intellectual who served as prime minister for less than a year after succeeding Monti. As soon as he moved into the prime minister's office at Rome's Palazzo Chigi, Renzi pledged to carry out the kind of comprehensive reform agenda that Italians had long been promised but never saw implemented by its ruling establishment.

Renzi called himself a *rottomatore*, a kind of demolition man who would scrap the old decaying system in favor of a dynamic new order. Within his first year in power, he surprised pundits by challenging the country's union leadership that was a core supporter of his party. He quickly pushed through a series of far-reaching labor reforms that make it much easier to hire and fire employees. Renzi's Jobs Act was designed to help create more openings for young people, who had become disillusioned with their dismal job prospects ever since recession first struck Europe in the wake of the 2008 global economic crisis. For nearly a decade, about 40 percent of Italians under age thirty have not been able to find sustainable jobs, forcing many of them to take part-time work, join the underground economy, or else emigrate to faster-growing economies in Britain or the United States.

When refugees entering Europe shifted their main crossing point from Turkey to Libya, Renzi was dismayed when he asked for but did not receive help from his European partners. Instead, he proposed a "migration compact" with the leaders of African countries in which he offered to increase development spending and investment if they would help curtail the flow of illegal immigrants seeking to cross the Mediterranean Sea to the islands off Sicily.

Italy's EU partners, particularly Germany and Sweden, which have been the main destinations for many immigrants in recent years, were impressed with the results. They gave their blessing to what became a Europe-wide policy by rallying around Renzi's barter arrangement of granting development aid in exchange for tougher controls by African countries on outward migration toward Europe.

Finally, Renzi decided to capitalize on his success by becoming much more assertive in challenging German Chancellor Angela Merkel, whose dominant, almost monopolistic control over European policies had been magnified by the weakness of France and other EU partners.

"I realized that Italy had to clean up its own act before we could challenge the Germans and start making demands on our own for Europe to change its policies," Renzi told me. "Once we showed that we could create 580,000 jobs within two years with the Jobs Act, we gained the credibility to argue for change across Europe. It was only then that I could start pushing back against Merkel and Germany's misguided policies for Europe."

Renzi surprised EU leaders with his brazen willingness to confront Merkel over what he described as failed economic policies that Germany had imposed on its EU partners, which he blamed for having suppressed jobs and growth in Europe. He criticized Germany's selfish vision and insisted the tough austerity measures that Merkel was advocating would permanently damage the economies of southern EU members and fuel the rise of political extremism. He warned that Germany's policies were causing deflation across Europe, which would only worsen the plight of debt-ridden states like Italy.

Renzi's bold defense of Italy's national interests paid off. He won support for a more flexible jobs policy and greater assistance in coping with refugee flows into Italy from North Africa. He also demanded special assistance for Italy's beleaguered banks, warning that failure to do so could trigger another financial crisis that could spread from Europe to the rest of the world. He was also willing to stand up to Merkel in questioning whether economic sanctions imposed against Russia in retaliation for its aggression in Ukraine are inflicting serious harm on European business. Since the sanctions went into effect following Russia's seizure of Crimea in 2014, Italy is estimated to have lost more than $3 billion worth of cancelled exports to Russia.

At the final European Union summit meeting of 2015—the fif-
teenth over the course of a year filled with almost constant crises—
Renzi shocked his peers by accusing Merkel of blatant hypocrisy on
the issue of sanctions against Russia. He said he would no longer
tolerate "being lectured by the schoolteacher" even if she was more
than two decades older than he was. Merkel had insisted for months
that in order to send a stern message to Vladimir Putin, Europe
needed to project a united front against Russia.

Merkel had urged Italy, Bulgaria, and other nations to cancel the
South Stream pipeline that was intended to bring Russian gas to
southern Europe, saying that to proceed with the project would send
the wrong signal to Putin. Renzi resisted, but finally accepted her pleas
to cancel the project, and Italy started looking for new supplies from
Africa. But then, shortly before their encounter in Brussels, Renzi
learned that Merkel had quietly approved a second North Stream
pipeline that would bring Siberian gas directly to the German port of
Greifswald—without bothering to inform other EU leaders.

"Enough is enough, Angela!" Renzi shouted. "You made us follow
your line on austerity at the cost of great pain for our people. You cannot say you are giving your blood to Europe when actually we are the
ones who are suffering." He went on to warn that the EU's sanctions
policy would damage income and employment to such an extent that
it would fuel the rise of political extremism on both the right and the
left wings of the political spectrum across the continent.

"Your policies will cost some of us here our jobs as presidents and
prime ministers," Renzi went on to say, according to summit participants. "But that may not matter in the long term. What does matter
is that if Europe is going to succeed, it needs to serve all twenty-eight
countries and not just one." Merkel meekly replied that the North
Stream project was just "a normal business deal" and that it should
not represent a break in the sanctions regime against Russia. But
Renzi would not accept her explanation. "We went along with you

and said no to South Stream. OK, fine, but then all of a sudden we discover you are making a quiet deal on the side with a second North Stream pipeline. The first one is not even at full capacity. So why do you need to do a second one? Who decided? Is that what you call an EU energy policy? One that serves only Germany and not the rest of us?"

Merkel was taken aback by the vehemence of Renzi's argument. For once, she could not persuade the other European leaders to accept her point of view. Renzi won the sympathy of all other leaders gathered around the large table in Brussels, except for Merkel's close ally, Mark Rutte, the Dutch prime minister. Merkel said she would review the terms of the North Stream deal and make sure that it complied with EU sanction rules against Russia. But Renzi had served notice that the emotional toll of Berlin's austerity regimen and Germany's cavalier approach to Russian gas shipments was endangering Europe's fragile consensus.

He also criticized Merkel for her open-door policy toward Syrian refugees and complained that Germany had failed to do what was demanded of Italy, namely to take the fingerprints and systematically process all migrants. In his emotional rebuke to the powerful German leader, Renzi emerged as a counterpoint to Merkel even though he was one of Europe's youngest and least experienced leaders. His brash challenge highlighted the north-south divide that was threatening to tear Europe apart, pitting highly indebted southern European states against their flinty creditors of the north.

Despite his display of political courage abroad, Renzi soon ran into trouble at home. After pledging dramatic changes in the way Italy would be governed, his reform efforts stalled. He staked his political future on a major overhaul of Italy's political structure with a referendum on constitutional reforms designed to transform the electoral and legislative systems. Renzi had entered office with a blaze of activity and a strong reformist record as a popular mayor of

Florence. But he later acknowledged he had pushed his people too far and too fast. He had vowed to resign as prime minister if he lost the referendum. When the results from the December 2016 vote were tallied, his slate of amendments was rejected by a resounding 60 percent of the voters. Renzi resigned the next day, allowing his friend and foreign minister, Paolo Gentiloni, to assume his position as prime minister.

As one of the youngest and most unorthodox leaders in Europe, Renzi lost his impetuous gamble but still retained the leadership of his party, in hopes of making a comeback. He had felt supremely confident that he could break Italy's governing pathologies and transform its politics by changing the way the country chooses its leaders. Something had to be done, he told me, to stop the revolving-door governments that had led to sixty-three prime ministers over the past seventy years. He admits it was a mistake to personalize the vote because it provided an excuse to voters who wanted to register their displeasure with him or his government. But he still believes "that one day it will be possible to unlock the dynamism and creativity of the Italian people and convince them to support a peaceful revolution in the way they are governed." That opportunity could rise again if his party wins the next national elections.

Many Italians believe Renzi was doomed because he had embraced an impossible mission. For many years, the empty promises of political and economic reforms that would unlock the country's hidden resources, ingenuity, and dynamism have left much of the population deeply cynical and frustrated. Italians lament the persistent failures of the reform process by often citing Giuseppe Tomasi de Lampedusa's novel *Il Gattopardo* (*The Leopard*) which describes the enduring power of the nineteenth century aristocracy through the motto "everything must change so that everything can remain the same."

Those Italians who do believe in radical change have become convinced that the entire ruling establishment must be dismantled if the country hopes to break the endless cycle of political turmoil, economic weakness, and endemic corruption in public administration. In recent years, many of them have rushed to support the populist insurgency known as the Five Star Movement, which has blossomed in less than a decade into one of the leading political forces in the country. The movement first emerged as Italy's biggest party in 2013 elections, scoring 26 percent of the vote. Since then, the leadership of the party has evolved and its share of the national vote has increased.

Founded in 2009 by the satirical comedian Beppe Grillo, the Five Star Movement has backed a wide range of causes, including tax cuts for small business, greater help for the poor, and larger investments in renewable energy and high-quality agriculture. It has also promised to slash the pay and privileges of all politicians and to curtail corruption by making government services more transparent. The movement defies ideological categories and insists it does not fit into the traditional political order. All policies and candidates for office must be selected and endorsed through extensive online vetting by its members. Like Renzi and his center-left Democratic Party, Grillo's supporters have been sharply critical of Europe's austerity policies. But they go even further in demanding to hold a referendum that will decide whether Italy should remain within the eurozone or bring back the lira as the national currency. If Italy were to abandon the European single currency, many economists believe it would soon trigger the total collapse of the euro.

Unlike other populist parties, such as leftist groups like Syriza in Greece and Podemos in Spain or right-wing parties like the National Front in France or Austria's Freedom Party, the Five Star movement considers itself to be liberated from all political labels. It has attracted disaffected voters from both the right and the left. Grillo and his late political guru, Gianroberto Casaleggio, an Internet entrepreneur from Milan, launched the movement by capitalizing on popular despair over Italy's recession and growing disaffection with the European Union. They envisioned the Five Star Movement as a total rejection of Italian party politics, one that would create a more egalitarian type of democracy based on direct participation of supporters by having them approve all policies and candidates through voting over the Internet. Five Star has always placed great faith in what it calls the "cyber utopia" that can employ the powerful instruments of the Internet to protect the honesty and integrity of its brand of direct democracy.

Casaleggio died from a brain edema in early 2016 and Grillo then retreated from day-to- day politics. Because of a manslaughter con-viction resulting from a car accident in which three people died, he is banned under his movement's rules from holding public office. But after grieving over his friend's death and fearing the party was losing momentum, Grillo soon resumed a prominent role in guiding the Five Star Movement's policies. He was not shy about using his celebrity status to mobilize voters and even swam two miles across the Messina Strait separating Sicily from the mainland to publicize pollution of the sea.

A new generation of youthful and well-disciplined activists plans to take the protest movement to the next level by entering the halls of power. They have already enjoyed success at the local level and hope to gain control of the national government perhaps in the next election. But their lack of experience in governing has frightened investors and mainstream politicians, who believe that Five Star's economic policies would lead to chaos. Their ascendancy could become yet another major crisis for Europe.

In June 2016, Five Star candidates Virginia Raggi and Chiara Appendino won mayoral races in Rome and Turin, the country's largest and fourth-largest cities. Despite being political novices, both women crushed more traditional opponents by pledging to carry out innovative yet pragmatic change, clean and transparent government, and effective job creation. On the heels of their victories, nationwide polls showed the Five Star Movement had reached its highest-ever levels of popularity, achieving over 30 percent support among all Italian voters.

The meteoric rise of the Five Star Movement reflects widespread public disgust with the way Italy has been ruled for decades. Despite frequent promises of broad reforms, the mainstream parties continue to lose support because they are seen as perpetuating rather than eradicating such public scourges as endemic corruption, wasteful spending, and inefficient tax collection. Meantime, organized crime has flourished by exploiting the forces of globalization and expanding its control over Italy's vast underground economy, which is estimated to be as large as one-quarter of the nation's gross domestic product. Despite convictions that have sent some of their most prominent leaders to jail, Italy's various crime syndicates still control public tenders for everything from toxic waste disposal to thermal spas, in addition to more conventional sources of revenue like trafficking in drugs and prostitutes.

The real test for the Five Star Movement will be to prove that it can govern effectively and not just identify the sources of the country's problems. Nobody is more aware of that challenge than Raggi, a lawyer and single mother who took over as mayor of Rome at the age of thirty-seven. She is the youngest person—and the first woman—to be elected to the post. Some consider the herculean mission of running Rome to be impossible, but Raggi said she hoped to make a positive impact simply by banishing old practices in which politicians and mobsters controlled municipal operations. She vowed scrupulous enforcement of open bidding on all public tenders. A study by the country's anticorruption agency showed that of the 1,500 contracts signed by city authorities in recent years for garbage collection and street cleaning, nine out of ten were awarded without due process to companies with links to organized crime.

Raggi won more than two-thirds of all votes, reflecting the intense outrage felt by many Roman citizens toward the corrupt old guard. Her surprisingly large margin of victory enabled her to assume office with a great reservoir of goodwill because disenchantment with the old guard and its corrupt habits was so acute. One of her first tasks was to renegotiate the terms of Rome's debts, which have soared to more than $13 billion. She encouraged the use of washable diapers to decrease the amount of garbage and return to a barter system for low-income families. Raggi also canceled Rome's bid to host the 2024 Olympics, to the consternation of Renzi and business groups that saw the Olympics as a potential boon for the nation. But she insisted that solving everyday problems in Rome must take priority over the pursuit of grandiose dreams like playing host to the Olympics.

Raggi was also confronted by the city's staggering housing problems and ensuring that city services can be put back on track after the recent Mafia Capitale scandal revealed the extent of neglect. Rome is plagued not just by entrenched corruption but also breathtaking inefficiency that could defy the most diligent efforts of any activist mayor. Shortly before Raggi took office, it was discovered that the municipality owned more than 28,000 residential properties on which unpaid rents amounted to about $400 million a year at current market prices. For years, tenants were allowed to live in villas or apartments either rent-free or at a fraction of what they are worth. One villa with a view over the Colosseum was being rented out for $36 a month and a small apartment on the popular Campo de' Fiori carried a monthly lease of only $6. The shocking revelations of so many cheap residences subsidized by the city were all the more galling to many Romans because they pay the highest property taxes in Italy.

Raggi also decided she would challenge the powerful Roman Catholic Church. She claims the Vatican has failed to pay back property taxes worth up to 400 million euros on the church's massive real estate holdings and other assets. Raggi says previous mayors were afraid to confront the church over the tax issue, but she has received assurances from Pope Francis that in the future the Vatican under his leadership will be willing to pay its fair share, including income taxes for all shops doing business on Vatican property. But Italian politicians have learned to their chagrin that attacking the Catholic Church and its hierarchy can be a perilous undertaking. Many believe that Raggi's pledge to pursue tax payments from the Vatican is yet another reflection of her political naïveté.

Raggi says her lack of experience in the dark arts of Italian politics will ultimately prove beneficial. One of the few women in Italy to achieve high-profile political office, she believes her rise will encourage other young women to become involved in government. She also hopes to prove the Five Star Movement is more than just a protest outlet, but represents an enduring political alternative that will provide honest and efficient government that has been sorely lacking in Italy.

Born and raised in Rome, she didn't become involved in politics until 2011, shortly after the birth of her son. She says she could no longer tolerate the graft and mismanagement she saw all around her and launched her career in politics by getting involved in a neighborhood group before joining the Five Star Movement. She served for three years on the city council before running for mayor. On the strength of her strong mandate in winning election as mayor of Rome, she had emerged as one of the brightest hopes of the Five Star movement's quest to take over the national government in a country yearning for a new era of honest and effective politicians.

But Raggi soon discovered that her positive reception as mayor wore out quickly. She got off to an incredibly rocky start. In her first

months in office, garbage continued to pile up on the streets during
the sweltering summer, exasperating many residents who were desperate for relief from the putrid piles of waste. She hired a consultant, Paola Muraro, to help design a plan to clean the city, only to get
rid of her after learning that Muraro was under investigation for conflicts of interest during previous consulting work for Rome's waste
management authority. Her chief of personnel, Raffaele Marra, was
arrested and detained on corruption charges dating back to 2013,
when he was in charge of housing under a previous administration.
While trying to sort out the garbage crisis, Raggi had trouble forming an administrative team. She was forced to fire her chief of staff,
who refused to take a cut in her huge salary. That prompted a spate
of resignations from the city council, leaving nobody in control of the
city's finances and thus able to help find ways to cope with Rome's
enormous debts.

Roman citizens have grown despondent from the many promises
of reforms that have gone unfulfilled in the past. The magnitude of
the challenges in repairing Rome's decaying infrastructure, cleaning
up its garbage, repairing its streets, and reviving the local economy
may prove beyond the capacity of any human being. Raggi knows
well Rome's reputation for chaos and realizes she faces an uphill
struggle to transform Rome into "a normal and livable city."

She has called on her fellow Romans to assume their own responsibility to make the city better. Besides the capital's poor record of
management, many problems come down to a lack of civic respect
by the citizens themselves. One in four passengers on buses, trams,
and the subway does not buy a ticket. One in five citizens does not
bother to pay the local tax that funds garbage collection. Illegal park-
ing is rarely penalized because of chronic absenteeism among traffic
cops. Despite a difficult start that critics attribute to her lack of experience, Raggi's plight has drawn sympathy. "You can't ask for mira-

cles," said Virginio Carnevali, head of the anticorruption campaign group Transparency International Italia. "Rome is ungovernable."

Then there is the omnipresent role of the mob, which never seems far from the various strands of public life. Raggi has promised to eradicate Mafia Capitale and uproot its presence inside the city's public administration, but the criminals themselves are confident that they will sustain their power and influence over Rome. Shortly before he was taken into custody in what police call the "mondo di mezzo," or underworld investigation, Carminati was recorded by a police wiretap telling a friend how he became known among his peers as "the last king of Rome."

In the conversation, he described in graphic detail how his criminal syndicate had come to occupy such an essential role in Roman life. He said the mob was indispensable in helping the world of rich and important people like businessmen and politicians solve their problems by connecting them with the underworld of criminality that could carry out the dirty work. "It's what I like to call the Middle Earth theory," Carminati said. "The living are above us, and the dead are below. And we are in the middle, making sure everything works just the way we want."

CHAPTER SEVEN

WARSAW

BETWEEN EAST AND WEST

O N A FOG-SHROUDED DAY IN APRIL 2010, A POLISH AIR FORCE plane carrying then-president Lech Kaczyński, his wife, and ninety-four members of the country's governing and security elite flew toward Smolensk in western Russia. The delegation was traveling to a memorial service that would pay homage for the first time on Russian soil to 22,000 Polish victims, many of them young army officers, who were massacred seventy years earlier in the nearby Katyn Forest on the orders of Soviet dictator Josef Stalin.

As the plane approached the small airport outside Smolensk, the pilot announced in a nervous voice that visibility was too poor and that he needed to abort the landing. But some members in the delegation, apparently including the president himself, insisted the ceremony was too important to miss and ordered the pilot, against his better judgment, to proceed with the dangerous landing attempt. The Russian-made Tupolev jetliner clipped some trees and then crashed in a forest less than a mile short of the runway, killing all those aboard, including many members of the political and military elite, in one of the worst aviation disasters to afflict Poland since World War II.

The Smolensk tragedy continues to haunt and divide the country. Jarosław Kaczyński, the deceased president's identical twin brother, believes that a dark conspiracy involving Russia and his brother's political opponents has obscured the real cause of the crash, which investigations in Poland and Russia blamed on pilot error. Kaczyński's Law and Justice party has suggested that Russia engaged in an act of state terrorism by bringing down the plane in order to decapitate Poland's leadership.

The ultraconservative movement, which took power after winning national elections in October 2015, attacked the previous centrist government led by Prime Minister Donald Tusk and his Civic Platform party for accepting Russia's explanations at face value. His critics accused Tusk of negligence in refusing to examine evidence that they claim may have pointed to sabotage or a midair explosion caused by a bomb or a ground-to-air missile. Their suspicions of Russian subterfuge only grew when Moscow refused to hand over the wreckage of the plane to Polish investigators.

One of the new government's first acts upon taking power after the 2015 elections was to commission a fresh investigation into the crash. Like the debate over what to do with former Communists when a new era of democracy arrived in Poland in 1989, the investigation has split the country over whether to close the books on a painful chapter of the country's history or to dig further into a tragedy that could reopen old wounds at home while further damaging Poland's relations with Russia. Defense Minister Antoni Macierewicz, who commissioned the new inquiry, says he is convinced that hidden explosives brought down the plane but has offered no persuasive evidence that Russia may have been involved.

Macierewicz and his team of experts have even suggested that Russia pumped artificial fog over the runway to confuse the pilots.

They tried to prove this theory by boiling sausages and noting that the split along the length of a cooked sausage matched the shape of the gash in the plane's fuselage, indicating that high heat was involved. But all evidence amassed so far still points to a tragic accident. Audio recordings from the Polish Air Force plane showed the two pilots clearly under duress because they were being urged by senior officials on board to overrule cockpit warning systems to attempt the landing in treacherous conditions.

Opponents of Law and Justice assert the new ruling party is striving to inflame emotions about the crash as a way of deflecting any blame away from Lech Kaczyński, who may have ordered the pilot to land the plane in difficult circumstances and could thus be held accountable for the catastrophic accident that devastated the country's ruling elite. The ultimate outcome of the investigation, which could affect the political atmosphere for years to come, may rest in the hands of the deceased president's brother.

Jarosław Kaczyński holds no public position other than a seat in parliament, but his dominant role as chairman of the Law and Justice party, which he founded in 2001 with his deceased brother, makes him the most powerful man in the country. He previously served as prime minister but has chosen this time around to run the country from behind the scenes. He personally selected the country's president, Andrzej Duda, as well as the prime minister, Beata Szydło, and other members of her cabinet. Like his hero Józef Piłsudski, the mustachioed revolutionary who led Poland to independence in 1918, Kaczyński prefers to shy away from public office and maintain a low profile, which enables him to dictate policy through his surrogates without exposing himself to any direct responsibility.

In his spartan office in central Warsaw, located above a pool hall and next to a Japanese restaurant, Kaczyński sits hunched behind a heavy dark desk, receiving a steady stream of visitors who keep him informed about every aspect of political life. From there, he conveys his decisions to the ruling cabinet's ministers and their deputies, who carry out his wishes to the letter. In no other Western democracy is government business conducted in such a manner, with complete power invested in a single personality who holds no formal place in government.

Kaczyński's philosophy is rooted in traditional Catholic values, an abiding distrust of Poland's historical enemies Russia and Germany, and intense disdain for the vision of a more united Europe that would erode the sovereignty of nation-states. Those views resonate with millions of conservative Polish voters who applaud his crusade to fortify Poland's sense of national identity and to restore the primacy of Christian values in a country that is more than 90 percent Catholic. While a majority of Poles favor membership in the European Union, they fiercely resent any intrusions on their daily lives from decisions imposed by liberal, secular institutions in Brussels or by any other outside powers. In Kaczyński's view, the growing domination by Germany over the European Union must be resisted just as much as the claims of a newly assertive Russia.

In the wake of Britain's vote to leave the European Union, Poland will be the largest EU member state that retains its national currency and has no intention of joining the eurozone. With Britain's looming departure, Kaczyński has tried to defuse any initiative by Germany and France to make a quantum leap toward a United States of Europe. After winning the support of other Eastern European countries, he has issued an appeal for a new European Union treaty that would transfer more powers back to member governments from EU institutions in Brussels.

At home, Kaczyński is determined above all to eradicate the lingering influence of those he sees as his most implacable enemies: the secular centrists in the Civic Platform party who served under Tusk and the former Communists who he claims have accumulated vast wealth and influence over modern Poland under capitalist dis-

guises. His ruling party has taken such brazen steps toward con-
trolling the media and the judiciary that it drew a sharp warning
from the European Union's executive commission that the party
was transgressing the bounds of democratic behavior by jeopardiz-
ing the rule of law.

Since his brother's death, Jarosław Kaczyński has dressed in
black every day and visited Lech's grave every Saturday. He attends
a memorial service outside the presidential palace on the tenth day
of every month and says he will be in mourning for the rest of his
life. Lech and Jarosław were extremely close and spoke on the telephone at least ten times a day. As young boys growing up in Communist Poland, they enjoyed a comfortable life. They became popular
child actors, starring in a highly successful film in 1962 called *The
Two Who Stole the Moon*.

They later went on to study law in Warsaw before becoming
involved in the Solidarity trade union movement headed by Lech
Wałęsa. The twins enjoyed a close rapport with Wałęsa as they
climbed the ranks of the movement and helped the future Nobel lau-
reate bring down the pro-Soviet Communist regime and usher in a
new era of democracy. But they broke with Wałęsa and other Solidarity leaders in an ideological dispute over how to deal with the former
Communists in Poland's new democracy.

The Kaczyńskis took a hardline rejectionist approach, saying
there should be a clean rupture with the past and that any officials
who worked for the Communist regime should be ostracized. But
Wałęsa and other leaders in Solidarity took as their example the conciliatory model adopted by Nelson Mandela in forging peace between
black and white communities in postapartheid South Africa. Like
Mandela, the Solidarity leadership favored compromise and rehabil-
itation as a way of engendering a spirit of national unity in the tumultuous early days of the 1990s.

It was too much to bear for the revenge-minded Kaczyński brothers. As they watched former Communists enrich themselves by getting involved in running banks and security services in the new capitalist democracy, the Kaczyńskis believed that the true Polish patriots who battled communism were being sold out in favor of the traitors they sought to overthrow.

The brothers accused Wałęsa of collaborating too closely with the Communists not only after 1989 but much earlier. They came to believe in persistent rumors that Wałęsa's sympathetic approach was rooted in a hidden past that he had acted as an informant for the Communist security services under the pseudonym "Bolek" during the 1970s, a claim that Wałęsa denies to this day. As a result of their extreme views, the Kaczyńskis were pushed out of the Solidarity movement and found themselves isolated on the conservative fringes of Polish politics as the country went through its wrenching transition from communism to capitalism. In 2001, they founded the Law and Justice party, which they claimed would be devoted to the Polish ideals of faith and family. The party soon established close ties to the powerful Catholic Church and the rural heartland that continues to serve as its main base of support.

The following year, Lech was elected mayor of Warsaw, and the Kaczyński brothers started to build a broader national front. They capitalized on growing disenchantment with accounts of corruption within the ruling class and a yawning income gap between the poorer classes and a newly enriched elite that capitalized on Poland's entrance into the European Union. In 2005, Jarosław led the Law and Justice party to victory in parliamentary elections. He turned down the job of prime minister, preferring his customary role as power broker behind the scenes.

But soon afterward, Lech won the presidency. He asked his brother to take over the government, which Jarosław did reluctantly. Together, after nearly a decade in the political wilderness, the Kaczyński brothers had emerged from the sidelines to take control of the governing hierarchy in the largest and most populous nation in Central and Eastern Europe.

The brothers wasted no time in exercising their extraordinary power. They launched a program of "lustration" that was intended to expose former Communist collaborators who had used their old connections to accumulate fabulous wealth. They sought to exploit public resentment with Germany's encroachment through property purchases in the western Polish provinces of Silesia and Pomerania, which formerly belonged to Germany.

Kaczyński also waged a campaign seeking extra voting powers in the European Union as compensation for the millions of Poles who were killed by Nazi Germany during the war. The Polish demand was rejected as an outlandish request by all other EU countries. In particular, it caused shock and outrage across Germany where the population felt that Poles showed a lack of gratitude for Germany's political and financial backing for Poland's EU membership. Poland's bold request for more clout in EU councils reflected a new brand of nationalism that was surfacing in Central Europe. Post-Communist governments, having gained their independence after decades of Soviet oppression, were determined not to surrender their sovereignty again, whether to powerful neighbors or to faceless EU institutions in Brussels.

Jarosław's rough-and-tumble manner sowed dissension in his own coalition. In 2007, the ruling coalition headed by Law and Justice collapsed, and in the ensuing election the party lost to the liberal, pro-European movement known as Civic Platform. Even though Lech stayed on as president, Law and Justice was banished to the fringes once again as Tusk and his Civic Platform coalition began moving the country back to the political center.

During his two terms in office, Tusk had restored strong political and business connections with Germany and established a close personal friendship with Chancellor Angela Merkel. Merkel and Tusk

Germany's Chancellor Angela Merkel with Russia's President Vladimir Putin at his residence near Sochi. She has a phobia about dogs, which Putin claims he didn't know when he allowed his black Labrador to prowl around the room. *(Sputnik / Alamy Stock Photo)*

Refugees stranded at Keleti train station in Budapest. They were allowed to proceed after Merkel insisted Europe's borders should remain open. Later, she would regret the political consequences of her decision. *(Zuma Press, Inc. / Alamy Stock Photo)*

Refugees disembarking from trains halted at Hegyeshalom, Hungary, on the Austrian border before seeking asylum in Germany or Sweden. Hungary erected wire fences along its frontiers to obstruct refugee crossings. *(Radek Procyk / Alamy Stock Photo)*

German police in Berlin set up a cordon around a Christmas market at Breidsheidplatz following an attack by a Tunisian immigrant who drove a truck through a crowd, killing 12 people and injuring 50 others. *(Agencja Fotograficzna Caro / Alamy Stock Photo)*

Merkel haggles with Greece's leftist leader Alexis Tspiras over terms of a resolution to the Greek debt crisis at a European Union summit in Brussels in October 2015. *(Newzulu / Alamy Stock Photo)*

A Syrian refugee clutches his two children as he climbs out of a raft after crossing from Turkey to the Greek island of Lesbos. More than 850,000 refugees passed through Lesbos on their way to northern Europe in 2015. *(Reuters / Alamy Stock Photo)*

Tsipras waves to cheering supporters at Syriza party headquarters after winning reelection in September 2015. He vowed to reject austerity measures demanded by creditors but relented to secure a third bailout. *(Elias Verdi / Alamy Stock Photo)*

Merkel caricatured with a Nazi swastika and a Hitler mustache on a wall with graffiti in Athens. Anti-German protests erupted after she insisted Greece must raise taxes and cut pensions despite a painful economic depression. *(360b / Alamy Stock Photo)*

Jarosław Kaczyński kisses Merkel's hand during a visit to Berlin. The right-wing Polish leader dismayed EU partners by cracking down on political opponents and the media, raising fears about the future of Polish democracy. *(Sueddeutsche Zeitung / Alamy Stock Photo)*

(*above*) Kaczyński attends a ceremony at a Warsaw military cemetery marking the sixth anniversary of the 2010 plane crash near Smolensk in Russia that killed 96 people, including his twin brother Lech. (*Chen Xu / Xinhua / Alamy Stock Photo*)

(*left*) Merkel hosts British prime minister Theresa May in Berlin in July 2016, shortly after May replaced David Cameron, who resigned in the wake of Britain's referendum vote in favor of leaving the European Union. (*dpa picture alliance / Alamy Stock Photo*)

(*below*) EU Commission president Jean-Claude Juncker and his nemesis, the leading British Euroskeptic, Nigel Farage, appearing together in Brussels. (*Andia / Alamy Stock Photo*)

The European Parliament building in Strasbourg, France, known as the "Tower of Babel," which along with Brussels and Luxembourg serve as rotating venues for the EU assembly. *(Stéphane Gautier / Sagaphoto.com / Alamy Stock Photo)*

Marine Le Pen, France's leader of the far-right National Front, speaks to a party congress held in the southern French town of Fréjus. She has emerged as a leading voice of populist nationalism in Europe. *(Francois Pauletto / Newzulu / Alamy Stock Photo)*

Emmanuel Macron, who never held elected office before running for president of France in 2017, greets supporters at a campaign rally in Pau, in southwestern France. He defied the country's ruling party structure by launching a reformist movement that channeled voter frustrations with France's "stalled society." *(ASK Images / Alamy Stock Photo)*

Riga mayor Nils Ušakovs speaks at a press conference following a meeting of the city council. Ethnic Russians, like Ušakovs, now make up about half the population of Latvia's capital. *(ITAR-TASS Photo Agency / Alamy Stock Photo)*

Merkel and Italy's prime minister Matteo Renzi engage in heated debate at an EU summit in Brussels. They clashed over Germany's insistence on austerity measures that depressed jobs and growth across southern Europe. *(Leo Cavallo / Alamy Stock Photo)*

Beppe Grillo, the actor-comedian and charismatic founder of Italy's Five Star Movement, speaks at a rally in Palermo. Within seven years, Grillo's radical group became Italy's leading opposition party. *(Antonio Melita / Alamy Stock Photo)*

Rome's mayor Virginia Raggi greets the media after the Five Star Movement won control of the capital. But she soon ran into political trouble by failing to clean up Rome's notoriously corrupt administration. *(Reuters / Alamy Stock Photo)*

Garbage piles up in Rome's Campo de' Fiori. The Eternal City has endured a deterioration in public services amid revelations that crime syndicates have seized control of municipal contracts in return for political bribes. *(Fabrizio Troiani / Alamy Stock Photo)*

Pablo Iglesias, leader of the left-wing Podemos movement, walks past Spain's conservative prime minister Mariano Rajoy after parliament voted to end a yearlong political vacuum and give Rajoy a second term in office. *(Reuters / Alamy Stock Photo)*

Tens of thousands of demonstrators march down one of Barcelona's main boulevards waving the Estelada flag of Catalonian independence and demanding secession from Spain. *(Jordi Boixareu / Alamy Stock Photo)*

Danish cyclists heading to work during the late-morning rush hour in Copenhagen, which aims to become the world's first carbon-neutral city by 2025. About 65 percent of all Danes commute to work or school by bicycle. *(Niels Quist / Alamy Stock Photo)*

The Little Mermaid statue and wind power turbines are Denmark's signature landmarks. The melting of Greenland's ice sheet has awakened Danes to the risk that rising sea levels may inundate their country. *(Peter Holibaum-Hansen / Alamy Stock Photo)*

shared a similar political outlook, and she would help him become the president of the European Council, one of the most powerful positions in the EU hierarchy since it chairs and sets the agenda for all of the EU summit meetings that determine all key policy decisions for the twenty-eight-nation bloc.

After his brother's death, Jarosław became depressed and withdrawn. A lifelong bachelor, his close political alliance with his brother had dominated his entire adult life. Following his mother's death in 2013, Jarosław threw himself back into the political fray with gusto. He decided that the best way to honor his brother would be to double down on their mutual commitment to carrying out a new political and cultural revolution in Poland.

Once Tusk left the prime minister's job to move to Brussels as president of the European Council, the centrist ruling coalition under Civic Platform began to bow beneath the weight of corruption allegations and voter disillusionment after more than eight years in power. Kaczyński could not hide his satisfaction as he watched the erosion of power among his secular political enemies. He still harbors a keen dislike for Tusk, whom he has accused of covering up what he believes was negligence or sabotage in the plane crash that killed his brother.

Kaczyński also saw that his populist and nationalist ideas were starting to gain traction elsewhere across the continent. At that time, he shrewdly decided to step back from day-to-day politics and personally selected younger, more telegenic personalities in Law and Justice to run as presidential and prime minister nominees in the 2015 elections. Kaczyński's decision to give his party a youthful cosmetic makeover paid off. The more attractive slate of ultra-conservative candidates won landslide victories that gave the party unfettered control over the country's key institutions.

Kaczyński absorbed important lessons from the party's mistakes during its earlier stint in power. He believes he and his allies were too slow in pushing ahead with their aggressive right-wing reforms. This time, he vowed that Law and Justice would move rapidly to promote its radical legislative agenda. Soon after the party took power, it acted with a speed and boldness that surprised and alarmed its opponents, at home and abroad. Within its first one hundred days, the right-wing government canceled a series of appointments to the country's highest court made by the previous Civic Platform government and replaced them with its own candidates. It also passed a law that would make it exceedingly difficult for the court to block legislation. The court ruled that the new law was unconstitutional, but the government refused to recognize its decision.

The EU Commission stepped in and warned the new Polish government that its actions undermined judicial independence and posed "a systemic risk to the rule of law." Frans Timmermans, the Commission vice president, dispatched an official letter to the Polish government saying that EU law required absolute guarantees of judicial independence. In the letter, he said he wanted to act in a "dispassionate and legal" manner but the Commission was obligated to uphold the rule of law. "The European Union is built on common values enshrined in the treaties," he said. "Making sure the rule of law is observed is a collective responsibility of all EU institutions and all member states."

Timmermans insisted that unless the new legislation was rescinded, Poland could be subject to unprecedented sanctions since the Commission was empowered by all member governments with the right to take punitive measures to protect the democratic nature of the union. That right to impose sanctions was granted to the Commission after Austria's anti-immigrant Freedom Party was brought into government for the first time by the ruling Christian Democrats in the late 1990s. Yet that instrument is less menacing than it would seem. Any punishment, including the removal of voting rights, against a country that violates "rule of law" political criteria would require a unanimous vote by EU member states. Orban promised to veto any action against Poland, just as the Warsaw government would undoubtedly reject any EU action taken against Hungary.

Nonetheless, the Polish government was outraged by the EU action and accused the Brussels authorities of trying to blackmail Poland in an attempt to force the country to take in more refugees. In Warsaw, Kaczyński was furious over what he described as unacceptable intrusion into the country's domestic affairs and declared that "Poland will not be treated as a colony." Prime Minister Beata Szydło reacted with a combination of scorn and ridicule. She banished the European Union flag from government briefings, where its gold stars and blue banner once stood side by side with the red and white Polish national flag. Szydło insisted her decision was not intended as a show of disrespect toward her country's European partners, but rather a symbolic demonstration that the new government would place Poland's national interests at the forefront of all decisions.

The United States was also troubled by Law and Justice's actions that it feared could lead to the dismantling of Poland's constitutional order. Chancellor Merkel and other allied leaders urged President Obama to exercise Washington's strong political leverage and close ties with the Polish people in a bid to persuade Kaczyński's party to stop interfering with the rule of law.

During a NATO summit conference held in Warsaw in July 2016, President Obama held a tense private meeting with his Polish counterpart, Andrzej Duda, and lectured him about the dangers of tampering with the judiciary. Duda, who takes his orders from Kaczyński, objected to Obama's criticism but promised the government would enact steps to address such concerns. Obama was not satisfied with Duda's response and delivered an unusual public rebuke after the meeting. "As your friend and ally, we've urged all parties to work together to sustain Poland's democratic institutions," Obama said, addressing the Polish people. "That's what makes us democracies, not just by the words written in constitutions or in the fact that we vote in elections, but the institutions we depend on every day, such as rule of law, independent judiciaries and a free press."

Undaunted by criticism from Brussels and Washington over its changes to the Constitutional Court, Law and Justice ministers then launched a purge of the security and intelligence services. Top career civil servants in other departments were also forced to leave office as a way to eliminate what a government spokesman called the "social pathology" of the Civic Platform era.

The moves shook financial markets and Poland's debt was soon downgraded because of fears that the new government was eroding the country's institutional checks and balances. But Kaczyński and his allies were undeterred and pushed ahead with what they proclaimed as a new Polish revolution that would bolster a patriotic national identity infused with pious Catholic values. They started chipping away at press freedoms by demanding that the state-run broadcasting channels and news programs must reflect the conservative and nationalist views of the new government. More than 160 journalists, including the most prominent news anchors and reporters in Poland, were fired or quit their jobs in disgust. Meantime, Culture Minister Piotr Gliński vowed to exert government control over artistic performances and sought to block theatrical showings of a play by the Nobel Prize–winning Austrian author Elfriede Jelinek on the grounds that it might be considered pornographic.

To the chagrin of Germany and other EU partners, Law and Justice declared that it would not honor the commitment made by its predecessor to accept more than 7,000 refugees from Syria under a quota system devised for all EU member states. Kaczyński has insisted that Poland must remain a homogenous Catholic nation and warned that refugees coming from the Middle East would bring "parasites and highly dangerous diseases that have not been seen in Europe for a long time."

Kaczyński received enthusiastic backing from the Polish Catholic establishment for his adamant opposition to accepting Muslim refugees into Poland because of the clergy's fears that the country's Catholic identity could be diluted. The church wields extraordinary political clout in Poland, not least because of Pope John Paul II (who was canonized as a saint in 2014) and his inspirational role in defeating communism.

While revered as a political revolutionary who helped bring down what Poles really believed was an Evil Empire, John Paul II was regarded as a social conservative and an absolute rejectionist when it came to issues like contraception, abortion, divorce, and accepting women into the priesthood. He still enjoys cult-like status in his native homeland, and his doctrinaire social views are overwhelmingly shared by the Polish Catholic hierarchy.

Despite being chastised by Pope Francis, who warned the Poles during a visit in July 2016 that they were becoming isolated, the Polish clergy have resisted the Argentine pontiff's pleas to be more open to a changing world, particularly in accepting large numbers of Muslim refugees. Some members of the Polish clergy have publicly criticized Pope Francis's progressive agenda, which includes a more welcoming attitude to homosexuals and remarried divorcees. Polish bishops have rejected any softening of church orthodoxy and reaffirmed their backing for Law and Justice's conservative social policies, including tougher restrictions on abortion and stricter controls on in-vitro fertilization.

The close relationship between the church and Kaczyński's party is mutually beneficial: Law and Justice attracts millions of voters because of the church's endorsement, and the Catholic clergy sees its conservative views enshrined into law and its influence in soci-

ety magnified even though church attendance is dropping and young
people are embracing secular lifestyles.

Kaczyński has reached out to other leaders in Central and Eastern Europe to build political alliances for his ultraconservative
policies and enlist their support in his battles with EU institutions.
Within three months after Law and Justice took power, he held a
secret meeting in southern Poland in early 2016 with his close friend
and ally, Hungary's prime minister Viktor Orban. They agreed to
do everything possible to undermine any European Union plans to
transfer Syrian refugees to their countries. In building razor-wire
fences along his borders, Orban had said all along that the refugee
crisis should be considered a "German problem" and not a "European problem."

The two leaders held frequent discussions about how to forge an
Eastern bloc that would defy German-driven policies by cooperat-
ing more effectively in building a transnational conservative agenda.
They both shared an illiberal vision that taking what might be considered autocratic measures was justified in pushing through necessary reforms in nascent democracies. That view was bound to
run into opposition from ruling centrist parties in the West and the
European Commission in Brussels. Orban had already clashed with
EU authorities over his own efforts through his ruling conservative
Fidesz party to establish an "illiberal new state" since he returned to
power in 2010. Since then, in defiance of EU wishes, Hungary's government under Orban has tightened its grip over the central bank,
the judiciary, and the country's data protection agency.

Poland and Hungary now seem to be rapidly retreating from the
liberal democratic ideals of the 1989 revolution that both countries
pursued in their successful struggle to topple Communist regimes.
Once anti-Communist dissidents, Kaczyński and Orban now advocate a highly intolerant form of nationalism that distrusts outside

intrusions, whether in the form of Middle Eastern refugees or European Union regulations.

They appear contemptuous of Western standards of political pluralism, civil liberties, and the rule of law. They believe that the liberal version of democracy has been a failure, pointing to political stalemate and income inequality in the United States and the dysfunction afflicting the European Union in its handling of the refugee influx and the euro debt crisis. But they are not just voices of the anti-immigrant right. They portray themselves as champions of social justice who want to protect the poor and disaffected classes from the brutal forces of globalization through government subsidies, such as special assistance for those citizens with large families. By centralizing power in their own hands at the price of curbing individual freedoms, they believe that voters are willing to accept their promises that government can be more efficient, fulfill a collective purpose, and instill a sense of national pride among their people. Indeed, Orban says that to be successful in the twenty-first-century global economy, Hungary should no longer look for its model among Western democracies but rather in the direction of authoritarian states like Russia, China, Turkey, and Singapore.

In Hungary and Poland, a new kind of populism has taken root that defies the classic left-right divide. Orban and Kaczynski have vowed to protect their countries from terrorism by rejecting Muslim refugees and abhor what they call "gender ideology" such as gay marriage and transgender rights. But they also embrace leftist positions in fighting the tide of globalization by opposing trade agreements that may cost jobs, as well as calling for tough restrictions on the behavior of foreign-owned banks. They favor cutting the retirement age despite rapidly aging populations and also offer subsidies to parents who have more than one child. Both policies will impose huge strains on national budgets and defy the prescriptions of most experts who believe that Hungary and Poland need to extend the retirement age and slash family subsidies in order to put their economic policies on sound footing. But Orban and Kaczynski spurn such criticism and believe the conventions of liberal democracy need to be adapted to the demands of the twenty-first century. Nation-states, they believe, need to be more assertive in fighting what they perceive as the abusive tendencies of globalization.

The backlash against liberal democracy across Europe is also evident in the electoral gains of right-wing populist parties like France's National Front, Italy's Five Star Movement, and Austria's Freedom Party among the prosperous societies who fear the social and economic gains they have achieved over the past half century may soon vanish. Indeed, discontent with democracy amid slipping living standards and dismay with corrupt ruling elites seems widespread across much of the Western world. In 2014, a European Commission poll showed that 68 percent of Europeans distrusted their national governments, and 82 percent distrusted the mainstream parties, such as Christian Democrats and Social Democrats, that produced such governments. In the United States, a Gallup Poll in the same year found that 65 percent of Americans were dissatisfied with their system of government and how it works—a striking increase from only 23 percent in 2002. Other surveys taken in recent years show that support for democracy is dwindling among Western populations.

The sudden turn against liberal democratic ideals by former Communist states in Central Europe has come as a surprise to original members of the European Union like Germany, France, and the Benelux. They anticipated that the eastern states would become staunch advocates of greater European integration since they benefited so greatly from sustained progress in their political stability and economic affluence, largely thanks to becoming members of key Western institutions like the EU and NATO.

Poland, in particular, has long been considered the poster child of successful transformation from a repressive Communist state into a thriving free-market democracy. Living standards have nearly tripled since it joined the EU in 2004. Poland's strong economic performance has created more jobs over the past decade than anywhere else in the EU, making it the only country in Europe to avoid recession since the global economic crisis of 2008. Nearly 40 million Polish citizens now enjoy a quality of life that was only a distant dream when the Communist regime collapsed in 1989.

More than any other EU member, Poland reaps huge benefits from the largesse of its EU partners through regional and structural funds that will pour more than 100 billion euros into the country through 2020. Hungary, with only one-quarter of Poland's population, is scheduled to receive about 22 billion euros of EU aid during that time frame. Yet the leaders of Poland and Hungary do not seem to have any qualms about biting the hand that feeds them.

Mikhail Gorbachev once said he could not understand why Poland and other eastern states would embrace membership in the European Union after life under Soviet communism because he believed they would just be trading one kind of despotism for another. Gorbachev predicted that they would eventually grow disenchanted with their decision to join the Western "country club."

When the Soviet Union was dissolved, there was jubilation among the populations of former Communist states who felt they would finally be allowed to reconcile with their past and rejoin the West. They embraced free speech, free markets, and free elections after being deprived of those hallmarks of democracy for more than half a century. But having adopted democracy, many voters in the East became reluctant to surrender their newfound national sovereignty in favor of a vaguely defined United Europe.

Today a wave of disillusionment is spreading through Central Europe with the dysfunctional governance perceived in EU institutions. Indeed, the democratic revolutions of 1989 appear to be going in reverse, with Slovakia, Croatia, and the Czech Republic all showing authoritarian leanings that could propel them along the same path being followed by Poland and Hungary. The new rallying cry of these apostate democracies seems to be that "Brussels is the new Moscow."

Orban has enjoyed overwhelming approval at home for his truculent disregard of Brussels and European policy on the refugee crisis. He enjoys a two-thirds majority in parliament, which has enabled him to introduce a new constitution and reshape the country's courts, media, and political system in what he openly describes as an "illiberal state." He has snubbed the Schengen principle of open borders and erected barbed-wire fences around his country's frontiers that have been applauded by his compatriots.

When asked about the irony of Hungary erecting new barriers today to thwart refugees after it was praised in 1989 for cutting down the barbed-wire fence that served as an Iron Curtain dividing East and West, Orban gave a dyspeptic answer. "The first fence . . . was against us. This one is for us. That is the difference." He justified his decision to reject Chancellor Merkel and the EU policy of internal open borders by insisting the refugee crisis had become a security threat to his country's Christian civilization. "I think we have a right to decide that we do not want to have a large number of Muslim people in our country," he said.

Impatient with the messiness of democracy, Orban has praised Russian president Vladimir Putin and suggested his model of authoritarian rule should be emulated more often in the West. In the Czech Republic, during the long reign of President Vaclav Klaus, who was a strong advocate of the Margaret Thatcher school of Euroskeptics, many citizens developed antipathy toward EU institutions. Many Czechs embraced Klaus's criticism of Brussels despite evident benefits they were able to enjoy, thanks to EU investments such as being able to travel along safe, modern highways, and through gleaming new airports built with EU money.

Before joining the European Union, applicants were required to pass legislation incorporating up to 80,000 pages of conditions ensuring loyalty to European values. Yet the recent restrictions imposed on the media and judiciary by Eastern European states who should be among the EU's most enthusiastic members suggests an ominous turn against liberal democracy. Not surprisingly, other EU member states are asking aloud why illiberal eastern governments like Poland and Hungary should continue to receive EU funds when they snub its basic values.

Why has modern Central Europe, including Austria, become such fertile ground for the renunciation of civil liberties, the rule of law, and political pluralism that serve as the foundations of democracy? Some experts contend that the roots of democratic governance in the region are still fragile less than three decades after the end of Communist rule.

Before Soviet domination, Eastern Europeans were ruled for centuries by successive empires of Ottoman, Russian, Hapsburg, and fascist regimes. Local populations inevitably became resentful of these outside oppressors, who sought to eradicate any signs of national identity. In Hungary, people still bitterly recall how their first elected prime minister was executed by the Hapsburgs in 1849. In Poland, hostile memories are passed down through generations about the terrible suffering caused by foreign domination, perpetrated mainly by Russia and Germany. For that reason alone, suspicions still run strong about the risks of surrendering their sovereignty to a faceless bureaucracy in Brussels.

Orban and Kaczyński claim that recent Islamic State attacks in Belgium, France, and Germany, some of which involved terrorists who had infiltrated Europe posing as refugees, have vindicated their staunch opposition to accepting more refugees. Both leaders were dismayed by Britain's decision to leave the European Union. Orban had even published a full-page advertisement in British newspapers urging voters to remain within the European Union. For Poland and Hungary, Britain was a strong ally in fighting against the emergence of what they feared could become a United States of Europe. They also found Britain's stand against uncontrolled immigration to be a welcome source of support for their own policy battles against Angela Merkel and the EU Commission.

Neither Poland nor Hungary wants to leave the European Union. Public support for EU membership remains high in both countries. A survey carried out by the Pew Research Center in 2016 showed that 61 percent of Hungarians and 72 percent of Poles held a favorable view of the European Union, higher than in any other EU member states. Orban and Kaczyński say it is not a matter of being for or against the European Union; they claim they simply want to make it better and more responsive to the wishes of their citizens.

They lament the fact that Europe has failed miserably to find effective solutions to a multitude of recent crises. These include the catastrophic debts that produced economic depression in Greece, repeated attacks by Islamist terrorists in France and elsewhere, Russia's unchecked aggression in Ukraine, the failure to create sustainable employment for young people, and to find a humane solution to the largest influx of refugees since World War II. "The European Union is incapable of defending its own citizens, its own external borders and is unable to hold its community together, as seen in the United Kingdom's exit," Orban told his Fidesz party congress during an annual summer retreat in July 2016. "What else is needed to state that Europe's current political leadership has failed?"

Orban was elated by the election of Donald Trump, whose hostile attitude toward illegal immigrants is very much in line with the restrictive asylum laws that Hungary has passed under his leadership. Orban strongly backs Trump's views on Islam and terror and also shares his criticism of the liberal international order. "Trump has called for an end to the policy of exporting democracy," Orban said. "I could not have said it better myself."

Within Europe, Orban says much of the blame can be laid at the foot of Europe's institutions, whose democratic deficit poses "a serious lack of legitimacy" in the eyes of European voters. He believes the constant search for policy responses at a European level is a sign of intellectual laziness. "Wanting an EU solution to everything is like the reflex of Pavlov's dog: there is no meaning behind it."

Other European leaders are frustrated that the confrontational attitude taken by the illiberal governments in Poland and Hungary appears to have paid off. The ungracious methods employed by Kaczyński and Orban in rebuking EU institutions and leadership while accepting billions in aid money have worked without any detriment to their governments. Both have succeeded in consolidating power by undermining the rule of law and other democratic values. But there is a risk that their selfishly critical approach toward the European project may not succeed in the long run. If more leaders are tempted to follow their example, at some point there may be no European Union left to blame.

CHAPTER EIGHT

COPENHAGEN

THE GREEN WELFARE STATE IN PERIL?

D URING THE 2016 DEMOCRATIC PRIMARY CAMPAIGN, BERNIE Sanders offered an unequivocal response when asked about his ideal vision for the United States. America, he said, should become more like Denmark. This small homogenous nation of 5.6 million people consistently ranks as the happiest society in the world. Who could disagree with aspiring to emulate the attractions of this prosperous, well-educated, and caring society?

Danes consider themselves open and egalitarian, with perhaps the world's highest degree of social mobility and gender equality. They enjoy some of the world's highest per capita income levels and lowest rates of crime and poverty. Anybody can receive free health care, and university education is available without cost. Parents are sent quarterly checks to pay for child care, college students receive a monthly stipend of about $900 to cover room and board, and elderly people get free maid service.

Danes have always taken pride in their reputation as a progressive and generous nation. Besides constructing their elaborate network of cradle-to-grave social protections at home, they have funded one of the world's largest development aid programs, which has helped improve education and curb starvation and disease in many impoverished regions around the globe.

They are also masters of work-life balance. They enjoy working hard, yet leave plenty of time to revel in the company of family and friends. *Hygge* (pronounced "hoo-gah") is an untranslatable word that conveys the Danish art of cozy conviviality, similar to the German term *Gemütlichkeit*. It conjures up a lifestyle of bracing walks in the forest, sitting by a warm fire with mulled wine, orderly bicycle commutes, uncluttered interior spaces suffused with bright sunlight and minimalist pine furniture. Luisa Thomsen Brits, the best-selling author of *The Book of Hygge*, says one key to Danish happiness is finding comfort and contentment in the absence of material junk. "Hygge is an experience of selfhood and communion with people and places that anchors and affirms us, gives us courage and consolation."

The Danish utopia sounds too good to be true—and perhaps it is. Danes are among the world's heaviest consumers of antidepressants, and alcoholism is not uncommon during the long Nordic winters. The country's reputation for tolerance and understanding is coming under attack because of what critics call a growing hostility toward multiculturalism and Muslim immigrants who dilute the blond, blue-eyed homogeneity of their native society. Many Danes fear their remarkable social welfare edifice that has been perfected over generations could soon be trampled by the forces of globalization, including the revolution in cheap travel and digital efforts in communications.

Danes are worried about the tide of refugees surging out of Africa and the Middle East in search of a better life among the peaceful and prosperous societies of northern Europe. They see the bountiful stocks of fish that once served as a staple of the Danish diet being rapidly depleted in polluted oceans. They watch as the planet-wide phenomenon of climate change melts the vast ice shelf of their col- ony Greenland and realize it may be only a matter of time before ris- ing sea levels threaten to inundate their peninsular homeland.

But the Danish culture is activist by nature, and the entire nation seems to have mobilized behind efforts to stave off a looming exis- tential challenge to their cherished green welfare state. More than any other country in Europe, this small Nordic nation is taking dras- tic measures to preserve one of the most affluent and successful soci- eties in the world. In many respects, Denmark has become a social laboratory conducting radical policy experiments to cope with diffi- cult twenty-first-century challenges that could set trends for the rest of Europe and the West.

Denmark is widely regarded as having some of the most innova- tive social policies in the world. Danes pioneered "flexicurity," the concept of providing a social safety net to assist the poor, disabled, and unemployed while devoting huge resources to teach them the necessary skills to integrate back into the workforce. Danes have a lot of faith in this model. One out of four workers switch jobs every year, more frequently than any labor force in the developed world. Employers are given much leeway in terms of hiring and firing in order to adapt to the vicissitudes of a highly competitive global economy. Denmark spends proportionately almost eighteen times as much as the United States on worker training, according to the Organization of Economic Cooperation and Development.

A strong work ethic also helps push jobless levels to the lowest in Europe; keeping many people employed is necessary to cover social welfare spending that amounts to 30 percent of gross national product, one of the highest rates in the world. Ove Kaj Pedersen, an economist at Copenhagen Business School, believes Denmark's wel- fare state is a boon and not a burden to the economy. "I guarantee the welfare state is going to become even larger five years from now, because for Denmark, it is our main competitive advantage."

Denmark's generous social welfare provisions attract great admiration around the world, which is a primary reason why the country has lured so many migrants and refugees seeking to settle there. Pensions and medical care are considered among the most generous and highest-quality in the world; the exorbitant costs are covered by high income-tax rates. The Danes jealously guard their quality of life and have always insisted on special terms to ensure that their membership in the European Union does not intrude on their national traditions.

While being part of the world's biggest commercial power bloc has paid great dividends because of Denmark's status as a historic trading nation, Danes have balked at any further surrender of their sovereignty. They rejected the 1992 Maastricht Treaty and refused to join the euro, which was considered too ambitious a leap toward creating a United States of Europe. While signing the Schengen treaty for passport-free travel within the European Union, they have spurned other treaties calling for closer cooperation on police and security matters. They also vowed not to embrace the common European currency by joining the nineteen-nation eurozone. They still insist on the right to impose occasional border controls when they feel their national interests are at stake.

Denmark has drawn criticism for some of the strictest immigration policies in Europe. Politicians across the political spectrum—not just from the far-right—seem to compete to see who can devise the most stringent rules about who should be allowed to live in their cosseted welfare state. In contrast to their progressive ideals, Danes have moved sharply to the right in dealing with Europe's refugee crisis; even leftist parties believe that accepting large numbers of Muslim immigrants would undermine their unique brand of social democracy. Meantime, the world refugee population has grown to 60 million—larger than at any time since World War II—and many are looking for ways to escape war, drought, and extreme poverty and find their way to affluent havens in Germany, Sweden, or Denmark.

As elsewhere across the continent, Europe's refugee crisis has triggered a xenophobic turn in Denmark, compelling the nation's right-wing government—in cooperation with the opposition Social Democrats—to follow public opinion by taking extraordinary measures to deter the flood of migrants that have poured into Europe from North Africa and the Middle East. When more than 1 million refugees arrived in Germany and another 200,000 came to neighboring Sweden in 2015, Danes panicked, fearing that their small Maryland-sized nation could be overwhelmed by the influx of Syrians, Iraqis, and Turks fleeing turmoil in the Middle East. First, the government paid for an advertising campaign in Lebanese newspapers urging all refugee camp inhabitants to stay away from their Scandinavian paradise. When a senior Danish diplomat complained that the campaign was damaging the country's reputation, the government's Integration Minister, Inger Støjberg, told him, "I know, and I think it's great if it keeps too many people from coming here."

Then, the Danish parliament ignited further controversy when it enacted a so-called "jewelry law" in January 2016. The law would allow authorities to search the clothes and luggage of all refugees and to confiscate valuables worth in excess of $1,500, ostensibly to help cover the costs of their accommodations and health care. Legislators also voted to slash social benefits by nearly 50 percent for new refugees and stretched the family reunification process for asylum seekers from one year to three years. The United Nations refugee agency warned that the law "could fuel fear, xenophobia and similar restrictions that would reduce, rather than expand, the asylum space and put refugees in need at life-threatening risks." Bent Melchior, Denmark's former chief rabbi, said the jewelry law seemed to have "the character of what was actually in force during the Nazis' persecution of minorities."

The punitive measures were criticized abroad as cruel and heartless. Many Danes were embarrassed to see their strong humanitarian record so tarnished amid the international outcry. But within Denmark, the measures enjoyed widespread support across the political spectrum. Even though Denmark is proud of its tolerant traditions and its vaunted protection of religious minorities, many Danes believed that protecting their social welfare must take priority over hospitality toward refugees.

The jewelry law and other measures to discourage the arrival of refugees and asylum seekers stood in sharp contrast to a more courageous era in the country's history. In 1939, the Danish parliament passed a law against "any threatening, insulting or degrading speech" to protect its Jewish population from anti-Semitism. During World War II, Denmark was the only country occupied by the Nazis that managed to rescue nearly all of the country's Jewish inhabitants, by smuggling them into Sweden. It was also the first state to sign the 1951 United Nations Convention Relating to the Status of Refugees.

But widespread fears among Danish voters that their homogenous society might crumble under the weight of refugees seeking safe harbor in their affluent homeland have pushed public opinion and government policy sharply to the right. In the June 2015 elections—well before the refugee crisis reached its peak—the mainstream parties clashed over who could be tougher in curbing the flow of asylum seekers. In the end, the center-right Liberals managed to drive the ruling Social Democrats from power.

The biggest victor, however, was the Danish People's Party, a right-wing anti-immigration party, which captured 21 percent of the vote. The Liberals formed a minority government that depended on support from the DPP, which declared that its goal was to preserve Denmark's social welfare state and even expand its benefits while at the same time making the country as unattractive as possible to foreigners. The founder of the DPP, Pia Kjaersgaard, was appointed to the powerful position of speaker of the Danish parliament. Kjaersgaard, who was a caretaker of elderly invalids before entering politics, claimed that Muslims should be kept out of Denmark because they are "at a lower stage of civilization."

Under DPP prodding, the Danish government of Liberal prime minister Lars Løkke Rasmussen enacted laws viewed as more xenophobic than many of those passed elsewhere in Western Europe. In most instances, the new laws also were endorsed by the opposition Social Democrats, reflecting a strong national consensus among voters of all political stripes behind the crackdown on immigration. The government has even cracked down on its own citizens who have simply wanted to offer token forms of humanitarian assistance to refugees. In a celebrated case that sparked controversial debate about the nature of Danish hospitality to foreigners, Lise Ramslog, a seventy-year-old grandmother, was convicted on charges of human smuggling and fined more than $3,000 for driving two young refugee couples, a small child, and a newborn baby in her small sedan 120 miles to their destination in Sweden.

Bo Lidegaard is a renowned Danish historian who has also served as chief editor of the nation's leading daily, *Politiken*, and as a security advisor in the prime minister's office. He acknowledges that the "jewelry law" was a clumsy attempt to deter immigrants from coming to Denmark, yet he also notes that it has rarely been enforced. He feels that the Ramslog case and other instances of Danes getting in trouble for doing what might be considered acts of human decency reflect a sense of vulnerability and desperation among Danish authorities about having to devote too many resources to offering care and sanctuary to asylum seekers.

"There is a strong temptation to say this law suggests something is rotten in the state of Denmark," Lidegaard told me. "It was simply an ill-conceived attempt to manage the flow of migrants by signaling that Denmark is not the place to go. The deeper problem is that it shows a serious lack of trust among the people toward Europe-wide solutions to the challenges of our time. And I fear the jewelry law is just one example of how far Europe could sink if we are not able to address our problems together."

The British referendum vote in favor of leaving the European Union led to widespread speculation that Denmark might be the next member state to pull out. Denmark joined the EU only because of its close trading ties at the time with Britain, which purchased half of all Danish exports. The country's Euroskeptic faction, led by the Danish People's Party, has agitated for a referendum because of its opposition to what it sees as a creeping European superstate that will intrude on Denmark's sovereignty. But in the months following the British vote, opinion polls showed that Danish support for the EU actually increased to a record 69 percent of voters.

The conservative government of Lars Løkke Rasmussen depends on support from the DPP, which blends xenophobia with left-wing socialism in its use of anti-immigrant rhetoric coupled with a staunch defense of Denmark's social welfare provisions. Following the British vote, DPP politicians said a referendum was necessary to uphold Denmark's national interests in fighting for more powers to be returned to national capitals from the Brussels EU institutions. "The cornerstones of Europe—the euro, the Schengen policy, its institutions—are breaking up, and if the politicians of the European Union will not begin to listen to the population maybe the whole thing will fall apart," says Morten Messerschmidt, a leading DPP member who serves in the European Parliament. "We do not want to withdraw from Europe, but we do want a new deal that will respect our national sovereignty."

But Messerschmidt, who won more personal votes than any other candidate in the 2014 European elections, was soon caught up in a scandal involving the misuse of European funds. EU investigators found he had contravened Parliament's rules by spending as much as $400,000 on DPP summer camps and vacation cruises. It was all the more embarrassing because he had built his political reputation on vowing to combat EU fraud. He was forced to resign from the party leadership, damaging his party's standing with the voters. The DPP scandal helped fuel the rise of the more extreme New Right party in 2016 which has demanded even stricter controls on immigration and wants to ban all asylum seekers. The New Right secured the required 20,000 signatures to run in national elections and hopes to lure supporters from the DPP.

Støjberg, the tough-minded integration minister, who is most closely associated with the government's antirefugee policies, disparages critics who claim Denmark is turning xenophobic. She prefers to employ the term "asylum austerity" to describe the series of laws passed by parliament to discourage immigrants and refugees. She points out that Denmark took in more than 21,000 refugees in 2015—more than the EU average—and that an additional 75,000 refugees will come as part of the family reunification program. On that basis, she notes, it would be equivalent to the United States taking in as many as 1.3 million refugees. What Støjberg fears most are future waves that would bring unconstrained flows of refugees that could overwhelm Europe, particularly small countries like Denmark.

At one point in 2015, Støjberg's nightmare seemed like it might become reality when as many as 6,000 Syrians per day were crossing from Turkey into Greece on their way to northern Europe. She is particularly alarmed at what has happened in neighboring Sweden, where the government opened its doors to hundreds of thousands of Iraqis and Syrians and now is desperately trying to deal with the consequences. That effusive hospitality has abruptly changed as Swedes have taken stringent measures to thwart further immigration in the wake of violent attacks against refugees by Swedish skinheads.

The alarming proliferation of immigrant ghettoes in Sweden has frightened many Swedish voters and caused a surge in support for the far-right Sweden Democrats, which has emerged in recent years as the country's biggest party, with 28 percent of the vote. Even though Denmark has managed to keep out many potential immigrants, the xenophobic message of the New Right and the Danish People's Party has enjoyed strong public support commensurate with the Sweden Democrats and the far-right nationalist Finns Party, which is now part of the government in Finland. Danish politicians say their restrictive actions have curtailed the proliferation of immigrant ghettoes; while Sweden is estimated to have as many as 180 of such enclaves, Denmark has kept its "ghetto list" to no more than 30.

Denmark has also raised barriers to immigrants by making it significantly more difficult to acquire Danish citizenship. A new test introduced in 2016 poses questions that are so complex that two-thirds of the applicants who took it for the first time failed. The forty questions included in the test cover subjects as diverse as Viking legends, astronomical discoveries, the life span of musical composers, and even obscure trivia about Danish cinema. Applicants must also pass an oral and written exam in Danish, whose abundance of vowel sounds makes it a difficult language to master. They must also prove that they have been able to support themselves financially for the previous five years. The Danish People's Party was a leading advocate of the tougher test, but Støjberg makes no apologies about raising the bar to citizenship. She insists that becoming Danish is a very special privilege, "something you have to earn."

Some immigrants have thrived in Denmark. Those that do succeed in becoming Danish citizens pay tribute to Denmark's cosmopolitan history as a major trading and shipping nation that has always been open to the rest of the world. Nearly 20 percent of greater Copenhagen's 1.2 million residents are considered first- or second-generation foreign immigrants, mainly from Turkey and the war-torn Balkans.

René Redzepi rose from a humble background as the son of a poor immigrant from Macedonia to become one of the most celebrated chefs in the world as the founder of the restaurant called Noma, which is a conflation of the Danish words for "Nordic" and "food." He recalls juggling ten newspaper routes with his brother to help the family finances, and grew up with a keen appreciation of the most essential foods that could be grown locally. He had problems concentrating in school and wound up in a vocational school for hotels and restaurants, where in his first week he won a competition for creating the most interesting dish.

He later served as an apprentice to top chefs in France and Spain before returning to Copenhagen to launch Noma under the guidance of his mentor, the Danish chef Claus Meyer. Redzepi was intrigued by the idea of creating a top-flight restaurant focused on Nordic ingredients. "The whole experience has been trying to understand our region, the soil, the seasons, what the weather gives us in southern Scandinavia. I see our restaurant as having some kind of pact with nature. That is simply the essence of it."

But Redzepi is clearly the exception. He has adapted well to Danish life and its cultural mores thanks to his success as a renowned chef. Most immigrants find themselves shunted into ethnic enclaves around Copenhagen and other cities that, while clean and well tended, are effectively foreign ghettoes that inhibit contact with the daily lives of most Danes. Denmark's Muslim population is estimated at 260,000, or less than 5 percent of the country's total inhabitants. But the country's recent embrace of right-wing political attitudes in terms of its treatment of foreigners suggests there is a growing domestic consensus that preventing large-scale Muslim immigration is absolutely essential to preserving the social welfare structure so prized by the Danes.

Anti-Muslim sentiment in Denmark has been reinforced by the country's recent experiences with jihadist terrorism. Nearly a decade before the terrorist attacks in Paris and Brussels, the publication of so-called Mohammed cartoons by the Danish newspaper *Jyllands-Posten* turned Denmark into a target of vehement criticism from Muslim extremists. For its September 2005 edition, the culture editor Flemming Rose invited forty-two illustrators to draw the prophet Mohammed as they perceived him. Twelve artists accepted the challenge, and the newspaper published the editorial cartoons under the title "The Face of Mohammed." The most controversial showed the prophet with a bomb in his turban. Another depicted him in heaven, pleading with suicide bombers to stop because "we have run out of virgins!"

As an exercise in freedom of expression, it quickly backfired. Four months later, the Danish and Norwegian embassies in Syria were set alight amid protests against the cartoons. A mob burned down the Danish embassy in Lebanon a day later. A total of 139 people were killed in demonstrations from Nigeria to Pakistan. Rose was forced to live under armed guard, later appearing on an al-Qaeda hit list that included the novelist Salman Rushdie and Stéphane Charbonnier, the editor of the French satirical weekly *Charlie Hebdo*, which also had published the Mohammed cartoons. Charbonnier was murdered along with 11 others by Islamist terrorists who attacked the magazine's Paris office in January 2015.

An elaborate plot to attack the *Jyllands-Posten* office in Copenhagen and kill all of its journalists was thwarted when its ringleader, the Pakistani-American extremist David Headley, was arrested in the United States before the plan could be carried out. Just weeks after the *Charlie Hebdo* attack, a young Danish-Palestinian named Omar Abdel Hamid el-Hussein shot a Danish filmmaker at a meeting of a free-speech group to which a Swedish cartoonist, also known for his drawings of Mohammed, had been invited. The attacker escaped and was shot dead by police hours later after he killed a security guard at Copenhagen's main synagogue.

The terrorist attacks on Danish targets had a chilling effect and undoubtedly contributed to the government's decision to clamp down on Muslim immigrants. While supportive of the restrictive policies, many Danes are ashamed to see their country portrayed as a bastion of racism and anti-Muslim attitudes. Yet xenophobic attitudes are not a new phenomenon. A 1997 study of Denmark by the European Center of Racism and Xenophobia concluded that Danes were simultaneously among the most tolerant of foreigners but also among the most racist of all populations in the European Union.

To the outside world, Denmark is regarded as one of the world's most generous countries in terms of humanitarian aid, and its innovative development programs in the Middle East, Africa, and Asia are considered to be some of the best in practice. Within their own country, Danes offer no apology for their fierce desire to keep foreign immigrants from overrunning their welfare state, which is so entrenched that it is seen as part of their DNA. While German chancellor Otto von Bismarck is widely regarded as the founder of Europe's modern welfare state in the nineteenth century, Danes trace the roots of their system back three centuries earlier to King Christian IV, who provided generous housing and living subsidies for the wives and children of his sailors. "It's an extremely expensive model, but one that Danes see as a basic part of their lives," said Lykke Friijs, a former government minister in charge of climate-change policy who is now rector of Copenhagen University. "We like to think of ourselves as a national tribe. In many ways, that makes us suspicious of outsiders, whether they be immigrants or EU bureaucrats. And we Danes will do whatever we think is necessary to prevent disruptions to our way of life."

While Denmark imposes some of the highest marginal income-tax rates in the world, many Danes accept this burden as a fair price for a generous cradle-to-grave welfare system that is the envy of the world. "Money is not as important in social life, as for example in

Britain or America," says Christian Bjørnskov, an economics professor at the Aarhus School of Business and Social Sciences who wrote
his doctorate on the Danish happiness phenomenon. "We probably
spend our money differently here. We don't buy big houses or big
cars, but rather like to spend our money on socializing with others."

Even before the refugee crisis raised alarms about the sustain-
ability of their welfare state, Danes were becoming worried about
the rising costs of their proliferating benefits in an era of slow economic growth and an aging population. Nearly one in five Danes is
over the age of sixty-five. But politicians from both the left and the
right are extremely reticent to impose cutbacks in a cradle-to-grave
system that includes free health care, free university education, and
large subsidies even for the wealthiest of citizens. Danes have come
to embrace these benefits as fundamental human rights that must
not be abrogated.

As a result, the state has been limited to tinkering around the
edges, searching for incentives that will push students more quickly
into the workforce and encouraging older workers to continue in
their jobs beyond retirement age. The state has also started pursuing welfare cheats after a notorious case involving a middle-aged
man known as "Lazy Robert," who was happy to acknowledge on
television that he felt no need to work when he could earn enough on
welfare to dine out in posh restaurants and even purchase his own
apartment. Following the ensuing uproar, the government cut back
the number of years that an unemployed person could receive state
payments from four years to two.

That case, and others, led to an examination of the Danish welfare
state and whether the expansive array of benefits was undermining the country's work ethic. The review also served to awaken the
country to the fact that Muslim immigrants, who make up about 5
percent of the population, were not being effectively integrated into
society. Instead, they were being shunted into ghettoes where they

collected state benefits but were not sufficiently encouraged to learn Danish or join the workforce.

A 2010 study led to the creation of the "ghetto list" of thirty neighborhoods, which are the focus of intense efforts to build new channels of contact with Danish communities. Denmark now employs a tough-love attitude toward unemployed immigrants; the "flexicurity program" offers generous income support and training, but if immigrants do not find a job or accept one that is found for them, they can lose their benefits within four months. Many Danes believe their "flexicurity" system has rescued the welfare state from runaway costs by getting more people back into the workforce and keeping them off welfare rolls and away from criminal mischief. The work training programs may be expensive, but Danish officials point out it helps keep their prison population at a very low level compared to the 2 million people imprisoned in the United States, where it can cost on average $31,000 per year to keep an American behind bars.

While worried about the immigration crisis and the fate of their welfare state, many Danes are even more troubled about the impact of climate change on their lives. Perhaps more than any other country, Denmark has confronted the threat of rising sea levels to its vulnerable coastlines by embracing some of the most creative and farsighted policies on climate change. Denmark has mobilized its "national tribe" to adopt some of the world's most innovative efforts to abandon fossil fuels, expand the use of alternative energy forms, and demonstrate global leadership by making the necessary sacrifices to hold back the rising seas.

Danes feel they stand on several front lines in battling the effects of climate change. The rapid erosion of the Greenland ice sheet—which scientists say has already lost more than 9 trillion tons of ice in the past century and whose melting rate is accelerating as temperatures keep warming—evokes the specter of sea levels that within decades could conceivably inundate Denmark's islands and Jutland Peninsula. Danes have watched anxiously as their territory of Greenland has rapidly turned into one of the prime exhibits of global warming. NASA estimates that the Greenland ice sheet is now losing about 287 billion tons of ice every year due to surface melting and ruptures of large chunks of ice. A recent series of warm summers has exacerbated the risk, scientists say, starting with the very intense melt of the summer of 2012.

Many Danes believe the loss of glaciers and ice shelves in Greenland has progressed so far so fast that their country may face extinction in the not-too-distant future. And partly because of climate change, the Arctic region so intimately tied to the security interests of Denmark and its prized territory of Greenland is now emerging as a new area of geopolitical tensions between Nordic countries and a Russia seeking to shore up its former superpower status by gaining control of the Arctic's vast resources and vital shipping lanes.

The twin threats of refugee flows and climate change are so complicated that they demand a global consensus for effective action, but Danes have decided they cannot afford to wait. They have struck out on their own in the absence of a coherent response by the world community and embarked on a set of policies that, for good or ill, may set a leading example for the way Europe and the rest of the world copes with the dilemmas raised by these challenging issues.

Despite its cold and blustery climate, Denmark consumes far less energy on a per capita basis than other European countries. It has become the avatar of developing wind energy and passive solar architecture as an alternative to fossil fuels, and gasoline is taxed so prohibitively that most people move around on bicycles. Nearly half of all power on the electric grid is based on renewable sources of energy. But while making such dramatic strides toward energy independence, Denmark is now finding that its policies encouraging alternative sources threaten to undermine all remaining conventional forms of power, which could lead to severe disruptions. How

Denmark resolves such challenges will hold great importance for the rest of the world.

Copenhagen's lord mayor, Frank Jensen, has even more ambitious plans to transform his city into a global model for clean power. He has enlisted the support of all political parties in promoting policies that will make Copenhagen the world's first carbon-neutral city by 2025. Besides the large amount of power generated by offshore wind farms, Copenhagen has built an enormous biomass energy plant that essentially will heat the capital by burning up its garbage.

The plant is so clean that the city is building an artificial ski slope on top of the biomass plant for recreational purposes. Thanks to the efficiencies of the biomass heat generator that will serve 800,000 people in inner-city Copenhagen, all coal-fired plants will be shut down, dramatically reducing the consumption of fossil fuels. The city's public transportation fleet is already powered by electricity, but the most popular means of getting around is still the bicycle. Copenhagen has some of the best organized routes for commuting by bicycle, and more than 65 percent of the population use their bikes daily to commute to work or attend school.

As a major port serving one of Europe's busiest shipping channels, Copenhagen faces immense problems in maintaining the quality of its water supply. Until the 1990s, storms would regularly spew sewage-polluted rainwater straight into the city's harbor. Copenhagen decided to invest in a massive $1 billion infrastructure program that quickly began to turn things around. The city cleaned up its harbor by building new rainwater reservoirs and special conduits that channeled the storm overflows away from the docks. A new wastewater treatment system has been so successful in cleansing the harbor of pollutants that the water is now perfectly safe for swimming. The city has also poured funds into shoring up dikes, dams, and other protective measures that will help Danes cope with the threat of rising water levels. Like everything else, Denmark's water infrastructure is funded through high taxes that have encouraged citizens to conserve the use of water in their residences, so much so that bathtubs are now considered highly uncommon in Danish homes.

Jensen gave up a promising career as a rising star in national politics to run for mayor because he strongly believes that only "local politics are close to the everyday lives of people." During his two terms as mayor, he has earned an international reputation as a progressive urbanist who has transformed Copenhagen into the world's greenest and most livable city. With more than half of the world's population now living in cities, Jensen believes that mayors have an obligation to their citizens to find solutions that will maintain a clean and healthy environment but also provide them with healthy incomes through strong economic growth.

Mikkel Hemmingsen, Jensen's chief troubleshooter, manages a group of more than fifty economists who explore all possible ways to deal with urban problems in cooperation with the private sector and the national government. Copenhagen's innovative methods have attracted so much interest around the world that China alone sends on average one delegation a week to examine how Copenhagen's methods can be employed in various Chinese cities.

"Around the world, cities have become without a doubt the primary engine of national economies," Hemmingsen said as he sipped espresso in his Town Hall office during a rare break from his usual fifteen-hour-a-day work schedule. "But cities also serve as a kind of laboratory for how we should deal with all kinds of social and economic problems, such as reducing class inequality and integrating immigrants. Most of all, we need to find more effective ways to sustain economic growth without worsening the effects of climate change. We live that challenge every day of our lives here, and so we are always conscious that we are fighting not just for our lives but that of our future generations."

He and Jensen are convinced that cities will assume greater power and responsibility than national governments in serving as the key lever of societies in coping with refugee problems, climate change, and other existential threats to the human condition. Hemmingsen says Copenhagen has managed to resolve some of its most intractable conflicts because it maintains a decentralized system of government that lets municipal leaders operate with much greater independence than the political parties squabbling at the national level. "When you are directly responsible to voters for collecting garbage, educating children, providing clean water and cheap electricity, you realize how true leadership means you cannot afford to engage in the polarized partisanship that you see at the national level." It is a lesson that other Western capitals should learn to apply as effectively as it has been done in Copenhagen.

CHAPTER NINE

RIGA

IN THE SHADOW OF THE BEAR

T HE MUSEUM OF THE OCCUPATION OF LATVIA IS ONE OF THE most popular sites for visitors in the capital of Riga, a majestic harbor town dating back to Hanseatic League days in the thirteenth century that is now the largest city in the Baltic region. The museum offers graphic documentation of three stages of brutal oppression endured by two generations of the Latvian people under the Soviet and Nazi regimes of the twentieth century. The first phase depicts how Latvia's brief period of independence between two world wars was ruptured by invading Soviet forces in 1940 following the Hitler-Stalin pact that carved up much of Eastern Europe. The second phase shows the wartime suffering during three years of Nazi rule from 1941 to 1944, when most of Riga's 24,000 Jews were isolated in the ghetto and systematically massacred. The third phase reflects more than four decades of Communist rule that ended with the dissolution of the Soviet empire in 1991 and the restoration of Latvia's independence.

From his spacious office in the municipal headquarters across the main town square, Riga's mayor Nils Ušakovs plays with his two cats and gazes out the window at the museum with mixed emotions. "It's very complicated," the forty-something politician says as he tries to explain the maelstrom of cultures, languages, and history that has defined his life and that of his country. As a popular two-term mayor who is of ethnic Russian origin, Ušakovs is deeply conscious of the identity crises that afflict the lives of many Latvians and other Baltic peoples, particularly in their turbulent relationship with a powerful eastern neighbor. "I would prefer to let historians decide about the past, and whether what happened should be called an occupation or annexation," Ušakovs says. "But nobody doubts that Latvia's independence was violated and that it was forced to become part of the Soviet Union against its will."

Riga was an imperial port in czarist days and many ethnic Russians can trace their family presence back more than two centuries. Such iconic figures as the ballet dancer Mikhail Baryshnikov and the film director Sergei Eisenstein were born and raised in Riga. Russians have played an important role in the culture of the Baltic region and have always regarded the Baltic seaports as a vital gateway to the outside world. Ušakovs's parents were part of a massive influx of nearly 1 million Russian laborers, administrators, military personnel and their dependents who were dispatched there by Stalin's regime to "Russify" Latvia and other countries incorporated into the Soviet Union. On the day that Latvia declared its independence in 1991, many of them woke up to find they were stateless because the new government decided that only descendants of people living in Latvia before 1940 would gain automatic citizenship.

Today nearly half of Riga's 700,000 inhabitants are Russian speakers who have no strong desire to return to their ancestral homeland. But they also insist that they should be treated as equals with their Latvian compatriots. They have lived in peace and relative prosperity with their native Latvian neighbors since the collapse of communism a quarter century ago. Nonetheless, ethnic Russians continue to complain about their second-class status as noncitizens who are not permitted to vote or hold state positions. They chafe at the state's refusal to accept Russian as a second official language. Most of all, they resent the fact that their parents helped rebuild Latvia's factories, roads, and rail networks after the war but then suddenly found themselves in limbo when the Soviet Union collapsed. Despite clear divisions within Latvian society toward Russia, there are no obvious signs that separatist sentiment is growing in ways that might lead to Russian intervention in Latvia.

That has not stopped growing speculation that World War III could break out here. The election of U.S. President Donald Trump and his ambivalence about America's defense commitments to its NATO allies have stirred alarm that Vladimir Putin might launch a quick strike to secure hegemony over former Soviet territory in the Baltic states. Russia's intervention in Ukraine and its annexation of Crimea has awakened the Baltic peoples to the risk that Putin might want to exploit what he sees as weak leadership in the West to push back against NATO expansion. One scenario: a demonstration by Russian-speaking Latvians in Riga is infiltrated by special forces sent by Moscow to stir up chaos. Concealed snipers shoot dead three protesters, creating the pretext for a Russian invasion that is over within hours. But by the time NATO can invoke a mutual security guarantee and organize an effective response, Russia declares that any attempt to wrest back control will be confronted by the use of nuclear weapons.

While it may sound like a plot from a James Bond movie, General Sir Richard Shirreff is convinced that a Russian invasion is highly plausible. He believes that Putin's Russia is prepared to employ all the cybertricks and -tools deployed in Ukraine and elsewhere in launching an invasion to reclaim Russian control of the Baltics, starting in Latvia. Shirreff was NATO's second-ranking officer as deputy supreme allied commander in Europe until he retired in 2014, and he has written a book that follows a similar script describing an imminent war with Russia. In his preface, Shirreff denies that his book is fiction and prefers to call it "fact-based prediction" that is closely modeled on what he knew as a senior military officer positioned "at the highest and best-informed level."

Ushakovs and other ethnic Russians in Riga deride Shirreff's book as a work of sheer fantasy. While proud of their Russian heritage and dismayed by what they say is discriminatory treatment, ethnic Russians in Latvia acknowledge they enjoy much better living standards than their brethren across the border. The vast majority of them prefer to be part of the West rather than Russia, and they are grateful for the improved living standards that Latvia has been able to achieve in recent years. This small Baltic nation of two million people has thrived since joining the European Union and North Atlantic Treaty Organization in 2004. Latvia also adopted the Euro in 2014, and even the most disgruntled members of the ethnic Russian community have embraced the material benefits that have come their way and say they are much better off since the fall of the Berlin wall.

Ušakovs was born in Riga in 1976 and only became a naturalized citizen of Latvia when he graduated from the local university in 1999. He was required to pass a rigorous language test showing his fluency in the Latvian language, demonstrate an extensive knowledge of Latvian history, and take an oath of allegiance to the country. More than 300,000 ethnic Russians living in Latvia are considered noncitizens, including Ušakovs's own mother, even though they have lived and worked there for their entire lives. Ušakovs grew up speaking only Russian, and decided to learn Latvian at the age of sixteen so that he could qualify to enroll as an economics major at university. After doing his graduate studies in Denmark, he became a prominent editor and television commentator and thought he would make a career either as a journalist or as an economics professor. But he was lured into politics when the Harmony party, which represents the interests of ethnic Russians in Latvia, was seeking younger, more charismatic leadership and asked Ušakovs to take over the party in 2005. He quickly began to broaden its base beyond ethnic Russian voters by transforming it into a center-left social democratic party that sought to attract Latvian supporters.

By 2011, Ušakovs had mobilized enough voters to make Harmony the largest party in the country. In the past two parliamentary elections, Harmony has won the most seats of any party but was unable to form a ruling coalition because it was blocked by an alliance of ethnic Latvian parties. He clearly harbors ambitions for higher national office and has emphasized his pragmatic approach to politics as he strives to win the support of young Latvians attracted to his social democratic views emphasizing jobs, growth, and new technologies. Ušakovs has cultivated close relationships with other Social Democrats across Western Europe and won the endorsement of the president of the European Parliament in Latvia's parliamentary elections. He claims to represent a new generation that wants to put an end to rival interpretations of history and instead serve as a bridge between Russia and the West. He is proud of the broader appeal that he has brought to the party by emphasizing center-left ideological values over ethnic issues and claims that 35 percent of Harmony's supporters are now ethnic Latvians.

Nonetheless, Ušakovs continues to be regarded with deep suspicion by the ruling Latvian elite, some of whom spread rumors that he may be a Russian agent, which he claims is ridiculous. "I was born here and I carry a Latvian passport," he says. "I may be an ethnic Russian but I am a Latvian patriot." Because of his ethnic Russian background, Ušakovs's words and actions are scrutinized more closely than those of most politicians. When he declared during a trip to Moscow that President Vladimir Putin might be the best possible Russian leader for the interests of Latvians, his remarks provoked howls of outrage. Once he returned home, he explained he was not in any way expressing support for Putin's actions but rather his own personal fears that more radical nationalistic alternatives to Putin among Russian politicians could prove much worse for Latvia. "The only point I was trying to make is that there are hard-core Russian nationalists waiting in the wings who would be much more danger-ous than Putin," he says. Ušakovs has only met the Russian president once and dislikes many aspects of Putin's authoritarian rule. None-theless, the Harmony party under his leadership has nurtured close political ties with Russia and signed a cooperation agreement with Putin's United Russia party in 2009.

Ušakovs would prefer to see Latvia and its Baltic neighbors move beyond their ancient struggles with ethnic and historical questions in order to focus on modern challenges like education, jobs, and adapting to new technologies. But he also remains acutely aware that this fragile, multiethnic society could easily fall victim to rising geo-political tensions between the West and a newly aggressive Russia under President Vladimir Putin. When Putin annexed the Crimea enclave on the Black Sea in March 2014 and stepped up military sup-port for Russian-speaking separatists in eastern Ukraine, a shudder of apprehension rippled across the three tiny Baltic states of Lithu-ania, Latvia, and Estonia. Even though these democracies now feel protected by a collective security shield provided by their member-ship in the European Union and the North Atlantic Treaty Organiza-tion, Baltic citizens still nurse dark memories of Russian domination over their lands, particularly during the Communist era when their nations were forcibly annexed to become part of the Soviet Union.

Putin launched his second term as Russia's president by declaring that NATO would henceforth be considered as the primary enemy of the Russian people. He also said he felt obligated to defend the rights of Russian people wherever they might live. Baltic leaders interpreted Putin's words as a direct challenge to their security and sensed they were being targeted for a new phase of Russian imperialism. Under Putin's rule, Russia has employed a sophisticated array of cyberattacks and intrusive media campaigns seeking to influence local politics. In January 2015, the People's Republic of Latgale was mysteriously proclaimed over the Internet calling for the independence of Russian-speaking communities in Latvia. The country's interior minister, Rihards Kozlovskis, said it did not take long to prove that Russian provocateurs were behind what he called a "criminal action" against Latvia's territorial integrity.

The Latgale declaration rattled many Latvian citizens because of its resemblance to the acts of rebellion by Russian-speaking separatists in Ukraine that quickly escalated into a civil war causing nearly 10,000 deaths. Besides the 180-mile-long border that Latvia shares with Russia, the region of Narva adjacent to the Russian frontier in eastern Estonia, where 80 percent of the population is ethnic Russian, is also considered a potential flashpoint where Putin might be tempted to stage a military incursion under the guise of protecting local Russians.

Latvian politicians complain that Putin's Kremlin disseminates a barrage of propaganda on local Russian-speaking television channels, which has created two separate information societies that serve to alienate the country's ethnic groups. A poll taken in 2014 after the Russian takeover of Crimea showed that 64 percent of ethnic Latvians perceived Russia as a threat to their nation, while only 8 percent of Russians speakers did so. In addition, 36 percent of ethnic Russians in Latvia said they strongly supported Russia's annexation of Crimea. The Latvian government believes that Putin will seek to exploit the grievances of ethnic Russians in their country through various forms of hybrid warfare—cyberattacks, media propaganda, and special forces disguised in green jumpsuits stirring up trouble— just as he has done in Ukraine.

Latvia's foreign minister, Edgars Rinkēvičs, accuses Russia of funneling money into various "compatriot" programs designed to win over the hearts and minds of young Latvians through lucrative study grants and expense-paid vacations at political camps inside Russia. "These are not just innocent boy scout activities but clearly an attempt to manipulate the thinking of our young people and make them more sympathetic to Russia's interests," he told me. Rinkēvičs says it is clear that Russia's activities in border states such as Ukraine, Moldova, and the Baltic region reflect a clever strategy to gain influence through the tools of hard and soft power that stop short of forms of aggression that could be labeled acts of war. It comes as no surprise to those living in the Baltic region to learn of Moscow's efforts to influence elections in the United States, Germany, and Bulgaria, which suggest Putin is escalating his below-the-radar efforts to disrupt and destabilize the West.

In the wake of its intervention in Ukraine's civil war, the Kremlin has stepped up its campaign to exploit ethnic tensions in Latvia and neighboring Estonia and Lithuania, which have smaller Russian minorities. A Moscow-based cultural fund, Russkiy Mir (Russian World) has channeled funds to Latvian organizations advocating the cause of ethnic Russians. Russia's foreign ministry has lodged protests at international conferences that the issue of noncitizens in Latvia was "a gross violation of human rights at the very heart of civilized Europe."

Moscow has also encouraged the rise of more extreme parties such as the Latvia Russian Union, which unlike the moderate Harmony party has strongly supported Russia's annexation of Crimea. Some of its members are also suspected by the Latvian government of enlisting to fight in eastern Ukraine with pro-Russian separatists in their civil war against the Kiev government. With its long history of Soviet occupation and simmering unrest in what is the largest Russian-speaking community in the European Union, Latvia feels that it may become the next prime target after Ukraine for Putin's various forms of hybrid warfare.

In response, Latvia's government has fought back on several fronts. It outlawed Russian state television programs that were broadcasting inflammatory reports about the Ukraine conflict and accusing the Kiev government of being a fascist government that must be destroyed. It has also canceled Russian cultural festivals and blocked the transfer of money from Moscow's so-called Compatriot Fund to finance the political rallies of ethnic Russian organizations. Andrejs Pildegovičs, Latvia's state secretary for foreign affairs and former ambassador to the United States, says such measures were necessary because the country is facing its most perilous crisis since the demise of the Soviet Union. "We lost our independence because of illegal acts by big powers in the past. Many bells start ringing when we hear about the legitimate right of Russian leaders to protect everyone who knows a word or a syllable in Russian."

Putin's expanded use of media information campaigns and cyber-attacks in the Baltics has caused particular alarm because they are so difficult to trace back to their source and disarm once they are put into use. At Latvia's request, NATO established the Strategic Communications Center of Excellence to devise countermeasures against Russia's broadcasting war and its cyber troll army that has been very active in the Baltic region. A NATO official called Russia's information campaign there "the largest and most intense NATO has faced since the end of the Cold War" and said it was designed to "confuse, divert and divide public opinion in the West."

While Ukraine is still the principal focus of Russian propaganda efforts, the Kremlin is devoting a much larger share of its media resources than in the past to disseminating news and entertainment programs designed to cultivate greater sympathy for the Russian per-spective. The rise of populist parties in the West with their overtones of disenchantment with the European Union, particularly in the wake of Britain's vote to leave the European Union, have also been a special target for Russian attempts to undermine the stability of Western democratic governments. Two state-owned Russian broadcasters, RT and Sputnik, serve up newscasts aimed at Western audiences that are permeated with subtle messages of support for far-right politicians challenging the establishment, such as Marine Le Pen.

Latvians say history has taught them not to dismiss Putin's threats as empty rhetoric, especially given the barrage of well-packaged nationalist propaganda on Russian television channels that now reach all populations across the Baltic region. In Latvia, 38 percent of the population consume their news from Moscow-based media, while the majority of ethnic Latvians get their information from Latvian or Western news outlets. Proposals to create a Russian-language television service within Latvia to counter Russian propaganda have won strong backing among other NATO countries, but the Latvian government has resisted moving ahead because it feels that ethnic Russians would thus be discouraged from learning Latvian.

As a result, Moscow retains a virtual monopoly over news and other programs shown on television to ethnic Russians across the Baltic region. This offers Putin ample opportunities to foment divisions within these societies if he so chooses, similar to what he did in Ukraine, where much of the population speaks Russian. There, Putin justified his aggression and armed support for separatists in the eastern part of the country by citing the need to protect the endangered Russian minority. It does not take a leap of imagination for Latvians, Estonians, and Lithuanians to believe this kind of exploitation could be used to ignite ethnic tensions and disrupt social peace to the point of encouraging conflict within their own societies. Such propagandistic drum-beating served as a precursor to outright military action by separatist rebels in eastern Ukraine who received arms, funding, logistical help, and training from Russian forces.

NATO officials have sought to reassure the Baltic countries that their security needs will be protected in the event of a military conflict. Under its European Reassurance Initiative, the United States has quadrupled its defense allocation in 2016 for the eastern flank to $3.4 billion in order to move more forces into position to counter any Russian aggression. While seeking to downplay the risks of outright war with Russia, NATO officials insist that such responses are necessary because there is "a real and present danger" of Russian military action in the region and they are obligated to help defend the Baltic states. Western allies have vowed to abide by their commitments under Article 5 of the NATO treaty to defend any attack on a member of the NATO alliance as an attack against them all.

But with the United States and its European allies eager to bring home their troops from Iraq and Afghanistan, the Baltic governments are grimly aware that there is little appetite among their Western allies for engaging in any kind of warfare with a Russia that possesses thousands of nuclear weapons and is rapidly modernizing its conventional forces. Baltic politicians believe it is only a matter of time before Russia's mounting economic troubles brought on by falling oil prices and Western sanctions could tempt Putin to take military action in their region.

Such anxiety has escalated since the election of President Trump, who set alarm bells ringing in the Baltics with his talk about making American support for the Baltic states conditional on their spending more on defense. His friendly words for Putin have also spread jitters through the region. "He's the first presidential candidate to question NATO and NATO commitments," said Ojars Eriks Kalnins, the long-time chairman of the foreign affairs committee in Latvia's parliament. "We are facing a great deal of uncertainty. For Latvia, for Europe, we have no idea what to expect in terms of foreign policy." Kalnins said he is troubled by misleading comments by Trump and influential Republicans like former House Speaker Newt Gingrich, who described Estonia as just a suburb of Saint Petersburg. "That kind of attitude is dangerous," said Kalnins, who led a group of Baltic legislators to Washington after the election to implore Republican leaders to take security responsibilities in the region more seriously. "It sends a signal that you can mess around on your borders and we will look at whether it's something worth bothering about."

Those worries have been compounded by the difficulty of defending NATO's northeastern flank that is exposed to Russian military forces in the Baltic region, which have been going through a ten-year $700 billion modernization program. A Rand Corporation study concluded after conducting a series of hypothetical war games that a Russian invasion could easily overwhelm the defenses of Latvia, Lithuania, and Estonia and consolidate an occupation of the three Baltic states within three days. In the event of a sudden Russian incursion in the Baltics, the United States and its allies would not have sufficient troops or tanks to slow the advance of Russian armor. A Russian seizure of the Baltic states would leave NATO with limited options, all of them bad, the Rand report concluded. The Western alliance could try to stage a bloody counterattack that might trigger a dramatic escalation by Russia, which would possibly see the allied response as a direct strategic threat to its homeland. A second option could involve the threat of massive retaliation, including the use of nuclear weapons. A third option would be to concede temporary defeat and embark on a new Cold War with Moscow while encouraging insurrection and guerrilla warfare against a Russian occupation of the Baltic region.

At their Warsaw summit in July 2016, the Western allies sought to deter possible Russian aggression by approving plans to station up to 4,000 troops on a rotating basis in Poland and the Baltic states that would buttress their defenses and serve as a tripwire for a much larger response by the alliance. Military tensions in the region have spiked as Russia has fortified the enclave of Kaliningrad with anti-ship and antiaircraft defenses. Besides leading a new battalion that will move into Poland, the United States has quadrupled its defense spending to $3.4 billion in the region, which is designed to reassure the Baltic members of NATO that the alliance will respond to any Russian aggression against them. Even with these additional forces, Baltic governments fear they could easily be overwhelmed by much larger and powerful Russian forces in the region. Lithuania, in particular, feels exposed to possible Russian aggression across a sixty-four-mile slice of its border with Poland that extends from the province of Kaliningrad to the territory of Belarus, Russia's close ally. This area, known as the Suwałki Gap, is now considered by Western military experts as the alliance's most vulnerable spot, since Russia could use its large forces and advanced missile arsenals in Kaliningrad to effectively cut off the region and sever the Baltic states from the rest of the alliance.

As East-West military tensions have increased in the Baltic region, American military officials have complained on several occasions that Russian fighter jets "behaved in an unsafe and unprofessional manner" by buzzing U.S. ships and planes. They warned that such provocative actions could easily lead to accidents that would escalate tensions between the United States and Russia. As the Russians respond in kind to the new Western military buildup there, such incidents seem likely to become even more frequent in the future. The nightmare scenario is that as the buildup on both sides continues, these kinds of exercises in the future will be carried out by larger land, naval, and air forces that could cause either side to misinterpret such actions as offensive in nature, leading to a serious military crisis.

Europe remains home to more than half of the world's nuclear weapons. Neither side is interested in seeing any military conflict

escalate to a level where the use of nuclear weapons might be con-
templated in an East-West confrontation. But the persistent sense of
military insecurity felt by the Baltic countries reflects their fear that
NATO capabilities being deployed in the region may not be sufficient
for deterrence to be credible. That, in turn, is creating a hair-trigger
sense of alert in which any disturbance could quickly lurch out of
control, especially with social media channels capable of spreading
false information. In addition to Moscow's sophisticated methods of
cyberwarfare and the constant drumbeat of media disinformation
campaigns, the Baltic governments believe their territorial vulnerability on NATO's northeastern flank to infiltration by Russia's "little
green men"—who seized control of Crimea overnight—is not appreciated by other Western allies.

They argue that the lesson of the past decade is that when Russia chooses to resort to all-out military action—as it did in Georgia
in 2008, Ukraine in 2014, and Syria in 2015—it tends to do so with
much greater speed than Western analysts ever anticipated. They
would like NATO to be more assertive in standing up to the Russian
threat by stationing permanent bases and deploying more forces in
the region to make any conventional assault by Russian invaders
more difficult. But Germany and other Western allies believe there
is a risk that NATO countermeasures against Russia's buildup could
provoke new deployments by Moscow that could cause the dangers
of military confrontation to spiral out of control.

Western politicians contend that NATO has always been a defensive alliance and that Moscow is vastly exaggerating any military
threat from the West. But the release of Soviet archives from the Cold
War era shows how easily any confrontation can lead to unintended
consequences. In the fall of 1983, at a time when the Soviet Union
was suffering a leadership crisis, a NATO military exercise in Europe
called Able Archer triggered fears inside the Kremlin that the West
was preparing a nuclear first strike to decapitate Russia's hierarchy.

Moscow placed some of its air force units in Eastern Europe on a high state of alert while KGB agents sought to find out if Britain and other Western countries had increased blood supplies in preparation for war. When United States intelligence picked up on the alarmist reaction in Moscow, NATO moved quickly to defuse the situation. Yet those early days in November 1983 are now considered, along with the Cuban Missile Crisis in 1962, to be one of the most dangerous episodes of the Cold War, serving as a vivid reminder of how East-West suspicions can lead to the brink of nuclear confrontation.

Ušakovs believes the rising military tensions in the Baltic region could create an "escalation dynamic" that would damage his political mission to build bridges between the ethnic Latvian and Russian communities. He has tried to take a middle road in criticizing Moscow's aggressive actions, as in Ukraine, but calling for more contacts and dialogue with Russia. The mayor's even-handed approach has not won him many political allies. He has angered some fiercely pro-Moscow supporters within the Harmony party by condemning Russia's invasion of eastern Ukraine and its takeover of Crimea. He insists that the United States and its European allies are right to challenge Russia for violating Ukraine's sovereignty and particularly for its unlawful seizure of Crimea. But like some German and Italian politicians, Ušakovs also objects to economic sanctions as a tool to punish Russia for its aggression, saying this will only make peaceful overtures more difficult.

He points out that Russia's retaliation against Western sanctions in the form of banning imports from the West has badly hurt Latvia's economy by blocking its dairy and food exports from reaching Russian consumers. The growing hostility also scares away Russian investment and tourism that he deems vital to Latvia's future peace and prosperity. In the past two decades, wealthy Russians have invested heavily in Riga's real estate market and flocked to the nearby seaside resort of Jurmala for their summer vacations. Ušakovs claims it is important to preserve the flow of trade, tourism, and investment from Russia and protect those sources of Latvian income from political tensions. He says those who accuse him of being too conciliatory toward Moscow overlook the fact that he is simply defending the interests of Latvians and not bowing in cowardly fashion to Russian belligerence. And those critics, he adds, should be prepared to explain why they are imposing economic sacrifices on Latvia's people as well as needlessly antagonizing their powerful neighbor.

"You cannot ignore the fact that we live in the shadow of a country that is much larger and militarily much stronger than we are," Ušakovs told me. "This is not about appeasement. Whenever there are tensions between Russia and the West, we in Latvia who happen to be located on the front line of another Cold War in all likelihood will be the first victims." While Latvia feels at risk from Russian aggression and has welcomed NATO support in bolstering its defenses, the country's close cultural and economic ties to Russia have also fostered a desire for renewed dialogue with Moscow in the hope of averting a conflict that could also rupture the nation's fragile ethnic peace.

Latvia and Estonia, which have large ethnic Russian populations, have taken a tempered approach in response to Russia's aggression in Ukraine. In contrast, Lithuania's president, Dalia Grybauskaitė, whose country has few ethnic Russians, has described Russia's actions as the behavior of a "terrorist state that must be stopped before it spreads its aggression further into Europe." Known as the Baltic Iron Lady, Grybauskaitė claims that Baltic nations should already be considered under attack from Kremlin propaganda and disinformation, which she believes could be the precursor to a possible invasion.

While Lithuania offered to provide lethal arms to Ukraine when civil warfare broke out with Russian-backed separatists, Latvia's prime minister at the time, Laimdota Straujuma, declined to do so and said her country would seek to show its support for Ukraine "in different ways." Latvian leaders are mindful of their country's economic dependency on Russia, which provides most of their country's energy needs and is the biggest market for Latvia's markets. If Russia were to cut off all economic ties with Latvia in the event of a crisis, the government estimates that Latvia could suffer a sharp drop in living standards. Already, because of the impact of sanctions from the Ukraine crisis, Latvia's farmers have been hurt badly because milk and vegetable prices have dropped by 30 to 50 percent with the collapse of demand in Russia.

Ušakovs believes that what matters most to young Latvians these days are issues like the economy, improved education, and how to build a better life for their children, not the prospect of conflict with Russia. He clearly aspires one day to become Latvia's first ethnic Russian prime minister, even though political convention still maintains that Latvia must be ruled by an ethnic Latvian. Perhaps it will take a decade or even more, but he foresees a time when that taboo will be broken and somebody of ethnic Russian background will lead a Latvian government. He thinks his message emphasizing ideology over ethnicity is winning adherents, especially among young people. Like all Latvians, he is conscious of the large shadow that Russia casts over their country, but he prefers to see it in a more positive light than many politicians.

"Whatever happens, we cannot change our geography," he told me. "We live next to a large and powerful nation that is not just a military power, but also one that has a deep and rich culture that we share. I'm not just talking about Dostoyevski and Tolstoy, but also pop music and television entertainment. Most Latvians would rather watch a police drama that takes place in Saint Petersburg rather than Los Angeles because it is more relevant to their own lives."

Ušakovs believes the best way to defuse potential hostilities with a resurgent Russia is to avoid the politics of ethnic resentment, since the nationalistic divide in the Baltic region only plays into Putin's hands. "Nobody wants what happened in Ukraine with its brutal civil war to happen here, especially the younger generation." He notes that their attitudes contrast sharply with those of their parents and offer grounds for optimism that Latvia can escape the ghosts of the past. Around 35 percent of all marriages today are mixed Latvian-Russian couples, and many young people believe the political class makes too much of the country's ethnic divisions. Ušakovs's third wife, his longtime chief of staff, Iveta Strautiņa, whom he married in 2014, is of Latvian descent. He says except on certain holidays that commemorate the past, their ethnic backgrounds rarely come up for discussion.

But Ušakovs is still struggling to get his country to turn the page of history. As mayor, he says one of his more frustrating duties is having to deal with wartime anniversaries. Those events offer a painful reminder of the difficulty he constantly faces in his uphill campaign to focus on the future and not the past. Every June, a somber parade of around 2,000 Latvians led by elderly war veterans winds its way through the medieval streets of Riga's historic center carrying flowers to be laid at the foot of the Freedom Monument, which serves as Latvia's symbol of national independence. The annual memorial service is highly controversial and arouses strong emotions because the war veterans fought for Nazi Germany against Russia. Many Latvians honor their service because in their eyes Hitler's soldiers were less evil than the Russian occupation forces sent by Stalin. In response, a crowd of several hundred Russian speakers usually gather behind police barricades near the monument to shout "Fascists and Nazis, go home!" Invariably, Ušakovs and his police force have to break up the gathering to keep the rival groups from coming to blows.

He also knows the impact of history in a personal way. When Ušakovs gave a speech to a mainly ethnic Russian crowd to celebrate the seventieth anniversary of the defeat of Nazi Germany, the Latvian state language board took its revenge by investigating him for speaking without Latvian translation. While charges were never filed, Ušakovs says it was clearly an act of resentment stemming from the fact that many Latvians still view the defeat of the Nazis as the start of the Soviet occupation. Both of his grandfathers fought in the Soviet army against the Nazis, while the family of his current wife was compelled to fight for the German side.

He and his wife make a point of not letting the past come between them. "We need to stop thinking so much about the past," he told me. "We have a lot of challenges in this country and young people are not so interested in all this talk about an ethnic divide. It's time to move on."

CHAPTER TEN

ATHENS

LIFE ON THE EDGE

"THEN IT'S OVER. GREECE WILL LEAVE THE EUROPEAN MONE-tary Union." With those words, a frustrated Angela Merkel stood up, gathered her papers, and began to walk toward the exit. It was nearly 6 a.m. as dawn was breaking outside the cavernous meeting hall at the Justus Lipsius Building in the European Quarter of Brussels. A sense of impending doom hovered over the twenty-eight leaders of European Union governments who had spent the past fourteen hours rehashing tortuous and emotional arguments over a third financial bailout for Greece.

For more than five years, Greece had been teetering on the brink of bankruptcy, its economy kept alive by infusions of billions of dollars in aid from its partners. But harsh reforms demanded by Germany and other creditors had simply become too much to bear. More than one out of three Greeks were living below the poverty line. National income had plummeted 26 percent, about the same as in the United States at the worst stage of the Great Depression. Greece's radical left-wing government, headed by Syriza party leader Alexis Tsipras, had been elected in January 2015 to bring an end to the suffering. As the price for getting a third infusion of $95 billion, Tsipras was told Greece would have to transfer $55 billion in assets to a trust fund in Luxembourg to pay down debt, or else leave the eurozone. He flatly refused.

Merkel feared the worst. She had fought with her finance minister, Wolfgang Schäuble, over what price to pay for keeping Greece in the eurozone. Schäuble had concluded that maintaining Greece on life support was financially wasteful and politically damaging. It was time to cut Greece loose and shore up the eurozone as a more homogeneous group. Merkel had staked her tenure as Europe's most dominant leader on the belief that if the euro fell apart, Europe would collapse.

She had persuaded the German Bundestag and her recalcitrant coalition partners to approve two previous Greek bailouts—worth $121 billion in 2010 and $143 billion in 2012—even though it was clear Greece would never be able to pay back the loans. But now, having struggled in vain with four different Greek governments to find a successful formula to get the Greek economy back on track, she was ready to concede defeat. She bowed to Schäuble's demands and seemed prepared to roll the dice with financial markets by having Greece become the first member country to drop out of Europe's nineteen-nation single currency zone.

Donald Tusk and François Hollande were determined to prevent her from making what they believed would be a disastrous mistake that would cause mayhem in Europe's financial markets on Monday morning. Tusk, the former Polish prime minister who had been appointed as president of the European Council at Merkel's behest, was responsible for chairing the EU summit meetings. As Merkel and her delegation walked toward the exit, he rushed ahead of her to block her way through the door. "Sorry, but there is no way you are leaving this room," Tusk told her.

With his arms crossed, he continued to bar the exit and insisted that nobody would be allowed to depart until a deal was concluded. Tusk's brazen defiance shocked Merkel's entourage, who wanted to push ahead out the door, but he cleverly knew how to appeal to the chancellor's sense of duty. He reminded her of Germany's responsibilities as Europe's paramount power and her professed desire not to see the euro collapse on her watch. Despite her obvious exhaustion, Merkel complied with his wishes and agreed to make one final effort to secure an agreement.

At the same time, Hollande sought to coax Tsipras back to the negotiating table. The French Socialist expressed sympathy with Tsipras's predicament and urged him to consider a possible compromise that would save face and prevent Greece from leaving the eurozone. Otherwise, Hollande said, the uncertainty of creating a new drachma in a chaotic situation, at a time when capital controls had been imposed and Greek banks had been closed for two weeks, could inflict unimaginable pain on the Greek people.

Tsipras looked shaken and subdued, like a "beaten dog," as one witness put it. He had summoned Greek voters to the polls a week earlier to seek their opinion in a referendum as to whether they would support more austerity in return for another bailout. The result was a resounding "No!" from more than 60 percent of the voters. Yet Tspiras, under Hollande's desperate prodding, now recognized the panic that could be unleashed at home and abroad if he did not cut a deal.

Tusk and Hollande hurriedly patched together a compromise that would preserve Greek sovereignty by allowing the $55 billion trust fund to be based in Athens instead of Luxembourg. Half the funds would be used to recapitalize Greek banks, a quarter earmarked for new investments, and a quarter to repay debt. Merkel reluctantly agreed, to the dismay of Schäuble, who had wanted Greece to depart the eurozone for up to five years while the Athens government tried to repair its economy. After one of the most contentious EU summits ever held, a leap into the abyss was averted just minutes before financial markets opened.

For Tsipras, the political challenge of defending the harsh terms of the bailout seemed insurmountable. He returned to Athens to face an uproar in his own government. Many ministers and parliamentary supporters were shocked that Tsipras had accepted terms that seemed even worse than those rejected in the referendum. He had founded Syriza in 2004 as an alliance of small left-wing parties that later became dedicated to breaking the stranglehold of austerity imposed by Greece's creditors. In January 2015, Syriza had jolted the political establishment by winning national elections. Tsipras then formed a government that vowed to secure debt write-offs and to gain some breathing room for the Greek economy so that jobs and growth could be restored.

Yet now Tsipras had come back from Brussels having performed a political U-turn. Instead of fighting for Greece's solvency through a debt write-off, he meekly accepted the bailout offer of fresh loans under harsh conditions that would only push the country deeper into debt. Yanis Varoufakis, Greece's flamboyant finance minister who resigned in disgust over Tsipras's capitulation, likened the terms to those imposed on Germany by the Versailles Treaty after World War I. Greece's crown jewels would be sold off to pay down debt. Just as Germany lost its merchant marine, its colonies, and its coal mines after the war, Greece would be compelled to sell off at fire-sale prices its shipping harbors, its airports, and even some of its most prized beachfront property.

The sales tax would be raised to 24 percent and all Greek companies would be asked to pay their estimated tax for the coming year ahead of time, crushing any hope for profits to be used as investments. Instead of EU partners giving Greece an opportunity to get back on its feet, Varoufakis lamented that "the odd principle of imposing the greatest austerity for Europe's most depressed economy lives on, spreading new misery through Greece and holding back recovery."

Remarkably, Tsipras managed to transform what looked like a humiliating defeat at the EU summit into a political triumph at home. He managed to win approval in parliament thanks to support from his pro-Europe opponents, who wanted Greece to stay in the eurozone at all costs. Many of Tsipras's left-wing allies voted against the deal. He used their betrayal as a way to jettison the radical leftist program he had proposed just seven months earlier to win office.

In an address to the nation, Tsipras admitted he had been forced to make difficult decisions under pressure. He said he had underestimated the country's economic troubles when he took control of the government. Under the circumstances, he declared that his mandate had run its course and that new elections would need to be held so the public could accept or reject his leadership. When the snap election was held a month later, he defied the polls and his critics by winning 35 percent of the vote. Syriza again emerged as Greece's leading party, well ahead of the conservative New Democracy opposition party which won 28 percent. Tsipras was able to solidify his grip on power by forming another coalition government with the right-wing Independent Greeks.

From his first days as prime minister, the former Maoist firebrand had been badly underestimated by his opponents, who ridiculed his radical ideology and unorthodox methods of government. Yet Tsipras has consistently outfoxed many of his opponents. He possesses extraordinary political instincts and struck a populist chord with many voters who were exasperated with the traditional ruling elite. In so doing, he has used his charisma to transform Syriza from what had been a marginal political movement into Greece's strongest party.

Despite his impressive political gymnastics, there are no signs that Tsipras or anybody else knows how to extricate the nation from its dismal plight. Greece hovers at the precipice of disaster on three of Europe's most troubling fronts: a prolonged debt and unemployment crisis in much of Europe, a rise in political extremism caused by the discrediting of mainstream elites, and the consequences of a massive influx of refugees that has been impossible to control for a country with so many porous frontiers.

The economic collapse that brought Greece to the brink of bankruptcy has devastated much of the country. Suicide rates have jumped 35 percent since 2012, as hundreds of Greeks decided to end their lives because of a deepening sense of despair about the downward spiral in their living standards. Greece has lost a quarter of its gross national product since the crisis first struck in 2008. Pensions for elderly retirees have been cut twelve times while joblessness among adults has climbed close to 30 percent, with youth unemployment double that figure.

Hospitals have reported soaring levels of mental depression as many Greeks who cannot afford to leave the country wallow in despondency about the imploding economy and their impotence to do anything about it. Given the refusal of Germany and other creditors to consider writing off massive amounts of Greek debts, as urged by the International Monetary Fund, there is no visible road back to solvency. None of the successive Greek governments—from right to left across the political spectrum—has proven capable of securing the kind of concessions from their European partners that might change such a gloomy narrative. As a result, Greece survives as a sort of protectorate of the Western world, with the surface trappings of a sovereign state but under the close and relentless supervision of foreign creditors.

The rise of Tsipras and his radical left-wing populist movement owed much to disenchantment with Greece's mainstream parties. For decades, the center-left Socialist party, or PASOK, and the conservative New Democracy took turns running the government.

During that time, both parties nurtured a culture of patronage and corruption that left the country ill prepared for the economic shock of joining the eurozone. Statistics were blatantly manipulated to show that Greece had met the criteria to join the euro when in fact its economy was not anywhere near capable of competing with its other EU partners.

When their country joined the eurozone in 2001, Greeks went on a spending spree that was subsidized by French and German banks, who were only too happy to loan money to their spendthrift Greek clients. For years, successive governments led by the two mainstream parties managed to hide their abuses of power because of the eagerness of European banks to loan them money, but when the global financial crisis struck in September 2008 after the U.S. Treasury refused to rescue the investment bank Lehman Brothers from bankruptcy, it soon became clear that Greece would no longer be able to meet its financial obligations. Within a year, the Greek government acknowledged it had been understating deficit figures for years, raising alarms about the stability of its finances. The country was shut out from borrowing in financial markets by the spring of 2010, just as it was lurching toward bankruptcy.

With the Lehman Brothers debacle still fresh in everyone's minds, nobody wanted to admit that a member of the eurozone should be declared insolvent. As the European financial crisis spread to other countries, including Ireland, Spain, Portugal, and Italy, there were desperate efforts to avoid any drastic remedial action that could undermine public confidence. In 2010, as it became clear that some kind of emergency support would be required in Greece, Jean-Claude Trichet, then head of the European Central Bank, warned that any declared bankruptcy or any attempt to forgive Greece's debts could trigger another global banking crisis just as the world was struggling to recover from the Lehman Brothers fiasco.

At that time, European banks held about $165 billion in Greek debt. Of that figure, $68 billion was owed to French banks and $40 billion to German banks. Chancellor Merkel and other European leaders feared that any large write-off of those debts could wipe out major European banks and possibly create a global financial panic. In addition, Germany feared that forgiving some debts owed by the Greeks would mean that Ireland, Spain, Portugal, and Italy (collectively with Greece known as the PIIGS) would insist on similar favorable treatment. Yet even then, as the IMF acknowledged in a self-critical 2016 report on its handling of the Greek debt crisis, everybody involved in the bailout negotiations realized the cumulative weight of those loans would be impossible to bear.

As a result, the nineteen eurozone governments adopted a policy that has continued to this day known as "extend and pretend," or postponing a day of reckoning. Greece would receive additional bailout money that would help pay off its international loans rather than make its way back into the Greek economy, which meant that an economic recovery that could reduce its staggering debt load would have to be postponed into the distant future. In return for fresh loans, Greece was forced to accept a painful regimen of deep cutbacks in public spending and steep tax increases that would prove incompatible with any hope of reviving growth and creating jobs.

The money loaned to Greece was used to pay off the reckless loans made by French and German banks, which EU leaders believed would defuse the risk of another financial crisis. In turn, European taxpayers would become responsible as the holders of sovereign debt. As a result, the first $132 billion bailout given to Greece, as well as two subsequent infusions of money, was seen as tantamount to a backdoor rescue of European banks and a transfer of those shaky debts from the banks to European taxpayers. In the process of working out this transfer of financial obligations, Greece evolved into the biggest rescue program in global financial history.

In total, Greece's three bailouts since May 2010 have provided almost $360 billion in aid supplied by the European Central Bank, the European Commission, and the IMF, known collectively as the "troika." Merkel and other leaders sold the idea of these controversial bailouts to their voters by promising that Athens would eventually pay off all debts, yet Greece's debt load has now ballooned to 180 percent of its GDP, or three times the level allowed under EU rules. "We will get every cent back, with interest," Merkel told the Bundestag before winning a vote of approval from German legislators to move ahead with the bailouts.

Yet it was all predicated on a fantasy. The IMF has been warning for years that it would be impossible for Greece to pay back its debts and that some form of restructuring—forgiving a significant portion of the debt—would be necessary for Greece to have any hope of regaining economic vitality. Yet neither Merkel nor any other European leaders wanted to acknowledge such an obvious reality because of the dangerous political impact that any debt repudiation would have among voters. In the most recent bailout approved in May 2016, Germany insisted that any further discussion about Greece's inevitable need for debt relief would have to be postponed until 2018—so that the issue would not become a factor in the 2017 national elections in France and Germany.

The Greek economy is likely to remain a basket case for years to come. Since the crisis struck in 2008, a massive brain drain has occurred as nearly half a million Greeks have moved abroad. By far the largest number of those leaving the country were well-educated young professionals who could easily manage to find jobs in Berlin, London, or America. The enormous tasks of reforming and restructuring the Greek economy as the conditions demanded by creditors to back up the loans have become even more difficult to achieve.

Any effort to shrink the payrolls will continue to be resisted since one in four people are still on the public payroll and cling to the state for their livelihoods. The draconian reductions in public spending have sucked more demand out of the economy and reduced unemployment benefits to the point that less than 10 percent of those without a job are getting any kind of state support. And while the close-knit Greek family network has helped three generations of Greeks keep their heads above water during the worst phase of the crisis, the economy has now deteriorated to the point where nearly half of all Greek families no longer include an adult who is employed.

For Tsipras, managing the growing human misery caused by unpayable debt burdens, a deteriorating health system, and the chaos resulting from a flood of Syrian refugees would seem an impossible task. Greece's fate could determine how soon Europe is plunged back into another financial crisis of the kind that nearly ruptured the European Union in 2015. Becoming part of Europe was once seen by Greeks as a way to exorcise the painful memory of military dictatorship and restore their proud history as the cradle of democracy. Now Europe is perceived as a brutal oppressor that turned their country into an international beggar. Europe's demands for a complete overhaul of Greece's economic structure in return for future loans has inflamed resentments toward its northern European creditors, who seem more interested in protecting their own special interests than helping Greece escape from economic depression.

Many Greeks, for example, could not comprehend why Germany and the Netherlands would demand that the government must abolish a law that declared fresh milk sold in shops must not be more than four days old. The reason, it turns out, is that German and Dutch dairy industries wanted further penetration into the local market by gaining sufficient time to transport their factory-farmed milk across Europe to sell to Greek consumers at much lower prices than local fresh milk. Rather than provide a boost to the local economy, such a measure was bound to lead to the ruin of the small Greek dairy producers. Growing public outrage over such actions in Greece and elsewhere has aggravated north-south tensions in Europe between indebted Mediterranean members and their wealthy creditors in Germany, Finland, and the Netherlands.

The huge exodus of Syrians trying to flee civil war through Turkey en route to northern Europe has only compounded Greece's economic mess. Since the summer of 2015, more than 1 million refugees have crossed the narrow straits in the Aegean Sea—at some points less than two miles wide—separating the Greek islands of Lesbos and Chios from the Turkish coastline. When the migrant surge first began, Greece acted merely as a conveyor belt as the vast majority of refugees were looking to travel to Germany or Sweden as their final destination. Ferry ships would bring them to the port of Piraeus near Athens, where they would board buses for the northern border with Macedonia before making their way along the Balkan route toward Germany or Sweden.

When Hungary, Macedonia, and Bulgaria erected fences along their borders to block the flow of people heading north, many of the refugees were stranded at the border post of Idomeni for months as they waited in vain for the frontiers to be reopened. When it became clear that they would no longer be allowed to travel freely through the Balkan route toward desired destinations, they were resettled into more permanent refugee camps built on former military bases. Those who continued to arrive on the islands were prevented from leaving for the mainland and housed in overcrowded settlements, with poor hygiene and insufficient food.

Within a year after the refugee surge began, Greece became transformed into a gigantic holding pen, with close to 60,000 desperate migrants and asylum seekers detained against their will. The refugee influx has placed enormous demands on Greece's fragile infrastructure, pushing government services that had already been sharply curtailed by the economic crisis to the breaking point. While the European Union promised to supply extra aid to help Greece cope with the refugees, little of the pledged EU support was forthcoming.

Greece was left alone to shoulder much of the burden; within two years of the arrival of the first wave of refugees, the government was spending an extra $45 million a month just to feed the tens of thousands of mostly Syrian, Afghan, and Iraqi refugees who had flooded into Greece hoping to continue their journey north, but soon found themselves holed up in Greek camps. Even though the daily flow of refugees arriving on rafts and rickety boats had greatly diminished, there was no guarantee that the surge would not resume if Turkey decided to cease its cooperation under the terms of a $3.3 billion deal with the EU by pulling out police and military units that patrolled the coastline.

Greeks at first showed a remarkable degree of hospitality toward the refugees at a time when their own families were enduring serious hardship. But their generosity soon began to wear thin as the growing financial burdens of caring for so many refugees caused further deterioration in their own lives. After praising his compatriots for their empathy and courage in coping with the refugees, Tsipras complained to his EU partners that their callous neglect of Greece risked turning his country into "a warehouse for souls."

Tsipras expressed grave anxiety about what would happen to his country after Chancellor Merkel reached an agreement with Turkey for its help to curb mass migration in exchange for a multibillion-dollar aid package. He feared that Greece would be turned into Europe's dumping ground for refugees and become overwhelmed by managing a new phase of Europe's migrant crisis as many EU nations refused to accept their fair share of the influx.

At first, the results of the EU-Turkey deal looked positive. The traffic in boats carrying refugees from Turkey to Greece nearly stopped after the deal went into effect on March 20, 2016. The migrant flows soon plummeted, with the number of refugees risking the dangerous voyage across the Aegean dropping from more than 6,000 per day at its peak in October 2015 to less than 50 per day nine months later. But

with the northward passage of refugees blocked, Greece was left struggling to process a cascade of asylum requests from tens of thousands
of refugees stuck in what they considered no-man's-land—unable to
move on from Greece to Germany or Sweden yet also unable to return
home to war-ravaged communities in Syria or Iraq.

Moreover, Turkey made it clear that unless it received visa-free
travel rights for its citizens, the deal to control migrant flows with the
EU could collapse. If that should happen, even Merkel agreed with
Tsipras that Greece would be plunged into chaos with the multiple
challenges of handling a large and growing population of refugees
while trying to appease creditors by carrying out austerity measures
and economic reforms. "I wake up every morning worrying that
the agreement will fall apart and the refugees will start arriving in
huge numbers again on our islands," said Ioannis Mouzalas, Greece's
minister for migration and refugees. "It is my biggest nightmare."
Mouzalas said without the deal with Turkey, close to 200,000 more
people would have come to Greece within three months.

For local residents on the five islands that have received most
of the refugees—Lesbos, Chios, Leros, Kos, and Samos—the initial
wave of sympathy has turned to anguished consternation about how
long they will be able to sustain their support of the migrants. The
Greek word for stranger, *xenos*, is also the word for guest, and many
locals have shown a remarkable generosity of spirit in welcoming the
Syrian refugees.

During a tour of the camps supervised by the United Nations refugee agency, many volunteer camp workers told me they were descendants of Greek families who had found safe haven on these islands in
the turmoil following the collapse of the Ottoman Empire. For over a
millennium, Christian Greeks and Muslim Turks have been waging
ferocious battles in the Aegean region that have shaped the destiny of
these islands. In 1922, after Turkish forces routed an invading Greek
army, hundreds of thousands of Greeks were forced to flee their

ancestral homes in Asia Minor and take refuge on Lesbos, Chios, and other islands. Muslim Turks who were living on the islands, in turn, were forcibly repatriated to Turkey.

"We all come from a refugee background, so we know what it is like," said Stavros Mirogiannis, who has served as the director of the Kara Tepe camp on Lesbos since it opened in April 2015. "Despite all the suffering we have experienced during our economic crisis, we are still willing to share our food and clothing with people who are so much in need. We do not think of ourselves as heroes, just servants of humanity."

Like other locals, Mirogiannis is proud of the fact that the people of Lesbos were saluted for their work by Pope Francis and were short-listed for the Nobel Peace Prize in honor of their generosity. But he acknowledges that the local economy, which survives largely on tourism, has suffered greatly, since weekly vacation charter flights from Europe dropped by 60 percent with the start of the refugee surge. The tight confinement in the camps created constant friction among the refugees, leading to fights between rival ethnic groups. There was a spate of hunger strikes over bad food and unsanitary conditions. The biggest irritation for the refugees seemed to be boredom as they await news about their asylum applications, a process which can drag on for more than a year.

The refugees are caught in a Catch-22. They are stuck in a crisis-ridden country with few resources to offer outsiders, while yearning for relocation to wealthier EU countries that are unwilling to accept them. Many of them regret ever trying to reach Europe. They express a desire to return to the camps in Turkey where they have family members rather than be stranded in Greece. Four asylum seekers even tried to swim back to Turkey, but were turned back by the Greek coast guard.

In some ways, this was all part of the cynical strategy behind the EU-Turkey deal: to deter new migrants by showing there is no way of getting to northern Europe by crossing from Turkey into Greece. The island camps are despised by many refugees as open-air prisons that serve as a buffer zone to keep them holed up in Greece—far away from Austria, Germany, and Sweden.

Under the terms of the deal, all refugees and migrants who arrive on Greek shores aboard smugglers' rafts are supposed to be sent back to Turkey, where they will be the last among those considered for resettlement in a European country in the future. In return, the European Union says it will accept one Syrian refugee from Turkey for every Syrian who is sent back there. While the deal may have discouraged some migrants from making the journey, Greece still faces an enormous challenge in figuring out what to do with the huge number of refugees who are still stuck in their territory with no place to go.

The European Union's institutions were slow to deliver the additional resources that had been pledged to help Greece serve as the de facto holding pen for many Syrian refugees. EU policy calls for refugees to seek asylum in the member state where they first arrive, which has saddled Greece with an enormous administrative burden in processing so many asylum applications at a time when it is trying to curtail government services. The financial weight of caring for the refugees has been even more difficult to sustain.

According to the immigration ministry in Athens, the cost of providing food, clothing, and shelter for the refugee population by mid-2016 had surpassed $100 million a month. Greece has pleaded with its EU partners for extra aid money to cope with daunting humanitarian and logistical challenges in sustaining the refugee population at a time when its economy is moribund because of the debt crisis that has lasted nearly a decade. But the international spotlight has shifted elsewhere, focusing on threats of further Islamic terrorist attacks, Russian aggression in Ukraine and possibly along Europe's eastern frontiers, and Britain's departure from the European Union.

Meanwhile, Greeks fear their fragile status and porous borders in a highly unstable part of the world leave them vulnerable to further disasters.

Some Greeks believe the only alternative for their country is to become resigned to its fate as a colony of Europe, depending for its survival on the generosity of its partners. But with populist nationalists gaining ground in many parts of Europe as the long-term crisis in jobs and growth shows no signs of abating, there is less willingness than ever before among European creditors to funnel more loans to Greece that everybody knows can never be repaid.

Within Greece, a large coterie of millionaires has managed to protect their fortunes by stashing money in foreign banks or purchasing property in London and Berlin. But as the middle and lower classes bear the brunt of suffering, income inequality has reached alarming proportions, to the point that Greece now reflects a social disparity between rich and poor that resembles the plight of Third World dictatorships. As can be seen from the many owners of luxury yachts sailing to their private island estates in the Aegean, much wealth in Greece escapes the reach of tax collectors. An estimated 55 percent of the country's adult population does not pay any income tax, either because they are below the poverty threshold of earning less than 9,000 euros a year or because they have found clever and ingenious ways to evade paying what they owe to the state.

Much of Greece's failure to learn the lessons of the financial crisis and adapt its political and economic culture can be attributed to a penchant for blaming others for problems that are largely self-inflicted. Throughout the crisis, Greeks staged frequent street protests denouncing what they claimed was the inhuman cruelty of Chancellor Merkel's government in Germany, the International Monetary Fund, and the European Central Bank for attaching draconian conditions to the loans offered to Greece.

While mistakes were certainly committed by its international creditors, as the IMF has admitted, some Greeks have slowly started to realize that their own excesses, under governments of both the right and the left, were mostly to blame. From 2004 to 2009, the government led by conservative prime minister Kostas Karamanlis ran up huge debts during Greece's free-spending years after joining the eurozone and then doctored official statistics to hide the true size of the budget deficit. When Socialist leader George Papandreou took over from Karamanlis, his government tried to heap blame on their conservative predecessors for deceiving the nation but they soon found themselves accused of buckling under pressure from creditors to accept unduly painful measures in return for a bailout.

When the Greek finance minister at the time, George Papaconstantinou, emerged from long negotiations with what he thought was the best deal possible, he was greeted as a pariah by his own compatriots. In his personal memoir, he recalls that the first question he was asked by a journalist after securing the bailout was how it felt to be the most hated man in Greece, which he said "felt like a punch in the stomach." He later was put on trial for allegedly erasing the names of relatives from a list of Swiss bank accounts, but was exonerated on all counts except one misdemeanor.

"It was a personal nightmare for me, but even more important is that it has become a total disaster for the entire country," Papaconstantinou told me. "We are now left with a broken society that may take at least a generation to repair. The political system has been blown apart, and there is a real danger that extremists will move into the void and take control of the country."

In particular, there is concern that Donald Trump's election will bestow a certain degree of legitimacy on xenophobic right-wing extremist groups like Golden Dawn, which is now Greece's third-most-popular party even though its leaders are facing trial for a series of crimes, including attacks on immigrants. Golden Dawn hailed Trump's election as a victory against "illegal immigration" and in favor of "ethnically clean states."

The fears about a turn toward right-wing extremism in Greece have become more plausible in the wake of Trump's election and the fact that other European countries are seeing a shift by voters toward right-wing nationalists, such as in France and the Netherlands. The popularity of the ruling leftist Syriza party has plummeted after two years in office produced little improvement in Greece's economic fortunes. The only moderate alternative that seems likely to replace Tsipras and his ruling leftists comes from Kyriakos Mitsotakis, the new leader of the conservative opposition New Democracy party.

As the forty-eight-year-old scion of one of Greece's most prominent dynasties, Mitsotakis came back to Greece a decade ago to launch his political career after a long self-imposed exile in the United States. After studying at Stanford and Harvard, where he earned a master's degree in business administration, Mitsotakis worked as an economic analyst at Chase Manhattan Bank and the international consulting firm McKinsey & Company in London.

He later took one of the most loathed jobs in a previous conservative government, serving as minister for administrative reform, yet he managed to push through performance reviews and streamline Greece's large bureaucracy by dismissing 5,000 civil servants. By doing so, he put his finger on one of the most serious structural problems plaguing Greece: that one in four Greeks is employed by the state and enjoys a substantial wage premium over the private sector, even though government jobs are rife with corruption and inefficiency and the quality of public services remains abysmal.

Mitsotakis was elected in January 2016 as the leader of the center-right New Democracy party and is seeking to rally supporters behind a free-market philosophy that encourages entrepreneurial zeal and seeks to slim down the size of the state, similar to what fellow conservative François Fillon has proposed for France. Most of all, Mitsotakis says Greeks need to change their natural disposition and start taking greater personal control over their lives.

"The fight with our creditors was always a way to dodge our own responsibility," Mitsotakis told me. "The genuine problem was that we had spent ourselves into the ground and that as a state we were bankrupt. Instead of addressing the basic cause of our troubles at home, we engaged in this long, useless game of finding somebody else to blame."

As the son of a former prime minister, Mitsotakis realizes that the desire to accept responsibility for one's own fate does not come easily to Greeks, who are imbued with all sorts of conspiratorial theories about why they should not be held responsible for their own shortcomings. "Rather than get on with life and do what is necessary to improve our situation, we prefer to sit around and blame all kinds of dark forces for what is happening to us," he says.

Where will Greece go from here? Despite the financial bailouts and austerity measures designed to streamline its bloated public sector, Greece still faces immense problems in transforming itself into a modern, well-functioning democracy. Much of the economy remains tightly controlled by clannish oligarchs, whose grip over the media and financial institutions gives them enormous leverage over politics. Syriza came to power promising to break up the stranglehold of oligarchs dominating much of Greece's political and economic life. But powerful individuals such as shipping magnates Vangelis Marinakis and Minos Kyriakou, media moguls Kostas Kimporopoulos and Yiannis Alafouzos, and building contractor Yiannis Kalogritsas continue to wield enormous influence.

At the urging of its EU creditors, the Greek government sought to raise $275 million in an auction by selling off private television broadcast licenses, which previously had been given away by political barons as favors to their corporate sponsors. Nikos Pappas, a close advisor to the prime minister who oversaw the auction of the licenses, said the sale surpassed expectations and came as "a positive surprise for everybody." Syriza's political opponents complained that reducing the number of television stations from seven to four would give the government too much control over how people receive news and information. But most Greeks applauded the much-needed overhaul of the television media, which is highly distrusted because of the heavy control exercised by political and business interests.

After two difficult years in office, Tsipras and his government finally seemed on the brink of a major success in its drive to claw back power from the incestuous political-corporate networks that control much of Greece. But the country's most powerful judicial body felt otherwise. To the shock and dismay of government supporters, Greece's highest court ruled the new law unconstitutional, insisting the government must not usurp regulatory authority over the licensing of commercial television stations. The decision dismayed many of those cheering the cause of reform. But it has pleased the powerful oligarchs who will be able to maintain their control of the media and thus continue to run the country behind the scenes.

CHAPTER ELEVEN

MOSCOW, ANKARA, TUNIS

EUROPE'S TROUBLED NEIGHBORHOOD

O NE OF THE MOST REMARKABLE ASPECTS OF GERMANY'S RISE from the ashes of World War II to its current dominance in Europe has been the achievement of peaceful and prosperous relations with all nine of its neighbors. Inspired by this success, the European Union adopted the German example as the guiding rationale behind its strategic ambition to project security and stability beyond its frontiers. In a twist on Robert Frost's famous poem, Europe believed that by cultivating and pacifying the territories beyond its borders it would create an environment where "good neighbors make good fences."

It started with the Balkans. A parade of European peace envoys watched helplessly as more than 200,000 were killed in a genocidal war that began just two years after the triumphant fall of the Berlin Wall. The arduous quest to bring peace to the blood-soaked lands of the former Yugoslavia in the 1990s eventually succeeded because Serbia and Croatia finally realized that the most optimistic route to the future was pursuing a path toward Brussels and the tantalizing prospect of eventual membership in the European Union. That became a vital incentive in convincing the warlords to lay down their weapons, abandon the autocratic rule of strongmen like Milošević and Tudjman, and embrace the idea of building a liberal democracy in partnership with the West.

Since then, Croatia and Slovenia have become full EU members, Montenegro has been accepted into NATO and is knocking on the door of the EU, while Serbia, Macedonia, and Bosnia-Herzegovina struggle to fulfill the criteria to be considered for EU and NATO membership. As Richard Holbrooke, the indefatigable American diplomat who negotiated the Dayton Peace Accords, told me, the most effective card he played in halting the fighting was to urge the protagonists to turn away from their deadly nationalistic rivalries that were rooted in the past and seize the opportunity of creating a future vision of peace and prosperity through the Western institutions based in Brussels.

The European Union tried to build on the Balkan peace agreement—which only occurred after years of diplomatic fumbling before the United States became directly involved—by establishing a new set of political and economic partnerships beyond its eastern and southern frontiers. The principal aims of the European Neighborhood Policy, which was launched in 2003 to serve as the cornerstone of a continental foreign policy, sought to establish close ties with Russia, Turkey, and North Africa.

First, the EU would seek to build a closer partnership with Moscow through energy cooperation, and eventually find ways to cooperate in dealing with China and the Middle East. Second, the Union urged Turkey to embrace democratic norms required for future EU membership and thus serve as a model for Islamic nations. Third, Europe would strive to accelerate economic development across North Africa through generous trade and investment programs designed to provide jobs for millions of young people who desperately wanted to immigrate to Europe because they could not find work at home.

Today, Europe's neighborhood policy stands in ruins. Instead of radiating stability beyond the Black and Mediterranean seas, Europe is now suffering blowback from hostile forces that have generated civil wars, anarchy, famine, and refugee surges along its periphery.

Russia has turned more belligerent toward the West, violating the postwar order by seizing Crimea and fomenting aggression in eastern Ukraine. In Turkey, President Erdoğan has consolidated power in the wake of a failed coup attempt against him and rejected Europe's appeals to restore a semblance of democracy. He warned European leaders that any outright rejection of Turkey's application for EU membership and failure to provide visa-free travel to his citizens would prompt him to open up the floodgates for the 3 million Syrian refugees on Turkish soil to stream into Europe. Across North Africa, the noble aspirations of the Arab Spring have evaporated in a brutal power struggle pitting Islamic insurgencies against military rule.

In the words of Sweden's former prime minister Carl Bildt, who worked closely alongside Holbrooke in forging a successful peace deal in the Balkans: "What was supposed to become a circle of friends surrounding Europe has turned into a ring of fire." A decade ago, the European Union entertained notions of becoming the world's first postmodern superpower, one that exercised power and influence not through military force but through forms of soft power like its generous aid programs, global commercial clout, and the compelling attraction of more than 500 million affluent consumers enjoying the world's highest living standards.

Even now, as the European Union struggles with existential crises on several fronts, many neighboring countries are still pursuing membership in an organization that they view as a desirable way to achieve enhanced political and economic stability in a chaotic world.

The Brexit crisis and other European troubles, however, have virtually paralyzed prospects for further EU expansion.

Some EU governments, such as those led by Hungary's prime
minister Viktor Orban and Poland's ruling party leader Jarosław
Kaczyński, have taken an illiberal turn and started to question the
open-society model that encourages respect for free speech and the
rule of law. While their voices are still in a minority, the Union now
finds it difficult to inspire democratic values in surrounding countries, hindering its ability to extend its zone of influence into Central
Asia, the Middle East, and North Africa. Russian aggression in eastern Ukraine, the prolonged civil war in Syria, the subsequent refugee
crisis, and the spreading threat of Islamist terrorism has turned the
concept of exporting stability beyond Europe on its head. Instead of
expanding its zone of peace and prosperity to its neighbors, Europe
is discovering that chaos and disorder on its periphery is now intrud-
ing on its own shores. Only yesterday, it seems, Europe had grand
hopes of transforming its neighbors; today it sees itself more as a
hostage to uncontrollable events taking place beyond its borders.

THE RUSSIA CONUNDRUM

In the East, Europe woke up late to the realization that parallel
efforts by NATO and the EU to extend membership to former Communist societies would trigger a backlash in Moscow and revive its
traditional paranoia about being encircled by the West. After the collapse of the Soviet empire, the European Union embarked on an historic wave of enlargement that absorbed ten nations and more than
100 million people into the West. At the time, Russia was prostrate
under the weak and erratic leadership of President Boris Yeltsin.
The post-Communist economy was in turmoil as Russians struggled
to adapt to the competitive world of free markets. Europe and the
United States sought to alleviate Russia's anxieties about pushing

EU and NATO toward its frontiers with separate partnership pacts concluded with Moscow. When the European Neighborhood Policy was established in 2003, the outlook for a new era of friendly cooperation with Russia could not have been more robust. The EU's first Security Strategy paper published that same year reflected this optimistic assessment of the security landscape across the continent. "Europe has never been so prosperous, so secure nor so free. The violence of the first half of the 20th century has given way to a period of peace and stability unprecedented in European history."

The European Union launched its Eastern Partnership program with six countries in Eastern Europe and in the southern Caucasus, who eagerly joined in the belief that it would serve as a way station toward full membership in the Union. Europe also believed it could work effectively with Prime Minister Dmitry Medvedev, who at first saw cooperation with the European Union as the most effective way to modernize Russia's economy. Medvedev, with President Putin's blessing, sought to promote Russia, with its rich oil and gas resources, as Europe's prime source of energy supplies. In return, Europe would expand investment in Russia, exploring new opportunities to build automobile factories to meet local rising demand for Western cars, improve the electrical grid and other forms of infrastructure, and invest in Medvedev's pet project of a high-technology cluster outside Moscow. But by 2007, as NATO and the EU considered further expansion into the former Soviet states of Georgia and Ukraine, Putin and his cohort of former KGB comrades began to feel they were being betrayed by the West, which they suspected as the hidden hand behind the Rose and Orange democratic revolutions emerging in those countries. Their deepest fear, it soon became apparent, was that the West's promotion of liberal democratic values would begin to threaten their own grip on power at home.

When Georgia pressed for early membership in NATO in 2008,

Russia soon provoked a short but intense war, which led to its recognition of the breakaway states of Abkhazia and South Ossetia, two Georgian territories located along Russia's southern frontier. Putin had by then become prime minister after trading positions with Medvedev as a way to retain power and still uphold Russia's constitutional term limits on the presidency. He flatly rejected Western criticism that Moscow was engaged in altering the borders of Europe by force. Russia claimed its recognition of the two secessionist governments was no different than what Western countries had done six months earlier when they endorsed Kosovo's declaration of independence from Serbia. "In international relations, you cannot have one rule for some and another rule for others," Medvedev said, accusing the West of hypocrisy in its treatment of Russia's efforts to protect its zone of influence.

In retrospect, Javier Solana, the former Spanish foreign minister who served as NATO secretary-general and then for ten years as the EU foreign policy chief, acknowledges that the West clearly underestimated the sense of humiliation that Russia endured during the Yeltsin years. The West also misjudged how Putin would exploit those sentiments in mobilizing support behind his campaign to revive Russia's power, confidence, and assertiveness on the world stage. As Solana recalled in several conversations, Western policy toward Russia was conceived with the perspective that the early phase of partnership, as endorsed by Medvedev and Putin, would continue indefinitely because it so clearly seemed in Moscow's political and economic interests to align with the West. In Washington, Brussels, London, and Berlin, foreign policy experts were nearly unanimous in the belief that the two biggest threats to Moscow came from China's encroachment on its eastern Siberian frontier and from Islamist radicalism in the south, such as the Chechen terrorists who staged several bombings in Moscow and were eventually ruthlessly suppressed. For those reasons, it was believed in Western capitals that

Moscow could not afford to alienate NATO and the European Union, which thus felt less constrained in pursuing alliances with the forces of democratic change in countries bordering Russia.

The Georgia crisis offered clear evidence that a new nationalism was taking hold in Russia that was overlooked in the West as Putin and Medvedev sought to restore their country to what they viewed as its rightful place as a global superpower. Putin attacked Western foundations, particularly the Open Society Institute funded by the billionaire investor George Soros, for trying to undermine Russia's government by encouraging the influence of dissident groups. As he moved Russia toward strict authoritarian rule, Putin intensified his criticism of what he called Western decadence that had flourished under liberal democracy. He chastised the West for its tolerance of gays and lesbians, its turn away from traditional religion, and the decriminalization of drugs. Putin suggested that such actions were not indicative of greater freedom but merely signs of a declining civilization.

Putin's resentment toward the West spiked in November 2013 when a wave of demonstrations and civic unrest erupted in Kiev's Independence Square among many young people demanding closer integration with Europe. The scope of the protests soon expanded, with demands growing for the resignation of President Viktor Yanukovych and his government. Transparency International, which regularly evaluates the honesty and integrity of governments around the world, named Yanukovych as one of the most corrupt leaders in the world. But what brought so many Ukrainians into the square was not so much his renowned venality but his controversial decision to bow to Putin's wishes and reject Ukraine's association agreement with the European Union.

Many Ukrainians saw closer ties to Europe as the best hope to improve their miserable quality of life, which two decades earlier had been on a par with neighboring Poland. They had followed with great envy the astounding improvement in Poland's economy, which since EU membership had seen living standards take off to the point where Poles were by virtually every measure at least three times better off than Ukrainians. Putin was well aware that similar comparisons might soon be drawn in Moscow with Russia's flagging economy if protests in Kiev were allowed to get out of hand. By February 2014, Yanukovych was forced to flee the country and seek refuge in Russia. He was replaced by a pro-Europe government that reinstated the terms of the EU agreement, which incited Putin to step up intervention in what he viewed as Russia's sphere of influence. Russian forces soon seized control of Crimea and shored up their support for pro-Russian rebels in eastern Ukraine. At home, Putin consolidated even more power as he cracked down on opponents who favored closer ties with Europe.

Since the Ukraine uprising, Putin has amplified his campaign to change the international order and undermine Western unity. He has intervened in Syria's civil war on behalf of its president Bashar al-Assad, where Russian warplanes have carried out widespread bombing attacks that have killed hundreds of civilians and caused refugee hordes to stream out of the embattled city of Aleppo.

He has also escalated his direct challenges to governments in the West. Russia has interfered brazenly in the domestic politics of Western countries through countless cyberattacks and hacking operations, including in the United States. Putin has reached out to far-right populists such as France's Marine Le Pen, offering a $10 million loan to fill party coffers for her presidential campaign. He has also sought to test the limits of NATO commitments, in which the allies pledge to respond to an attack on one as if it is an attack against them all. Russia has focused its propaganda efforts in the Baltic states that once were part of the Soviet Empire, particularly in Estonia and Latvia, where large Russian-speaking populations live. In a bold and spiteful affront to the European Union, Putin has embarked on building a Eurasian economic bloc that would link Slavic nations like Serbia, Belarus, and other parts of Eastern Europe with Russia, Central Asia, and China.

To the dismay of Chancellor Merkel and other critics, Putin seems to be making considerable headway in sowing disarray in the West. He strongly supported the referendum to take Britain out of the EU and Donald Trump's campaign to become president—and the Russian leader has won his bet in both cases. He also hopes to benefit from the rising influence of populist nationalists across Europe who favor greater accommodation with Moscow, in particular Le Pen. In an interview with BBC television, Le Pen said "there is absolutely no reason why we should turn systematically to the United States and why we should neglect Russia." She dismissed Putin's record of interference in Ukraine and in Western elections and instead placed the blame on the European Union, which she called "an oppressive model" that France should abandon once a referendum is held as was done in Britain. "Who is destabilizing Europe today and its neighbors? It's the European Union," she said. Le Pen also claimed Europe has much more to fear from America's aggressive tendencies and that she believes Russia, if treated fairly, would prove to be a cooperative partner for the West.

Le Pen said she shared many of Trump's views about the need for every nation to protect its national interests first. Trump's positive comments during the campaign about Putin's leadership have resonated throughout Europe, drawing support about the need for a more cooperative approach toward Moscow from right-wing populists like Le Pen and Russophile politicians like Hungary's Orban and Bulgaria's president, Rumen Radev.

With European voters more concerned about terrorism and immigration than the fate of Ukraine, there has been a profound political shift across Europe in which sentiment is moving away from further confrontation with Moscow toward a more realistic acceptance that Russia must be allowed to defend its national interests and maintain its proper zone of influence.

In wealthy Western nations like Italy and Germany, where Prime Minister Matteo Renzi and Chancellor Angela Merkel went along with punitive sanctions against Moscow despite the negative impact on their nations' lucrative export business with Russia, there is a growing realization that blocking trade and investment has failed to serve the purpose of getting Russia out of Ukraine. In addition, the conviction is spreading that if the United States and Britain retreat from their commitments to the continent's security, Europe needs to reach long-term understandings with Moscow.

Meanwhile, Russia continues to modernize its military forces under a seven-year, $700 billion arms program that Putin has launched. Through cyberwarfare and media disinformation campaigns, Russia has expanded its ability to assert its power and influence in spite of its shrinking population and weakening economy. Moscow's strategy seems intent on eroding the Western liberal democratic order in the hope that a new balance of power in Europe will continue to shift east, pulling France, Germany, and Italy in the direction of more sympathetic attitudes toward Russia.

Europe's future neighborhood policy will likely place greater emphasis on securing Russian cooperation in coping with what are seen as the most urgent threats coming from the Middle East and North Africa. Europe could also be propelled in that direction by a Trump administration that seems eager for a new era of détente with Moscow. But that kind of a transaction could also entail enormous hidden costs for Europe. With Putin likely to remain in power until 2024, will the price of accepting a more powerful Russia as a guarantor of its stability exact a toll in Europe's retreat from its own values and ambitions?

THE TURKEY DILEMMA

Over the years, Europe has invested high hopes and hefty sums of money in Recep Tayyip Erdoğan. He first rose to prominence as an energetic and effective mayor of Istanbul, a sprawling metropolis of 15 million people crowding the banks of the Bosporus. Taking charge of one of the world's most rambunctious cities, Erdoğan managed to clean the streets, collect the garbage, and weed out corruption that was rife within the city's administration. But his fervent religious views aroused suspicions among Turkey's powerful military leadership, which has often interceded in domestic politics when deemed necessary to maintain public order. After four years as mayor, Erdoğan was stripped of power, banned from office, and jailed for ten months on the charge of inciting religious intolerance. He then abandoned his avowed Islamist politics and formed the moderate Justice and Development Party (AKP) in 2001. The following year the AKP won a landslide victory in national elections and promised, despite its religious origins, to respect the secular traditions laid down by Turkey's founder Kemal Atatürk. Once his ban was annulled, Erdoğan became prime minister, a post he held until being elected president in 2014.

Erdoğan's early years as prime minister attracted admiring supporters in Europe and the United States. He carried his party to successive victories in national elections, on the strength of a booming economy, a surge in foreign investment, and the construction of new roads, airports, and high-speed rail networks. In 2010, President Obama hailed Turkey as a "great Muslim democracy" and "a critically important model for other Muslim countries in the region." Obama consulted Erdoğan about Middle East events on a frequent basis—calling him on the phone as often as twice a week—and cited him along with Chancellor Merkel as one of the very few leaders with whom he had forged a close personal relationship. In partic-

ular, Erdoğan served as an important interlocutor during the difficult negotiations to prevent Iran from developing nuclear weapons.
Obama, Merkel, and other Western leaders also believed that Erdoğan could use his party's ties with the Muslim Brotherhood to good
effect in relations with the Arab world. Turkey has always lived in a
rough and turbulent neighborhood, bordering countries in frequent
stages of turmoil such as Iran, Iraq, and Syria. But many Western
leaders took Erdogan at his word when he declared that Turkey would
become a stabilizing force as the dominant regional power because
it had "zero problems" with its neighbors. His foreign minister at the
time, Ahmet Davutoğlu, promised that Turkey "will lead the winds
of change in the Middle East" and help create a more secure world.

At last, the West seemed to have discovered an exemplary Muslim
ruler, who could find the right balance between Islam and democracy. But some secular critics warned that Erdoğan was a wolf in
sheep's clothing, an Islamic autocrat at heart who was patiently
playing along with the secular game until he might find the right
moment to steer the country toward his own brand of theocratic
rule. Erdoğan and his supporters scoffed at such accusations and
vehemently denied that he was playing a double game. They claim
there was no contradiction between his personal motivations and
the religious roots of Christian Democratic politicians in Germany,
Austria, and other European countries. When Chancellor Merkel
asked him during one of their first meetings about how Islam influ-
enced his political thinking, Erdoğan responded that he and his
party were just like Merkel's Christian Democrats: conservative on
social issues, free-market advocates on the economy, and religious
in personal choice only.

Turkey has long aspired to join the European Union and first
applied for membership more than five decades ago. Erdoğan's
success in modernizing the country during his first years in power
encouraged European leaders to believe that Turkey's time had

arrived to become fully integrated with the West. Turkey was already a long-standing member of NATO and now seemed determined to do what was necessary to become part of the European Union. The Ankara government abolished the death penalty, pursued peace talks, offered much greater autonomy to moderate Kurdish nationalists, and began adopting legislation designed to conform to EU requirements. Human rights issues were still a problem, including the incarceration of journalists on trumped-up charges of sedition. While skeptics in Europe believed Turkey was too big for the EU to swallow and should be considered part of Asia, its supporters claimed that embracing Turkey would prove the EU could help pacify the Middle East through the power of enlargement. For his part, Erdoğan insisted that Turkey was determined to do whatever was necessary to join the EU by 2023, in time to celebrate the centenary of the Turkish Republic.

But others saw darker motives behind Erdoğan's push for EU membership. He was particularly keen on fulfilling EU demands for civilian control of the military, which suited his key objective to thwart the military leadership from any future meddling in politics. Erdoğan's ally at the time was none other than Fethullah Gülen, the Islamic preacher who from his base of self-imposed exile in Pennsylvania had supported the rise to power of Erdoğan and his AKP. He had started his movement, known as Hizmet (Service) in the 1970s, and had expanded his reach through schools and charities around the world to embrace millions of followers. Gülen's well-educated supporters heeded his urgings to infiltrate the police, the judiciary, the civil service, and even the military as a way to help Erdoğan to break down the military's iron grip on state institutions. Others became influential members of the media and opened successful banks and businesses. Later Erdoğan and Gülen would become mortal enemies, but at the time, they were united in their determination to banish the "deep state" apparatus through which Turkish military leaders had exercised power behind the scenes. In the Ergenekon trials launched in 2007, hundreds of senior military officers were placed on trial on dubious charges based on doctored evidence. But the controversial trials seemed to inflame a growing rivalry between Erdoğan and Gülen, whose clashing egos and sharply different views about Turkey's future came into public focus in 2013.

By that time, Erdoğan's dreams of a new order in the Middle East with Turkey as the anchor of stability were starting to unravel. His personal alliance with Syria's strongman, Bashar al-Assad, fell apart when Assad spurned his advice to introduce reforms and instead allowed his military free rein to crush protests against his regime that soon turned into a violent civil war. As the fighting escalated and civilian casualties mounted, Erdoğan became infuriated that the United States and the European Union would not intervene to topple Assad. Feeling abandoned by the West, Erdoğan funneled arms deliveries to Islamic insurgents and allowed thousands of jihadist foreign fighters to transit Turkey into Syria, which raised serious tensions with Europe, which feared a blowback effect when the fighters would return home to France and Belgium. Many of those fighters joined forces with ISIS, or the Islamic State, which soon expanded its domain to become a direct threat as well to the governments of Turkey and Iraq.

Meantime, Erdoğan engaged in a nasty spat with Israel over its blockade of aid deliveries to Palestinians in Gaza, damaging military and intelligence cooperation with what had become a useful strategic ally. A truce with the Kurds also fell victim to the Syrian war, as Kurdish forces, with American support, took back territory in the fight with ISIS and were determined to press ahead with their own plan for an independent Kurdish state—at Turkey's expense. With Russia and Iran fully engaged in the battle to salvage the Assad regime, Erdoğan's "zero problems" policy with his neighbors had become "nothing but problems." He also remained sharply at odds with the United States and Europe, whose chief objective was to destroy the Islamic State, while Ankara wanted to focus on overthrowing Assad and preventing the Kurds from gaining more territorial control in Syria.

With his country inundated by close to 3 million refugees, Erdoğan turned a blind eye as traffickers began smuggling vast numbers of Syrian and other refugees across the narrow strait to neighboring Greek islands in the Aegean Sea. As the refugee exodus into Europe swelled to more than 1 million people in 2015, Erdoğan seemed to relish the fact that Turkey had become a vital key to Europe's own stability. He drove a hard bargain in negotiations with Chancellor Merkel, insisting that in return for stemming the outflow of refugees Turkey would receive more than $6 billion in economic aid, ostensibly to help care for the refugees. In addition, he won Merkel's support to redouble efforts to bring Turkey into the EU and to secure visa-free access for Turks traveling to Europe. But with Merkel and other European leaders facing a growing political challenge from anti-immigrant populist parties, there seems little likelihood that the European Union will act anytime soon on its promise to open its doors to 76 million Turks.

At home, Erdoğan was also showing signs of authoritarian tendencies. He pushed for constitutional changes to endow his presidency with full executive powers. He built a 1,000-room palace fit for an emperor that would become his new residence. When Merkel and other leaders warned him that concentrating so much power in his hands would run afoul of EU democratic norms, he insisted that such measures were necessary to deal with the security threats posed by the Syrian war and terrorist attacks from Kurdish separatists. Then, on July 15, 2016, rogue elements in the Turkish military and police forces staged a coup attempt that the government quickly blamed on Gülen's pervasive network of supporters. Erdoğan barely escaped arrest and managed to summon his backers into the streets through cell phone transmissions carried on television. His desperate appeals managed to defuse within a matter of hours a rebellion that killed 240 people and destroyed parts of the national parliament when air force jets strafed the building.

Erdoğan then wasted no time in waging a harsh crackdown against Gülen's followers. After declaring a state of emergency, Erdoğan used extraordinary powers to arrest and purge thousands of other suspected opponents, including journalists, professors, and Kurdish politicians. Some 37,000 people were packed into jails, and more than 100,000 others accused of ties with Gülen's movement were dismissed from their positions. About 150 media outlets were shut down after the coup attempt, including leading opposition newspapers like *Cumhuriyet*, and more than 150 journalists were placed in pretrial detention. Under Erdoğan, Turkey has incarcerated more journalists than any other country in the world, making a mockery of EU demands that Ankara must protect free speech and the right to dissent in order to qualify for EU membership.

Erdogan was incensed by the slow and tepid response by the United States and Europe in condemning the coup attempt. He also took offense at suggestions by European politicians that his crackdown was far too excessive in its abuse of human rights and merely a disguise for him to grab more power. When the European Parliament passed a nonbinding resolution seeking to cut off all negotiations with Turkey about joining the European Union, Erdoğan himself declared that perhaps it was time to call an end to the charade of the on-again, off-again negotiations to bring Turkey into Europe. He promised to call a referendum of his own to decide whether Turkey should reject once and for all the idea of EU membership. "What do we expect from people who kept us waiting at the door for 53 years?" he complained. "Let's not kid ourselves. Let's cut our own umbilical cord."

Once seen as the crucial player in Europe's vaunted strategy of cultivating good neighbors, Turkey and its relations with the European Union have never seemed so poisonous. With domestic politics in Europe turning strongly against opening the continent's frontiers any further, and particularly to Muslim countries, it would seem only natural to acknowledge the obvious conclusion that Turkey— after five decades of waiting—will never become a member of the European Union. But that irrevocable decision troubles leaders like Angela Merkel, who realize that in some ways Turkey is already inseparable from Europe's fate. More than 4 million people of Turkish origin live in Germany. Erdoğan has brandished a potent weapon to influence Europe's politics by threatening to open the floodgates for refugees to stream once again into Europe. He knows that if he took that step, it could have incalculable effects by promoting the cause of the xenophobic populists who are striving to topple mainstream parties from power—and plunge Europe into a new Dark Age.

THE NORTH AFRICA QUANDARY

When Mohammed Bouazizi doused himself with paint thinner and lit a match on a December morning in 2010, the flames that consumed him generated a firestorm across the entire Arab world. The Tunisian fruit vendor set himself ablaze in front of the local governor's office to protest chronic shakedowns by the authorities who had ruined his business. The horrible tragedy captured the pervasive rage and frustrations among many Arab youths who felt deprived of hopes for a better life. Soon, images of a young man immolating himself while police did nothing to save him flashed across Facebook pages in more than a dozen countries, infuriating populations from Morocco to Yemen. Bouazizi's death three weeks later ignited a contagious rebellion that soon toppled the twenty-three-year iron-fisted rule of President Zine el-Abidine Ben Ali and led as well to the demise of dictators in Egypt, Libya, and Yemen.

The promise of an Arab political revolution that would sweep away a culture of autocrats in favor of democrats also seized the imagination of many European leaders. For decades, the European Union had been struggling to find an effective policy that would encourage political and economic reform across the Mediterranean as a way to improve prospects at home for young Arabs and Africans so they would not be tempted to hop aboard dinghies to sneak into Europe. The Arab spring offered Europe the chance to atone for a shameful colonial legacy that left former subjects of French and British empires wallowing in misery long after they had achieved independence. So in early 2011, the European Union announced a new aid program for its southern neighbors to offer greater market access, easier mobility through visas, and large sums of money to improve schools, roads, and communication networks that would vastly improve their living standards.

As the cradle of the Arab democratic uprising, Tunisia was designated as the country that would become a showcase for European generosity. Since gaining its independence from France in 1956, Tunisia had maintained closer ties with Europe than most Arab countries through high volumes of tourism and cultural exchanges. With great fanfare, the European Union announced an immediate doubling of financial aid and established a "privileged partnership" with the fledgling democracy in Tunis. The main goals of EU involvement would focus on consolidating democratic institutions, bringing down high levels of youth unemployment, and defusing a rising terrorist threat. Tunisia has some of the highest levels of education and Internet usage in the Arab world, but it also has served as the largest source of foreign fighters joining the Islamic State. More than 5,000 Tunisians have gone abroad to fight with the Islamic State, according to the United Nations. The Tunis government fears once they return home they could fuel a wider Islamist insurgency, much like jihadists returning from Afghanistan did in Algeria two decades ago.

The political openness that followed the revolt against Ben Ali's

regime provided the space that allowed Islamic extremists to organize and attack secular institutions. The first parliamentary elections elevated a moderate Islamic party, Ennahda, to power, but
extremists launched a wave of bloody assaults of liberal politicians
that pushed the country close to collapse. Two prominent opposition
leaders, Mohamed Brahmi and Chokri Belaid, were assassinated.
Meanwhile, the economy was wracked by high inflation, and work
on creating a new constitution was paralyzed. The European Union's
"three M's" plan to provide the kind of massive assistance that would
transform Tunisia into a model democracy appeared to be stillborn.

As Tunisia's Jasmine Revolution hovered on the brink of violent
anarchy, an alliance of civil society groups intervened in 2013 to
mediate a set of political compromises between Islamist and moderate forces. The key actor was the country's leading labor union,
which held the power to call general strikes and had gained respect
throughout society. Its leader, Houcine Abbassi, became the key
negotiator and enlisted support from prominent industrialists,
human rights activists, and lawyers. The National Dialogue Quartet,
as they became known, thrashed out an agreement in which the Islamists surrendered power to a transitional government and created a
time frame for new elections and plans for a draft constitution. The
arrangements were less than perfect and did not succeed in quell-
ing terrorism. Extremists staged a dramatic attack at a museum in
downtown Tunis in March 2015; three months later, a gunman who
received training from Islamist groups in Libya murdered 38 people
at the beach resort of Sousse. But Tunisia managed to survive the
terrorist rampages and emerge as the strongest democracy in the
Arab world. For their heroic efforts in salvaging the nation's fragile
democracy, the Quartet was awarded the 2015 Nobel Peace Prize.

Elsewhere across North Africa, the picture still looks bleak. While
Morocco remains relatively calm, it now faces a serious threat from
Islamic extremism. Algeria is struggling with a collapsing economy

caused by plunging oil and gas prices and is plagued by disaffected youths tempted by the siren song of jihadism. Libya is in the throes of violent civil war involving Islamists, secularists, and tribal clans. Egypt's brief fling with democracy after banishing the regime of Hosni Mubarak has again reverted to a military dictatorship, led by Abdel Fattah al-Sisi, who spearheaded the coup that deposed the elected Muslim Brotherhood government, citing the need to restore public order. Egypt's economy is also floundering while it confronts a demographic time bomb as more than 650,000 young people enter the labor force each year.

The European Union has discovered that no amount of aid money and economic infrastructure programs seems effective in dealing with a breakdown of old social contracts. When oil and gas revenues were abundant, Arab governments could easily afford to provide basic services such as health care and education, create sufficient jobs, and sustain food and fuel subsidies. In return, the people were expected to stay out of politics. But that grand bargain started to erode at the turn of the century, as governments reached limits of their largesse and could no longer fulfill their part of the deal because of shrinking revenues and bloated bureaucracies. That failure, in turn, has fanned rage and frustration across the Arab world as surging youth populations demand a greater voice in running their own lives and society.

Paul Scheffer, a Dutch immigration expert at Tilburg University, predicts the Arab world's population will soar to 630 million people by 2050 from 360 million in 2010. The International Monetary Fund calculates that the region will need continuous growth of more than 7 percent a year just to prevent current levels of unemployment from rising further. The United Nations says that while the Arab world is home to only 5 percent of the world's population, it now accounts for half of the world's acts of terrorism and flows of refugees. Eleven Arab states are embroiled in violent conflicts, one of which is the

Syrian Civil War, which has killed more than 500,000 and produced close to 5 million refugees. Meanwhile, the Arab youth population (between ages fifteen and twenty-nine) has surpassed the 100 million mark but cannot find adequate employment opportunities, which is tempting many to join terrorist groups or smuggle themselves into Europe. The huge barriers to jobs, growth, and mobility are radicalizing many young Arabs and making them susceptible to extremist behavior propagated on jihadist websites.

In some ways, the situation is even more worrisome in West Africa, where an alarming decline in the availability of food and water caused by climate change, constant civil wars, and governing failures have created catastrophic conditions. While Europe, China, and India are poised for demographic decline, West Africa is entering an explosive phase of population growth. The United Nations predicts the number of people there will quadruple by the end of the century to more than 1.6 billion. By 2100, for example, Nigeria will have 750 million inhabitants, making it the world's third-largest country after India and China. Yet crop yields and water supplies are nowhere near levels needed to sustain such numbers of people. Food and water shortages seem likely to become worse since most climate models forecast that temperatures will rise faster there than for the rest of the planet during the twenty-first century. As many as 160 million people in West Africa could then seek to escape famine and drought through mass migration to Europe and other havens to an extent that would overwhelm the 65 million refugees now on the move around the world.

Even though Germany does not have the same historical ties to Africa as France, Italy, or Britain, Chancellor Angela Merkel has again taken the lead in demanding that Europe must come up with more effective policies to promote public and private investment in Africa so that its citizens will not feel compelled to emigrate to Europe. After learning that more than 160,000 people had crossed the Mediterranean from Africa to Italy and 4,220 had died trying in the first ten months of 2016, Merkel embarked on a major tour of African states. She promised that in return for West African cooperation to reverse the tide of migrants into Europe, Germany and its EU partners were willing to launch a new "Marshall Plan with Africa" that would resemble the huge American investment program that fueled Europe's economic recovery after World War II. "We have to invest in these countries and give their people better perspectives for the future," explains Germany's development minister, Gerd Müller. "If the youth of Africa cannot find work or a future in their own countries, it won't be hundreds of thousands, but millions of them who will make their way to Europe."

For Europe, the political and economic pressures are growing to find an urgent solution to the swelling tide of illegal immigrants trying to make the perilous crossing from Libya's shores to the islands off Sicily. While Europe managed to shrink the exodus of Syrian refugees from Turkey into Greece after the surge of 2015, the rickety boats carrying Arabs and Africans across the Mediterranean soon transformed southern Italy into the most besieged part of Europe. Now those fleeing the troubled regions wracked by poverty and war along the porous southern frontiers are fueling support for xenophobic extremist parties that threaten to destabilize Europe's own societies. Despite the best of intentions, the European Union has discovered to its chagrin that it lacks sufficient political, military, and economic leverage to alleviate the problems on its periphery that have so rapidly intruded on its own territory. The Arab Spring that blossomed in North Africa in 2011 has now turned into the Arab Winter, and Europe is learning there is little it can do to change the course of the political seasons.

CHAPTER TWELVE

WASHINGTON, D.C.

THE ILLUSION OF AMERICA FIRST

For SEVEN DECADES, THE ATLANTIC ALLIANCE HAS PROVIDED the crucial foundation for the security and stability of Western democracies. A common pledge to defend free speech, open markets, and transparent elections cemented bonds between the United States and its European allies throughout the Cold War and beyond. This partnership also became an inspiration for captive populations in Communist societies who yearned for a life of greater personal liberty and prosperity following the collapse of the Soviet Empire.

American leadership proved essential. It sustained the cohesion of the West through the Marshall Plan and economic recovery after World War II, the creation of the North Atlantic Treaty Organization to repel the threat of a Soviet invasion of Western Europe, and the expansion of democracy once the Cold War ended. Since 1945, twelve American presidents—six Democrats and six Republicans—gave unwavering support to a transatlantic alliance that defined the United States as the exceptional and indispensable nation to maintain world order. All twelve presidents fulfilled the role of commander-in-chief for a Western community of nations that looked to the United States to serve as the ultimate protector of its shared values and interests.

The election of Donald Trump has called that legacy into question. Even before taking the oath of office, Trump undermined America's long-standing promise to defend its allies. He suggested the United States would only abide by Article 5 of the NATO treaty—which commits members to treat an attack on one as an attack against all—if those countries under threat were deemed to be spending enough money on their own defense. He vowed to tear up past and pending trade pacts, including the Transatlantic Trade and Investment Partnership (TTIP), designed to revitalize Western leadership of the global economy in the face of challenges from emerging powers such as China and India.

Even before he took over the presidency, Trump's isolationist refrain that America was no longer willing to bear the costs of acting as the guarantor of global security and stability scrambled the dynamics of world power. By insisting the time had come to think about "America First" even if it meant disengaging from the world, Trump gave the impression that promises underpinning American leadership of the postwar international order would now be put on the negotiating table.

During the election campaign, Trump vacillated on any number of foreign policy issues, such as whether and when he supported or opposed the Iraq War. But on relations with Europe, Trump has delivered a consistent message for nearly two decades. He praised the strong leadership of Russia's Vladimir Putin and described NATO as "obsolete." As early as the year 2000, when his book *The America We Deserve* first appeared, Trump disavowed intervention in Europe by claiming "America has no vital interest in choosing between warring factions whose animosities go back centuries." He lamented the costs of stationing troops in Europe and said an American withdrawal "would save our country millions of dollars annually." He saw no reason why the United States should be devoted to keeping the peace among nations of Europe because "their conflicts are not worth American lives."

In his first major foreign policy address of the campaign, Trump made it clear that as president he would embark on a radical new departure for America's role in the world that would no longer emphasize global commitments but instead address America's own needs above anything else. "America First will be the overriding theme of my administration," Trump said. "Under a Trump administration, no American citizen will ever again feel that their needs come second to the citizens of foreign countries. My foreign policy will always put the interests of the American people and American security first."

In his inauguration address, Trump again emphasized that his administration would conduct its foreign policy on the basis of American interests above all else. The choice of America First as Trump's presidential mantra recalled the disastrous years in the 1930s when pro-German isolationists, led by aviation hero Charles Lindbergh and other anti-Semites, fought to keep the United States from entering the war to stop Nazi aggression in Europe. While Trump's message has appalled historians, it resonates among American voters who were disenchanted by the interminable wars in Iraq and Afghanistan and wanted their government to invest more resources to rebuild and repair their own nation.

For the first time since 1945, a major American presidential candidate endorsed the controversial path of nationalism and protectionism as a cure for the nation's troubles. Trump's vision, if put into practice, would jeopardize the vital role of the United States as the chief defender of the liberal democratic order. It would also erode faith in America's commitments on everything from climate change and international trade to mutual defense treaties and nuclear deterrence. Since taking the oath of office, Trump has given every indication that he intends to fulfill his campaign promises despite the consternation he has provoked abroad, including among America's closest friends

Trump's blunt solipsism has rocked American allies in Europe to the core. Even though populist nationalists have been on the rise across the continent for several years, few Europeans expected the backlash against globalization would drive Americans to elect somebody who was prepared to turn his back on seventy years of U.S. leadership of the Western democracies. Nonetheless, they hoped that the responsibilities of governing would temper some of Trump's rhetoric, including his effusive admiration for autocrats like Putin, his threats of triggering a trade war with China, or his insistence on building a wall to keep out Mexican immigrants.

But in the aftermath of his election, Trump reaffirmed his conviction that the time had come for America to stop bearing the heavy costs of defending foreign allies. He indicated that under his presidency, the United States would narrow the focus of its global security strategy to defending its own homeland against radical Islamic terrorism. Thus, Trump suggested that his foreign and security policy would be defined in terms of counterterrorism. His message struck fear in the hearts of many Europeans who may have become complacent in believing that the American military shield would always be available to protect them from outside threats. Now they've realized the day may soon come when their principal protector would abandon them.

"If you listen to what Donald Trump has been saying during and before his campaign, this is the end of the West as we know it," observed Carl Bildt, Sweden's former prime minister and one of Europe's strongest advocates of transatlantic partnership. "Europe is already confronted with the revisionism in the East and implosions in the South, but now there is a lingering feeling that the most dangerous developments could actually come from within the West."

Germany's former foreign minister Joschka Fischer is also convinced that Trump's ascendancy heralds the collapse of the entire conceptual framework of the Western liberal order and destroys an alliance of democracies that remains unique in human history. "We should not harbor any illusions; Europe is far too weak and divided to stand in for the U.S. strategically," Fischer said. "And without U.S. leadership, the West cannot survive. Thus the Western world as virtually everyone alive today has known it will almost certainly perish before our eyes."

Besides questioning NATO's relevance, Trump disparaged the European Union as a faceless supranational bureaucracy that had robbed people of control over their daily lives. He praised Britain's decision to leave the EU and even endorsed Nigel Farage, a leading Euroskeptic who spearheaded the Brexit campaign, as the person he would like to see appointed as Britain's next ambassador to Washington.

Like other critics, Trump overlooks the EU's extraordinary achievements, starting with peaceful reconciliation between France and Germany, which for five centuries had been fighting each other virtually every generation. The European project banished the risk of war among the twenty-eight EU member states and nurtured a degree of prosperity unmatched in the rest of the world among their 500 million citizens. Yet three generations after World War II, those accomplishments are taken too much for granted by young Europeans who have known nothing but peace, free education, universal medical care, and rising living standards largely because of achievements made possible by the European Union.

Those who cheered Trump's victory were mainly Europe's populist demagogues, who have been demanding that more powers be returned to the nation states even though their ancient rivalries contributed to Europe's history of bloodshed. Geert Wilders, who heads the Freedom Party in the Netherlands and aspires to become prime minister, hailed Trump's win as the start of a "Patriotic Spring" that would soon spread across Europe. He said it was only a matter of time before other populist nationalists, like himself, would achieve power and vanquish the forces of globalization, immigration, and corrupt ruling establishments. Marine Le Pen praised Trump for "liberating the American people" and inspiring "a great movement across the world."

Trump's rise to power was greeted with enthusiasm in Moscow, where the Duma, or national parliament, erupted in loud applause in anticipation that sanctions over Russia's annexation of Crimea might soon be lifted. While dismissing reports that the Kremlin approved cyberattacks that would benefit Trump's campaign, President Putin promised to work closely with the new president in building a more cooperative partnership between Russia and the United States.

Hungary's prime minister, Viktor Orban, who has drawn criticism for his anti-immigrant attitudes, his open admiration for Putin, and his suppression of dissent, expressed delight with Trump's victory. Orban praised Trump's policy agenda as just what Europe needs. He bragged about receiving an early invitation to visit the Trump White House after years of being ostracized during the Obama administration. "I told him that I have not been there (to the White House) for a long time as I was regarded as a black sheep," Orban said. "He laughed and said so was he."

One of Trump's biggest challenges will come in reassuring Europe's leaders about American support for international agreements that were reached by the Obama administration, including on climate change and Iran. Trump has castigated the terms of the Iran nuclear accord that was reached in 2015 after years of haggling between Tehran and an international coalition including the

United States, Germany, France, Britain, Russia, and China. The deal imposes strict limits on Iran's nuclear program that is designed to prevent the building of atomic weapons in exchange for the suspension of economic sanctions. But Trump and many Republicans have criticized the agreement as badly flawed and vowed to change its terms, or else abandon it. They have discussed applying new sanctions on Iran for activity unrelated to its nuclear programs, including ballistic missile testing and support for terrorism in the Middle East. The new sanctions could involve having the Treasury Department demand that foreign banks stop handling transactions involving Iranian firms. That measure could meet with staunch resistance from our allies.

But rejecting the Iran accord would have devastating consequences for American credibility. It would open the door for Iran to revive its uranium enrichment program, renew its pursuit of nuclear weapons, and provoke a damaging split with China, Russia, and our leading European allies. None of them would likely be willing to follow a unilateral American move and endorse fresh sanctions against Iran, particularly since they have initiated lucrative new investments there. And if Iran did renew its quest for nuclear weapons, the United States would then be left on its own, along with Israel, to take military action against Tehran. That, in turn, could trigger a new nuclear arms race in the Middle East as other countries in the region, notably Saudi Arabia, Egypt, and Turkey, would be tempted to acquire their own deterrent.

Trump's warm words for Vladimir Putin and his choice of Exxon's chairman and chief executive, Rex Tillerson (who has known Putin for more than two decades), as secretary of state suggest he will make reconciliation with Russia one of his top foreign policy priorities. Given Trump's transactional style, some experts believe he may be willing to turn a blind eye to Russia's annexation of Crimea and lift economic sanctions in exchange for Moscow's cooperation in waging a more effective campaign against Islamic terrorism. Trump sees Moscow as a potential ally in the war against radical jihadist terrorism and has insisted that as president he will aim to destroy the Islamic State and other extremist threats. In embracing a new course of collaboration with Russia, Trump might even be willing to drop America's long-standing demand of getting rid of Syria's strongman Bashar al-Assad as a prerequisite for peace.

But any shift in American policy toward Russia and the sanctions policy could spread disarray among the European allies. Several European countries, including Italy, Bulgaria, Greece, and France, already oppose Germany's insistence on maintaining sanctions against Russia and want to get back to business as usual with Moscow. The Baltic nations fear they might become victims of a new Russian-American entente and be left unprotected against Moscow's aggressive designs to roll back history. Even though, unlike Ukraine, the Baltic states joined NATO after the collapse of the Soviet Union, they are deeply worried that a Trump administration may not live up to the alliance's collective security pledges.

Any loss of faith in American promises could open up a Pandora's box of uncontrollable consequences, in Europe as well as in Asia. For example, hard bargaining by a Trump administration with Japan and South Korea over a reassessment of the American security mission in Asia could tempt those countries to pursue nuclear weapons. China, meanwhile, might be encouraged to expand its military presence in the South China Sea if and when the United States pulls back.

American presidents have complained for years about the persistent failure of European allies to assume a fair share of their defense burden. Only five countries out of NATO's twenty-eight members (the United States, Britain, Poland, Estonia, and Greece) have lived up to an alliance pledge to devote at least 2 percent of their national income to their defense budget. Besides doubts about whether they would come to the aid of another ally under attack, many Europeans seem reluctant even to resort to the use of military force to protect their own homeland. A 2014 WIN/Gallup International survey showed only 29 percent of French citizens, 27 percent of British, and 18 percent of Germans said they were willing to fight for their country (while 68 percent of Italians said they would outright refuse to do so).

To that end, Trump's warnings that America might not come to their aid if they do not abide by their NATO commitments may produce a salutary effect in reminding Europe that Uncle Sam will no longer play the role of "Uncle Sucker" in allowing them a free ride while America subsidizes their defense. The recent Russian military buildup and aggressive action in Ukraine has delivered a wake-up call to the allies and jolted them out of their sense of complacency about the need to do more for their own defense. Germany, one of the biggest laggards in defense spending despite its enormous wealth, recently approved a substantial hike in its military budget by 8 percent in 2017. Even so, Germany with its ingrained pacifist tendencies is unlikely to meet the NATO defense budget goal in the near future.

Trump's frequent allusions to "America First" contrast sharply with the eloquent promises made by every other American president since 1945 to champion democracy and an open world trading system and to honor security commitments to the allies. When he took office in 1961, John F. Kennedy left no doubt that the United States was prepared to defend the cause of freedom around the world. "Let every nation know," he declared, "whether it wishes us well or ill, that we shall pay any price, bear any burden, meet any hardship, support any friend, oppose any foe, to assure the survival and success of liberty."

Kennedy's vision restored faith in American leadership of the free world at a time when a young, untested president was being challenged by a Soviet Communist empire that seemed determined to take control of the entire continent. The Kennedy generation had learned through bitter experience what history taught their parents. The America First policies that sought to isolate the United States from the problems of the world during the 1920s and 1930s only aggravated the economic and military devastation resulting from the Great Depression and the Second World War. In the twenty-first century, the idea that Fortress America could find shelter behind two oceans from turmoil abroad is even less true than it was between the two world wars.

The notion of an impregnable American citadel shielded from the rest of the world is particularly misguided when it comes to international economic relations. Trump wants to renegotiate the North Atlantic Free Trade Agreement (NAFTA), which he describes as "the worst trade deal in history." He insists the deal that brought China into the World Trade Organization—which he blames for the closure of tens of thousands of American factories—must be thoroughly revised. He also intends to throw out the pending Trans-Pacific Partnership reached by the United States, Japan, and ten other Asia-Pacific countries. But already, China is stepping into the void with its own offer of a comprehensive trade agreement with many of the same countries, which would help Beijing solidify its regional ascendancy and deprive the United States of privileged access to Asian markets. Many Republicans, including former presidential candidate Senator John McCain, believe that Trump's withdrawal from the Trans-Pacific trade deal will backfire on American interests and accelerate China's rise as the dominant power in Asia, if not the world.

With Europe, Trump says he wants to reconsider the TTIP accord, which has been under negotiation between the United States and the European Union for the past four years. Sometimes called an economic version of NATO, the TTIP deal is designed to fortify the Western alliance by reducing regulatory barriers to expand the already enormous volumes of trade and investment across the Atlantic, which account for nearly half of all global economic activity. Perhaps more important, TTIP would ensure that the rules established by the United States and Europe would become the gold standard for world trade, reinforcing Western leadership of the global economy at a time when many people worry the United States is retreating from its responsibilities abroad.

Trump and his followers may think the best way to advance the interests of American workers and consumers would be to trash existing multilateral trade agreements and cut separate deals with individual nations. The new American president has said repeatedly that he believes the United States can curtail its dependence on other governments by imposing high trade barriers that will ensure that Americans buy products made at home. Yet as the Western world discovered in the 1930s, nothing could be further from the truth.

In today's global economy, fewer products than ever before in human history are made in one place. More than half the goods and nearly three-quarters of the services traded on a global basis include components from different countries. Even the most powerful nation in the world needs the cooperation of other governments in managing trade. American automobile, computer, and pharmaceutical companies are so deeply integrated in global supply chains that any moves toward national autonomy would disrupt industries that employ millions of Americans and impose staggering costs on American consumers.

Trump's rejection of these trade agreements would only invite retaliation from China and other major trading partners. The world's open trade and investment system has depended to a great extent on the hegemonic power of the United States to function smoothly. If the principal sponsor starts acting in a unilateral way to change the terms of the contract, there are many powerful players who would be happy to respond in kind. When Trump spoke about the prospect of 45 percent tariffs being slapped on Chinese exports, Beijing was quick to remind him that such acts of hostility might affect China's willingness to maintain its enormous holdings of American debt. At a time when populist nationalism is growing in many parts of the world, and not just in the United States, the risks of retaliatory economic warfare in the guise of protectionism have become ever more apparent.

If America decides to break the rules on its own, it could easily unleash the kind of economic catastrophe that led to the Great Depression. The volume of world trade is already shrinking and according to some measurements now hovers at levels no greater than that of two decades ago. A revival of protectionism could be a dangerous trend that drives the global economy into a deep recession. After all, the decisive blow that ushered in the Great Depression of the 1930s came when the Smoot-Hawley tariffs were approved by an isolationist-minded Congress.

While no trade deal can be perfect, international cooperation still offers the best way to manage global trade so that all sides can benefit. Even Trump's plans to bring jobs back to the United States through corporate tax reform will only work if other countries can be persuaded to avoid beggar-thy-neighbor tax policies designed to attract investment, such as the near-zero rate that Ireland offered to lure American technology companies like Apple. That sweetheart deal was deemed so outrageous that the European Union's antitrust authorities slapped a $14 billion fine on Apple for not paying sufficient tax.

The United States has been seduced by the siren song of isolationism in the past, yet the desire to wall itself off from foreign turmoil always ended in tragedy. The America First movement emerged in the aftermath of World War I, when the senseless carnage caused by trench warfare and toxic gas convinced many Americans they should never again become entangled in foreign conflicts. The painful sacrifice of 50,000 American lives in the last nineteen months of Europe's Great War, supposedly fighting a noble crusade to make the Western world "safe for democracy," appalled the entire country and infused strong anti-war sentiments among voters and the U.S. Congress.

In the wake of that horrible war, Americans decided their country should never again become drawn into the treacherous balance-of-power battles in Europe that many believed had very little to do with their own interests at home. They spurned the internationalist pleas of President Woodrow Wilson and refused to join the League of Nations. The United States turned its back on its own history as a nation of immigrants and rejected the appeals of many refugees fleeing Asia and Europe who were knocking on its doors. The disgust with having fought in "the war to end all wars" was so pervasive that Americans of every class and region were determined to withdraw from world affairs. Today similar sentiments of alienation reverberate across America in the wake of two failed military interventions in Iraq and Afghanistan.

The mood of retrenchment between the two world wars was reflected in hostility toward accepting a new wave of immigrants. The Quota Acts of 1921 and 1924 set strict limits on the number of foreigners allowed into the country. This kind of isolationist sentiment also suffused American trade policies. The United States decided to impose high tariffs on imports in a shortsighted attempt to keep out foreign products and encourage economic growth at home. Like other forms of protectionism, the measures had a pernicious impact, raising prices for American consumers and causing grave hardship for European exporters that lost access to the American market. In turn, European governments hiked their own tariffs in retaliation to exclude products from American farms and factories. America's nagging demands to collect war debts from its beleaguered allies and the issue of reparations from a defeated Germany fanned further resentment between Europe and the United States.

America's isolationist phase persisted for two decades despite a constant drumbeat of warnings about the dangers of neglecting the outside world. While America slept, the ominous rise of communism, fascism, Nazism, and Japanese militarism would soon pave the way toward another world war. Even as the world was collapsing around them, Americans told themselves it was simply none of their business to get involved again in conflicts abroad.

Their aversion to any foreign involvement was so intense that President Franklin Delano Roosevelt chose to disavow any plans for international action. During the 1936 election campaign, he promised to "shun political commitments which might entangle us in foreign wars" and told American voters that he would do everything in his power to "isolate ourselves completely from war." He continued to repeat his vow that there would be no American boots on European soil even as Hitler conquered ever-greater swathes of territory across Europe.

The painful effects of the Great Depression and traumatic memories from the First World War hardened the resolve of many Americans, who were convinced they should work to improve their own miserable predicament at home before worrying about the outside world. This disengaged view was shared by the leadership of both major parties in the U.S. Congress. It was also reinforced among the public at large by widespread reports that banks and arms manufacturers had racked up huge profits by pushing America into World War I. Many Americans were determined not to be tricked ever again by the banks and arms industries into making such enormous personal sacrifices through foreign military interventions.

The Neutrality Acts passed into law by Congress were designed to prevent American ships and citizens from becoming embroiled in outside conflicts unfolding in Europe and Asia. Even the Nazi declarations of war against Britain, France, and Poland did not generate sufficient alarm for the United States to intervene. It would take a brazen assault by Japan on U.S. naval ships at Pearl Harbor on

December 7, 1941, and the imminent threat of Nazi domination across Europe to convince a majority of Americans that their country's own future was suddenly at stake. The isolationist cocoon was shattered once Americans realized that their safety and security could no longer be guaranteed by two vast oceans and weak neighbors.

When the war ended in 1945, the United States recognized that an entirely different approach was necessary to prevent future catastrophes caused by the perpetual cycle of balance-of-power struggles that inevitably led to wars in Europe. As the world's new superpower, the United States could no longer remain aloof from the rest of the world and resolved to build a new order that would banish the ghosts of nationalism that had fomented military conflict in every European generation over the course of five centuries.

The mirage of isolationism that captivated Americans between the wars was replaced by the bold international idealism first enshrined in Wilson's Fourteen Points plan for universal peace. His failed project came back to life when the United Nations was established to wide acclaim just months after the wars with Germany and Japan came to an end. The Bretton Woods Agreement in 1944—put into place even before the war ended—laid the foundations for a global economic recovery through the creation of the International Monetary Fund, the World Bank, and the precursor of what would become the World Trade Organization. The generosity of the Marshall Plan, launched in 1948, would soon help Europe rebuild from the ruins of war. A year later, NATO was created as a collective security alliance to defend Western democracies from the expansionist designs of the Soviet Union and its Communist empire.

There were other enlightened initiatives as well. A young U.S. senator named J. William Fulbright, who would go on to a distinguished career as chairman of the Foreign Relations Committee, took note of the huge war debts owed to the United State that could never be repaid except in foreign currency. He also saw how similar funds could be raised through the sale of surplus U.S. military equipment. Why not use these idle resources to finance educational exchanges? Fulbright's bright idea spawned one of the most successful acts of international cooperation ever devised in bringing students to and from the United States and over 150 foreign countries. In the past seventy years, the Fulbright program has enabled more than 300,000 students to spend time studying abroad, learning languages, and acquiring an international perspective that has encouraged greater mutual understanding. Some three dozen former Fulbright scholars have become heads of national governments and over fifty of them have won a Nobel Prize.

The early postwar years transformed the United States into a farsighted paragon of internationalism. Instead of America First and its self-absorbed view of the world, President Harry S. Truman vowed in a memorable 1947 speech that the United States would provide political, military, and economic assistance to all democratic nations under threat from authoritarian forces. The Truman Doctrine declared the United States would invest heavily to prevent Greece and Turkey from succumbing to Communist subversion. It also foreshadowed the transformation of America's national security policy from a fortress mentality into a forward-leaning expeditionary posture, with U.S. soldiers poised to intervene in distant conflicts to combat the spread of communism and defend Pax Americana. America had learned its lessons from two world wars: there could be no escape by retreating from its international obligations.

The American initiative to assume leadership of the liberal democratic order when much of the rest of the world lay in ruins helped restore a sense of confidence in Western concepts of free markets, free speech, and free elections. It also mobilized the European allies and contained the spread of Soviet expansionism in Europe and the Middle East. Through four decades of the Cold War, the United States would maintain its costly alliance commitments on different continents because the country understood its own political and economic interests were at stake in upholding the free world. America is now so invested in its foreign relationships that retrenchment from the world, as proven in the 1930s, could produce disastrous consequences far worse than the costs of sustained engagement.

The success of Western democracy culminated with the collapse of the Berlin Wall in 1989 and the peaceful dissolution of the Soviet Union and its Communist satellites. America emerged as a benign hegemon whose powers in the world were uncontested. The United States and its Western allies seized the unipolar moment to promote the expansion of NATO and the European Union to embrace new members in Central and Eastern Europe. More than ever before, the United States was able to spread the gospel of free-market democracy through Europe, Asia, Latin America, and Africa. The number of democratic governments increased from forty-four to eighty-six in the two decades prior to 2015, representing 40 percent of the world's population and nearly 70 percent of its wealth.

But over the past decade, the liberal international order has lost its luster. The struggle to defeat radical jihadist terrorism since the 9/11 attacks led to unpopular wars in Iraq and Afghanistan that squandered much American blood and treasure. The 2008 financial crisis caused painful recessions in the United States and Europe and fueled the populist insurgencies against mainstream governing parties that seemed incapable of restoring jobs and growth. The political dysfunction in Washington, D.C., and other Western capitals sapped confidence in the democratic model. Illiberal and authoritarian styles of government attracted support as voters became more impatient for quick solutions to pressing social and economic problems.

The promise of greater prosperity through the disintegration of national boundaries and protected markets faded as globalization expanded the inequality gap between rich and poor. Many people in the West saw their living standards decline even as greater wealth was concentrated in the pockets of the 1 percent elites. Instead of making everybody better off, the forces of globalization that brought nearly 3 billion people—the populations of China, India, and the Soviet Empire—into the world economy caused massive disruptions. As a result, the disillusionment among many working-class people caused them to rebel against the ruling establishments and turn toward populist insurgents who promised them greater control over their lives.

Donald Trump's rise to power behind the momentum of a new wave of nationalism bears an eerie similarity to the situation in the isolationist era that prevailed between the two world wars. There is growing protectionism sentiment in reaction to widespread economic insecurity, particularly among the Tea Party movement and blue-collar workers who have seen factories close and jobs move to Mexico or China. There is a surge of xenophobia, reflected in calls for higher walls to keep out foreign immigrants. There is an expanding network of state surveillance, driven by security obsessions about hidden dangers from terrorists who may be hiding in our midst. And there is the perception of corruption and cronyism among professional politicians, which has allowed Trump to exploit his status as a businessman untainted by past experience in government.

Most of all, there is once again a strong desire in America to retreat from foreign economic and military engagements. Trump's vision suggests that in response to the wishes of the American public, the United States may soon pull back from defense and trade agreements, thus giving Russia and China unfettered control over their own neighborhoods. Exhausted by the forever wars in the Middle East and yearning to build a more equitable society at home, Americans seem eager to indulge in another phase of retrenchment.

Indeed, this mood is reflected in opinion polls that show American isolationist sentiment is higher than at any time in the past fifty years. Surveys by the Pew Research Center, which has been measuring U.S. public opinion since 1964, concluded that public support for an active American foreign policy has never been so low. A 2013 survey found that the share of Americans who believe "the United States should mind its own business internationally and let other countries get along the best they can on their own" had reached a record high of 52 percent.

In previous polls taken every year over four decades, that figure ranged between 20 percent and 40 percent of respondents.

Another metric confirmed the sharp rise in isolationist attitudes. When asked if they agreed the United States should "not think so much in international terms but concentrate more on our own national problems," an unprecedented level of 80 percent said they did. In addition, the inquiry showed record numbers of Americans now believe their country is "less important and less powerful as a world leader" than it was a decade earlier. A striking 70 percent of Americans also believed the United States is "less respected" abroad than it has been in the past.

For seven decades, the United States provided the security umbrella under which the liberal international system has flourished. But today, the United States is more inward-looking than at any time since World War II. While Barack Obama sought to recalibrate America's role abroad by encouraging allies to take greater responsibility for their own security, President Trump now promises to pursue transactional bargains. He wants the United States to become a mercenary power, protecting only those countries willing to pay for their protection, so he can concentrate on making America great again at home.

But the hard lessons learned throughout history suggest the best way for the United States to care for its own interests is by investing in the security of its allies. American primacy in the world has been assured by its outward projection of power in managing the international order, ensuring the rule of law through institutions such as the U.N., the IMF, the WTO, and the World Bank. But now, through a combination of neglect, mismanagement, and dwindling American support, these pillars of the liberal democratic order are crumbling.

The disregard the United States has shown toward these key institutions has eroded their power and influence. Too often, America has acted in a unilateral manner and only selectively respected the rules of the international order that it once vowed to preserve. It invaded Iraq under a dubious legal mandate that has been cited by Russia as justification for its own aggressive actions in Ukraine. The U.S. Congress has refused to ratify the U.N. Convention on the Law of the Sea, as well as other multilateral treaties. The overthrow of Libya's dictator Muammar al-Qaddafi in 2011 was carried out without a clear international mandate. While criticizing Russia and Syria for indiscriminate bombing of civilians in Syria, the United States has supported Saudi Arabia in pursuing its bloody bombing campaign in Yemen. Such inconsistencies have left the United States vulnerable to charges of hypocrisy by Putin and other critics, who claim the United States only respects international law when it serves America's strategic purposes.

While many Americans, Trump included, would reject such criticism, it is important to realize that when the United States applies only selective support for international laws and treaties that provide the foundation for the liberal democratic order, it provides an excuse for Russia and other potential foes to follow the same course of action. In his famous book *The Arrogance of Power*, Senator Fulbright argued that scrupulous respect by the United States for the reign of international law was vital to maintain peace and security in a liberal democratic order. Otherwise, the system can quickly unravel.

"It provides us with stability and order and with a means of predicting the behavior of those with whom we have reciprocal legal obligations," Fulbright wrote. "When we violate the law ourselves, whatever short-term advantage may be gained, we are obviously encouraging others to violate the law. We thus encourage disorder and instability and thereby do incalculable damage to our own long-term interests."

When President Trump says he intends to tear up trade agreements and walk away from American pledges under the Paris climate change pact or the Iran nuclear accord, he thus provides ammunition for our enemies to renege on laws and conventions designed to restrain their own transgressions. Trump says he feels obliged to renounce America's obligations because the government was duped into signing bad deals under the feckless or naïve leadership of his predecessors. That rationale has been used time and again by populist and right-wing demagogues seeking to justify behavior that breaks international law. D. W. Brogan, in his famous 1952 essay "The Illusion of American Omnipotence," observed that America First policies are often rooted in "the illusion that any situation which distresses or endangers the United States can only exist because some Americans have been fools or knaves."

The world stands at a hinge moment in history. The post–Cold War order is coming to an end. The Pax Americana that managed global security and world trade for seventy years is weakening. The era of unipolar American dominance has passed, but nobody can be sure what will emerge in its place. Will Russia assert greater control over its neighbors and project new influence in the Middle East even though its economy is decaying and its population rapidly shrinking? Will China and India fulfill their ambitions to become new superpowers even though they confront volatile social and economic tensions at home?

In the West, disenchantment with the ruling class and a growing chasm between rich and poor threaten to destabilize our democracies. Populist movements built on the myopia of economic nationalism, which has caused so many wars and other disasters in world history, are now resurgent in the United States and Europe. These grassroots uprisings have polarized societies on both sides of the Atlantic, creating hostile camps that espouse radically different philosophies about how our citizens should be governed.

In the United States, where Hillary Clinton won 3 million more votes in the presidential election than Trump, Democrats believe the electoral college disavowed the popular choice for the second time in less than two decades by ushering into power somebody they view as an illegitimate president. In Europe, the revival of populist nationalism has inflamed grievances toward a European Union seen as controlled by an elite class of unelected officials who ignore the will of the people. These internecine battles may damage the liberal democratic order and transatlantic unity at a time when Western leaders confront global challenges that require collective action as never before.

Today many Europeans fear that an absence of strong American leadership could unleash the demons of nationalism that have caused so much havoc on their continent and in the world. Liberal democracies can wither and die quickly, with disastrous consequences if the wrong choices are made in just two or three elections. Whether catastrophes of the kind witnessed in the previous century will occur again may depend on a possibly dangerous return to a transactional system of balance-of-power politics. Will the governments of Europe and the United States look inward, as many voters now seem to desire? Or will they realize their national interests are best served by participating in a liberal international order that shares common goals and values? In a fractured Europe and a divided America, the political struggle over this fateful choice will determine the road to peace or calamity over the course of the next century.

A POST-AMERICAN
EUROPE?

TWO WEEKS AFTER DONALD TRUMP TOOK THE OATH OF OFFICE, the leaders of the European Union gathered in Malta to consider how they should deal with America's forty-fifth president. The meeting on the fortress island in the Mediterranean Sea was supposed to serve as a brainstorming session about how to revitalize the European Union in the sixtieth-anniversary year of its founding Treaty of Rome. The ambitious agenda was aimed at finding a way that EU leaders could transform the manifold threats facing them in 2017 into a bold leap forward toward greater European unity.

Months later, the aura of crisis has only deepened. Europe confronts two years of arduous haggling over the terms of how Britain will leave the EU. While the refugee surge has abated from Syria, boatloads of illegal immigrants continue to cross treacherous waters from Libya into Italy. Meanwhile, the risk of further terrorist attacks keeps security forces on high alert across the continent. New financial troubles could erupt at any time at precarious banking institutions in Greece or Italy. Russia continues to foment turmoil in eastern Ukraine and has brazenly interfered in election campaigns in the United States, France, and Germany. And despite electoral setbacks, populist nationalists challenging mainstream governments across the continent still attract strong support.

Another troubling challenge now compounds Europe's anxieties: America under Donald Trump seems to be turning its back on the liberal international order it has led for seventy years. If the United States is relinquishing its role as leader of the free world, has the time come to start thinking about a post-American Europe? While Trump has disavowed his early claim that NATO is obsolete, his contempt toward the European Union and other international organizations has sown distrust and even fear among many Europeans. Within his first six months in office, Trump jolted Western allies by pulling out of the Paris climate change accord and vowing to impose protectionist measures that could spark an international trade war.

In a letter sent to twenty-seven EU leaders just before the Malta summit, Donald Tusk, the president of the European Council, who chaired the meeting, spelled out the sense of shock and alarm he took away from his ten-minute get-acquainted conversation with Trump. The new president expressed an antipathy toward Europe that Tusk had never before heard from the White House. Besides warning about European allies not doing their fair share in defense spending, Trump applauded Britain's exit from EU and asked if Tusk knew which other nations might soon leave in order to regain their sovereignty and escape what Trump considers their exploitation by Germany.

In his letter, Tusk noted that "the change in Washington puts the European Union in a difficult situation, with the new administration seeming to put into question the last 70 years of American foreign policy." He suggested that Trump's presidency posed a geopolitical threat to Europe no less severe than a newly assertive China, an aggressive Russia, and the "wars, terror and anarchy in the Middle East and Africa." He reminded the leaders that the European Union had nurtured an era of peace and prosperity unparalleled in Europe's history and that its demise would lead to tragedy. "We cannot surrender to those who want to weaken or invalidate the transatlantic bond, without which global order and peace cannot survive," Tusk wrote. "We should remind our American friends of their own motto: *United we stand, divided we fall.*"

Several EU leaders offered their own accounts of initial conversations with Trump and the traumatic impact they fear he could inflict on the Western world. They reprimanded Britain's prime minister Theresa May, who had rushed to Washington in her eagerness to become the first leader to meet with Trump in the Oval Office and shore up pretenses that the special relationship between Washington and London would prevail even after Britain leaves the European Union. France's outgoing president François Hollande warned against such transactional efforts to strike bilateral deals with Washington and declared "there can be no future with Trump if it is not defined together." He said it was time to think in terms of "a European concept for our future" and not pursue continued dependency on the United States.

Germany's chancellor Angela Merkel expressed her deep misgivings over one of Trump's first executive orders—halting immigration from seven mainly Muslim countries—which was later overturned by the courts. Merkel insisted that Western democratic values meant that "fighting terrorism should not be a reason for blanket stigmatization." Merkel also recounted her own testy telephone conversation with Trump, who had described her open-door refugee policy as "a catastrophic mistake" because, he said, it would allow terrorists unfettered entry into Europe. Merkel was exasperated by his criticism and pointedly reminded him of the international right to asylum embedded in the Geneva Conventions, which the United States has always supported. Despite her abiding faith in the transatlantic alliance, Merkel mused to her fellow EU leaders that perhaps the time had come "to take our destiny into our own hands."

Merkel's first dealings with Trump confirmed her worst fears. During a visit to the White House, she was appalled at his lack of understanding about Russia and its aggressive designs on its neighbors. Merkel pulled out an old map of the Soviet Union and showed him how Putin has not concealed his efforts to regain de facto control over much of the former Soviet empire through hybrid warfare methods involving cyber attacks and media disinformation campaigns. When she offered to shake hands with him in front of the cameras, Trump sullenly looked down and refused to extend his hand. Nonetheless, Merkel and her advisors still held out hope that senior officials such as Defense Secretary James Mattis and National Security Advisor H. R. McMaster would persuade Trump to embrace America's traditional leadership of the Western alliance. But at a NATO summit in Brussels in late May, Trump rejected their advice and declined to offer reassurances that America would live up to Article 5 commitments under the NATO treaty that call for an attack on one ally to be treated as an attack against them all. Then, at the G-7 summit meeting in Sicily, he attacked Germany for running a huge trade surplus with the United States as "bad, very bad" and warned that he was prepared to impose tariffs on German car exports to America.

Merkel and other leaders gathered in Sicily implored Trump not to pull out of the Paris climate change agreement. They insisted that the United States, as the world's second-largest emitter of greenhouse gases after China, held a moral obligation to the rest of the world to abide by the terms of the accord. Seeking a positive spin, Merkel tried to make Trump see that the agreement offered important economic opportunities for the United States to create new jobs in the renewable-energy sector. She also warned that by reneging on the agreement, the United States would abandon leadership on climate change to the Chinese and become one of only three countries—along with Syria and Nicaragua—that have refused to sign the Paris deal. But her pleas and those of other leaders, such as France's new president, Emmanuel Macron, and Canada's prime minister, Justin Trudeau, were spurned by Trump. Once he returned to the United States, Trump formally denounced the Paris agreement and declared that the United States could not accept its provisions, citing the need to sustain America's coal industry.

Merkel returned home despondent about the future of the transatlantic partnership that she has steadfastly supported throughout her entire political career. At a Bavarian beer tent festival convened by her governing partner, the Christian Social Union, Merkel went public with her concerns about future relations with Germany's postwar security guarantors, the United States and Britain. "The times in which we could totally rely on others are to some extent over, as I have experienced in the past few days," she said. Then, to prolonged cheers, she repeated the sentiments she had first shared with other EU leaders at their closed-door meeting in Malta: "We Europeans must really take our fate into our own hands."

The broad and fundamental disagreements between Trump and other European leaders indicate that the breach in the Atlantic alliance may not be repaired soon. In the past, disputes between the allies focused on a single issue that could be alleviated over time. Even the most difficult quarrels, such as the refusal by German chancellor Gerhard Schröder and French president Jacques Chirac to support President George W. Bush in his decision to invade Iraq, did not lead to prolonged alienation between the West's most important allies. But the acute differences between Trump and European leaders over fundamental tenets of democracy like free trade, free and fair elections, press freedoms, support for the rule of law, and respect for international agreements like that covering climate change, do not appear likely to be reconciled anytime soon.

The growing strategic divide between Europe and America was reflected in a striking op-ed published in the *Wall Street Journal* shortly after the NATO and G-7 summits by the chief White House security and economic advisors, McMaster and Gary Cohn. In what was branded as the new "Trump Doctrine," McMaster and Cohn declared the president saw the world not as a global community "but an arena where nations, non-governmental actors, and businesses engage and compete for advantage." They suggested the postwar global order and even the Western alliance could no longer be taken for granted in a world where national interests were paramount. "Rather than deny this elemental nature of international affairs, we embrace it," McMaster and Cohn said. European leaders reacted with almost universal dismay toward this America First manifesto by two senior advisors who were perceived as leading White House moderates. Following Trump's controversial performance during his first foreign trip, it was a ringing affirmation, in the view of America's allies, that they could no longer look to the United States for enlightened and dependable world leadership.

Will Trump's presidency instill a new sense of common purpose within the European Union? Has the estrangement across the Atlantic grown so acute that Europe may decide to cut the umbilical cord with the United States? In fact, both sides have been moving apart for many years well before Trump entered the White House. George W. Bush was seen by many Europeans as a reckless and misinformed leader intent on dragging America's allies into misbegotten wars in Iraq and Afghanistan for which Western democracies are still paying a heavy price. At the time, Chirac and Schröder warned about the folly of blindly following America's lead into Iraq. When the toppling of Saddam Hussein was followed by violent chaos that soon engulfed American forces, many Americans acknowledged that Chirac and Schröder had been proved right—even if they were never forgiven by Bush for their apostasy.

Obama was regarded in Europe as the first American president born and bred with a Pacific Ocean perspective instead of a European outlook. Europe's fears were reinforced by Obama's vaunted if ineffectual pivot toward Asia. For all of his popularity among young Europeans and his personal affinity for Merkel, Obama never evinced much visceral sympathy for Europe, deriding the allies as "free riders" in NATO for failing to live up to their promises on defense spending goals. Trump now seems prepared to go much further in putting America's interests first by curbing its NATO commitments and encouraging the disintegration of the European Union, which he views less as a partner than as a powerful economic rival. Any hopes of concluding the Transatlantic Trade and Investment Partnership agreement, which was painstakingly negotiated over five years and supposed to encourage greater trade and investment flows across the Atlantic, have been poisoned by Trump's protectionist threats and Europe's vows to retaliate in kind. The fact that Trump's main political cheerleaders in Europe are anti-EU extremists like Geert Wilders in the Netherlands and Marine Le Pen in France has further alienated him from the continent's mainstream leaders like Merkel and Macron.

With Britain leaving and America turning inward, continental Europe will be faced with perplexing strategic choices. Abroad, the waning of America's role in Europe may tempt some nations in the western part of Europe to seek long-term accommodation with Moscow. That, in turn, could deepen a cleavage between East and West within the EU: dividing Poland and the Baltic states, which distrust Moscow's intentions, from France, Germany and the rest of the continent, which want to avoid future conflict with Russia. Europe is waking up to the need to develop a more coherent and effective security and defense strategy since it may no longer be able to depend on America's security umbrella. But that will require a dramatic leap toward a more united Europe at a time when there is little enthusiasm among voters for bold new steps toward closer European integration since the public mood remains distrustful toward Brussels institutions and the forces of globalization.

The renewed ambition to create a stronger European foreign and security policy, and possibly even its own army, would require an enormous shift in resources at a time when the continent's economies are slowly recovering from a decade-long slump resulting from the 2008 financial crisis. Higher defense spending is not popular in Europe, even amid a resurgence of the Russian threat, as politicians and voters still favor preserving as much as possible of the generous social safety net, such as free higher education, universal health care, and child care subsidies. The need to escape security dependency on the United States may give rise to a new dynamic in which EU leaders can tell their voters that now is the time to do what is necessary to protect Europe's future peace. But this call will also require some hard choices for governments and voters alike. With its aging societies fighting over meager state resources, with fewer jobs being created for the next generation, and prospects for future economic growth diminishing, the European social model so envied around the world for the way it softens the rough edges of capitalism could begin to fall apart if massive resources are shifted to the defense sector. Like the clash in security outlooks between East and West, the split between Europe's wealthy northern creditors and its poorer debtor states in the south will become aggravated.

What course of action will Europe follow to salvage its future? The electoral triumph of Macron, who at thirty-nine became France's youngest leader since Napoleon, raised hopes that new governments in Paris and Berlin would soon launch fresh initiatives to revive the vision of a dynamic core Europe. Within hours after his crushing defeat of far-right leader Marine Le Pen in the May 2017 presidential election, Macron called German chancellor Angela Merkel to inform her that he would soon embark on radical reforms designed to invigorate the economy and restore greater balance to French–German leadership of the European Union. Merkel enthusiastically endorsed his plans and said she would do all she could, in spite of her own upcoming campaign ahead of September elections, to support his efforts. Having endured a succession of weak French leaders during her twelve years in power, Merkel was wary about whether Macron and his nascent political movement could build a legislative majority that would support a dramatic restructuring of the French economy in a nation so hostile to change. The success of Macron's new party, La Republique en Marche! (Republic on the Move!), in winning a crushing majority in the legislative elections barely a month after becoming president was reassuring to Merkel and other EU leaders who want to see France play a larger and more effective role in Europe. Above all, Merkel recognizes that for her Macron might be the last chance to salvage Europe. For if Macron fails, she fears the next French presidential election in 2022 could result in a breakthrough victory for Le Pen and her xenophobic, anti-Europe message.

While supportive of Macron's ambitious reform blueprint, Merkel worried that Germany would be asked to make painful changes of its own that would be hard to sell to German voters reluctant to bail out European partners. Germany has long resisted the idea of forgiving a large share of Greece's debt, as favored by the International Monetary Fund, and accepting shared responsibility for financial obligations to support the single European currency. But Macron has made it clear that he expects Germany to respond in a more flexible way after the September elections, just as he wants Berlin to drop its insistence on austerity programs in favor of growth-oriented programs across Europe that would help improve employment prospects for young people and diminish the frustrations that have fueled the rise of populist nationalists. Macron also wants Germany to join France in taking joint responsibility for Europe's defense and security needs to cope with new threats and reduce dependency on the

United States. While Germany has recoiled in the past from a more assertive military posture because of historical anxieties among its neighbors, the erratic nature of the Trump presidency has persuaded many Germans that now may be the time to pursue a multinational European defense force in tandem with France in order to prepare for the day when America departs Europe.

In response to the Trump administration's America First policy, a revitalized political alignment in France and Germany that seeks to strike a more independent course carries the risk that it could lead to further estrangement in the Atlantic partnership. Popular sentiment in Europe has already been moving in that direction. In Germany, Martin Schulz, the Social Democratic challenger to Merkel, has generated enthusiasm among voters with an anti-Trump message emphasizing the need for Europe to stand up for its own interests and diminish its reliance on the United States. A survey by the Infratest Dimap polling group found that in the aftermath of Trump's election, the share of Germans who believe the United States is a trustworthy partner dropped from 59 percent to 22 percent. Indeed, Schulz's theme about developing a louder and a more assertive European voice in the world is resonating not just in Germany but elsewhere around the continent.

A Pew survey in 2016 showed that despite the rising status of Euroskeptics, 74 percent of voters in EU member states want to see Europe play a more effective role on the world stage in defending the continent's interests against the United States, Russia, and China. In France, Gaullists have long been dubious about tethering Europe's fate to the United States. During the French presidential campaign, both Le Pen and Fillon argued in favor of renewed cooperation with Moscow as a way of nurturing a "European Gaullism" to create a more balanced equilibrium through a twenty-first-century global power nexus linking Europe with Russia, China, and the United States.

The rapid deterioration in the Western democratic order leaves Germany in a troublesome predicament. For several years, Germany has come under pressure from the United States as well as its continental partners to increase its share of spending to defend the security of Europe and bolster its economy. Merkel and other German politicians have promised to do more, but a strong pacifist streak inculcated since World War II has held back the need to invest more funds in defense as well as in the development of southern Europe. In 2015, Germany reaped a record amount of tax revenue from its booming economy, yet its proportion of defense contributions remains one of the lowest in the Western alliance. Germans are still not comfortable with becoming a robust military force, even in defense of European ideals. Nor are many of its neighbors, where memories and suspicions about wartime German aggression run deep.

Three generations after World War II, Germans are still reluctant to send their own troops beyond their national frontiers and remain acutely aware of the historic sensitivities of their neighbors. Even today, sixty years after joining NATO, a majority of Germans say they do not believe they should feel compelled by treaty commitments to rush to the defense of their allies bordering Russia if they were attacked. Such ambivalence undermines any notions of creating a pan-European army that one day could replace American security guarantees. Whether or not NATO survives in its current form during the Trump administration, Germany as the dominant power surrounded by nine countries in the heart of Europe will be required to make much greater costs and sacrifices in fortifying its military forces in order to assure a stable security environment. "We Germans need to prepare for turbulent times," warned Germany's federal president, Frank-Walter Steinmeier, shortly before taking office. "Trump means the old world of the 20th century is gone."

Germany also faces growing pressure to deploy its economic prowess in ways that will help its partners. In one sense, Trump's criticism of Germany's export prowess is accurate and echoed by other European partners. Germany recorded the world's largest trade surplus in 2016—nearly $300 billion—beating even China. Italy and other southern European states have urged Germany to invest at least $100 billion a year in its home market to boost their exports and help revive their own economies. But Germany, with an aging population bent on saving for retirement, has for years spurned those pleas to increase government spending in ways that could help the rest of Europe. The United States, which in 2016 ran up a trade deficit of more than $500 billion, the world's biggest, is also urging the German government to redress those imbalances or face protectionist measures that could further damage the Western alliance by provoking a trade war across the Atlantic. In the years to come, Germany will be compelled to realize it can no longer afford to sit back and enjoy its comfortable role as a pacifist mercantile nation insulated from the responsibilities of being Europe's most powerful and pivotal nation.

Will the Trump administration provide a kind of shock therapy that could invigorate the quest for greater European unity among Germany, France, and its EU partners? The entire continent has much at stake in preserving a liberal international order that has served as the basis for the longest period of peace and prosperity Europe has ever known. Indeed, the European Union was built on a foundation of consensus and understanding that has made it a paragon of the liberal international order. Yet in the absence of continuing American support for its defense and security, it is hard to see how a fractured continent can overcome its many fissures and sustain the cohesion that has ensured many of Europe's successful achievements over the past 70 years. As French president François Mitterrand observed in his farewell speech to the European Parliament in 1995, the ghosts of nationalist fervor that have stalked Europe's bloody history still linger and may come back to haunt the

world. "Nationalism means war!" Mitterand declared in his impassioned plea to make the leap toward a unified Europe. "War is not
only our past. It can also be our future." Without courage, states-
manship, and the active backing of the United States, it is difficult to
see how Europe can set aside its differences and bring the dream of a
unified continent back to life.

ACKNOWLEDGMENTS

This book is the result of more than a year of travel, interviews, and research across Europe, but also the distillation of four decades of personal involvement in the Atlantic partnership. During that time, I have benefited from the wisdom and experience of many people I have come to know and admire in government, business, nonprofit organizations, and the media on both sides of the pond. I am profoundly grateful for their generosity and patience in teaching me about the fascinating complexities of a continent that still serves as the cradle of Western civilization and the fulcrum of American interests in the world.

One of the most enjoyable aspects of this project was the ability to spend time in Europe with old friends and acquaintances cultivated over the years during my different stages in life. I first moved to Europe in the 1970s to play professional basketball. I had graduated from the University of Oregon and been drafted by the Golden State Warriors, but my playing skills were too limited to sustain a career in the NBA. I found a comfortable niche playing ball in Europe, where I encountered strange languages, great cuisine, amazing art, captivating literature, and warm hospitality from many new friends made while playing in diverse places across Italy, Spain, France, and Belgium. There, I decided to pursue graduate studies at the Collège d'Europe in Bruges, while continuing my playing career. Not much studying was done in Bruges, but it was an exhilarating time as Britain, Ireland, and Denmark were joining the community of nations that would become known as the European Union. In Bruges, I also met a young Belgian woman who would go on to serve her country as a distinguished diplomat and ambassador, but more important to me, would also eventually become my wife, lifelong friend, and mother of our three children.

After seven years of bouncing around Europe as an itinerant basketball player, I was interested in seeking a new career that would take me beyond the realm of sports. I learned that the *Washington Post* was looking for a part-time reporter in Europe and thought this might be an auspicious opening. The *Post* was the toast of the journalism world after exposing the Watergate scandal, and getting hired there as a neophyte reporter was practically impossible. I met the Paris bureau chief at the time, Jim Hoagland, who took a gamble in hiring a pro basketball player as a *Post* stringer in Europe merely on the basis of my persistence. It was the start of a great friendship and collaboration that continues to this day.

After a few months of reporting for the *Post,* I got a lucky break covering a prolonged siege involving Moluccan terrorists who held as hostages dozens of schoolchildren and train passengers in the northern Netherlands. The story made front-page headlines for three weeks. That brought me to the attention of editors at *Time* magazine, who offered me a job covering the State Department during the Jimmy Carter era. I would later move to Cairo and report from the Middle East at a time of tumultuous upheaval. I was constantly on the move, living out of a suitcase to keep up with a wide range of stories, including the aftermath of the Camp David peace accords between Israel and Egypt, the fall of the Shah of Iran and the Islamic Revolution, the Iran-Iraq War, the final phase of Lebanon's civil war, and the assassination of Egyptian president Anwar Sadat. It was an incredibly intense assignment and Sadat's passing was a fitting coda. I spent the days after his death writing the *Time* cover story while dashing back and forth to the hospital to assist in the birth of our son.

I circled back to the *Post,* where I received a welcome embrace from Hoagland, then in charge of the paper's international coverage, and executive editor Ben Bradlee. Hoagland wanted to send me to Germany, which seemed on the brink of turmoil because of the imminent deployment of Pershing II and Cruise nuclear missiles to counter a buildup of SS-20 missiles by the Soviet Union. But first I had to win Bradlee's seal of approval. It was just after the Janet Cooke scandal, in which a talented young reporter had lied about her background and fabricated a story about a young heroin addict. The *Post* was humiliated by Cooke's fake story; she had won a Pulitzer Prize and the paper was forced to surrender the award. As one of the first people hired by the *Post* in the wake of the Cooke scandal, I was subjected to a degree of scrutiny I never anticipated. Ben later told me he became suspicious when he heard about my basketball background and ordered the sports department under George Solomon to undertake a thorough investigation. Everything checked out, but when I went in to see Ben for the final job interview, he kept me in suspense before saying he wanted me to answer a question that bothered him: why had my free-throw percentage dropped during my senior year at Oregon? I breathed a sigh of relief and explained I had lost my powers of concentration because I was breaking up with a girlfriend. It was a lesson that showed why Bradlee was an inspirational leader who knew how to keep his reporters on their toes.

My time in Germany taught me how that pivotal nation was the key to understanding Europe. After later serving as foreign editor for four years, I would return to Germany as the paper's chief European correspondent in the aftermath of reunification, when the capital moved from Bonn to Berlin. I also spent several years in Paris and Brussels for the *Post*, but Germany remained at the heart of my reporting interest in Europe. After two decades at the *Post*, I decided to embark on a career in the nonprofit world that would help deepen my knowledge of Europe. I became the founding executive director of the German Marshall Fund office in Brussels, which organizes the annual Brussels Forum that brings together government leaders, business executives, and journalists to discuss the challenges facing Europe and the United States. Later, I would move to New York to become president of the American Council on Germany when my wife was assigned there as Belgium's consul general.

These cumulative roles and relationships formed the basis of my perspective when I decided to write about Europe's gravest existential crisis in seventy years. I am grateful to many people for the insights gleaned from countless conversations across Europe that inform much of this book. In Berlin: Angela Merkel, Wolfgang Schäuble, Christoph Heusgen, Lars-Hendrik Röller, Steffen Seibert, Joschka Fischer, Thomas Bagger, Markus Ederer, Norbert Röttgen, Niels Annen, Peter Schneider, Volker Schlöndorff, Stefan Kornelius, Marie Warburg, Michael Naumann, Horst Teltschik, Friedrich Merz, Mathias Döpfner, Wolfgang Ischinger. In London: Christopher Mallaby, Charles Grant, Robert Cooper, Mark Leonard, Lionel Barber, Philip Stephens, Gideon Rachman, Nicholas Clegg, William Shawcross, Steven Erlanger. In Paris: Alain Juppé, Hubert Védrine, Anne Lauvergeon, Dominique de Villepin, Alain Minc, Jacques Mistral, John Vinocur, Sylvie Kauffmann, François Heisbourg, Dominique Moïsi. In Brussels: Frans Van Daele, Étienne Davignon, Johan Van Overtveldt, Guy Verhofstadt, Karel De Gucht, Marc Otte, Simon Lunn, Alexander Lambsdorff, Giles Merritt, Peter Spiegel, Reinhard Bütikofer, Matt Kaminski.

In Madrid: Javier Solana, Manuel Marín, Pablo Sebastián, Ramón Navarro, Asunción Valdés, Fernando Puerto, Raül Romeva, Alberto Portera. In Rome: Matteo Renzi, Pier Carlo Padoan, Enrico Letta, Marta Dassù, Mario Monti, Giuliano Amato, Paolo Valentino, Maurizio Caprara, Carlo Bastasin, Cesare Merlini, Riccardo Perissich, Dennis Redmont. In Riga: Nils Ušakovs, Vaira Vīķe-Freiberga, Edgars Rinkēvičs, Andrejs Pildegovičs, Agnese Siliņa, Kristine Berzins. In Copenhagen: Frank Jensen, Mikkel Hemmingsen, Bo Lidegaard, Lykke Friis, Leif Beck Fallesen, Niels Mikkelsen. In Warsaw: Adam Michnik, Eugeniusz Smolar, Pavel Swieboda, Janusz Reiter, Michal Baranowski. In Athens: Kyriakos Mitsotakis, George Papaconstantinou, Alexis Papahelas, Andreas Papandreou, Michael Printzos, Peter Poulos, Eleni Kounalakis.

In particular, I wish to thank my friends at McLarty Associates, notably Mack McLarty, Nelson Cunningham, and Rick Burt, for their avid support of this project. I also appreciate the help I received from colleagues at the Brookings Institution, including Fiona Hill, Andy Moffatt, Martin Indyk and Strobe Talbott. Most of all, I owe a special debt of gratitude to family members and close friends who pushed me across the finish line: Renilde, Karen, Natalia, and Nick Drozdiak; John and Christina Ritch, Sid and Jackie Blumenthal, and Jim and Caroline Mann. Finally, I want to thank my editor, John Glusman, and my agent, Gail Ross, for their encouragement and confidence in me.

NOTES

CHAPTER ONE: BERLIN

1 After receiving the green light: "The Makings of Merkel's Decision to Accept Refugees," *Der Spiegel*, August 24, 2016.

3 But the ugly confrontation: Interviews with senior officials at the Federal Chancellery in Berlin, Germany, May 4, 2016.

3 The other heads of government: Interviews with European Union summit meeting participants in Brussels, October 2015.

10 CSU leader Horst Seehofer: Interview with former CSU leader Erwin Huber at the Bavarian state parliament about Germany's growing difficulties in taking in so many Syrian refugees, February 12, 2016.

12 It was reported that . . . German authorities: Guy Chazan and James Shotter, "Search for Berlin Terror Suspect Is Europe-wide, Merkel Says," *Financial Times*, December 22, 2016.

16 "It was a great opportunity": Interview with Italy's former prime minister Mario Monti in his Rome office at Palazzo Giustiniani, March 18, 2016.

CHAPTER TWO: LONDON

28 Taavi Rõivas: "Brexit Aftershocks," *Der Spiegel*, July 1, 2016.

28 "When I came here 17 years ago": "Why Are You Still Here?" Luke Harding and Haroon Siddique, *The Guardian*, June 28, 2016.

29 The man accused of her murder: "A Howl of Rage," Jonathan Freed-land, *New York Review of Books*, July 14, 2016.

29 On the day of the vote: "Talks with Turkey Will Start in Days," *Daily Mail*, June 23, 2016.

30 The turnout among young people: "Youth Turnout Higher than Initial Reports," Peter Yeung, *The Independent*, July 10, 2016.

31 Cameron enlisted economists: Tom McTague et al., "How David Cameron Blew It," *Politico*, June 25, 2016

32 He had long disdained: BBC News, April 4, 2006.

33 She insisted that if Britain: Interviews at Federal Chancellery in Berlin, Germany, June 2016.

34 After Johnson cast his lot: McTague et al., "How David Cameron Blew It."

35 A majority of British voters: "Obama Tells British Youth: Don't Pull Back from the World," Reuters, April 23, 2016.

39 "But if you keep telling people": "Europe Seeks Closure at Sad Supper with David Cameron," *Politico*, July 11, 2016.

40 Johnson raised the white flag: George Parker, "How Michael Gove Forced Boris Johnson's Surrender," *Financial Times*, June 30, 2016.

41 May attributes her desire: Steven Erlanger, "Theresa May's Style: Put Your Head Down and Get to Work," *New York Times*, July 13, 2016.

41 She emphasized that her government: Kate Allen, "Theresa May: Taking Control," *Financial Times*, July 15, 2016.

42 The impact on Britain's service economy: Simon Head, "The Death of British Business," *New York Review of Books*, October 18, 2016.

45 "Even, if today": David M. Herszenhorn, "Tusk Warns UK: No Compromises in Brexit Talks," *Politico*, October 13, 2016.

45 But she also realized: Interviews at Whitehall and Westminster, London, England, October 2016.

CHAPTER THREE: PARIS

52 "the anger, the anxiety, the doubts": Roger Cohen, "Macron and the Revival of Europe," *New York Times*, May 7, 2017.

57 He likened the relationship: "France and Germany Mark Elysee Pact's 50th Anniversary," BBC News, January 22, 2013.

60 Late into his five-year presidential term: Science Po opinion survey on President Hollande's popularity levels, published October 25, 2016.

60 "For the French": Anne-Sylvaine Chassany, "Tales of Two Presidents Speak of French Left's Woes," *Financial Times*, October 27, 2016.

64 While French Muslims represent: Ramzi Kassem, "France's Real State of Emergency," *New York Times*, August 4, 2016.

65 The study, which is the first: Interview with Hakim el Karoui in *Le Journal de Dimanche* about findings of the Institute Montaigne study of attitudes among French Muslims, September 18, 2016.

65 They were close friends: Adam Nossiter, "Two French Scholars of Radical Islam Turn Bitter Rivals," *New York Times*, July 12, 2016.

66 Kepel draws a straight trajectory: Gilles Kepel with Antoine Jardin, *Terreur dans l'Hexagone: Genèse du Djihad Français* (Terror in the Hexagon: The Genesis of French Jihadism) (Paris: Gallimard, 2015).

68 Alain Juppé denounced the proposal: Robert Zaretsky, "Sister Republics, Brother Authoritarians," *RealClearWorld,* September 28, 2016.

70 "That question is now being asked": Rachel Donadio, "Joan of Arc's Shaky Pedestal: France Battles over Its Identity at School," *New York Times*, September 27, 2016.

71 But images of police forces: "Ill-Suited: France Argues over Burkinis," *The Economist*, September 3, 2016.

CHAPTER FOUR: BRUSSELS

74 Of the EU's seven institutions: Giles Merritt, *Slippery Slope: Europe's Troubled Future* (Oxford University Press, 2016). An excellent account of why EU institutions lack legitimacy, credibility, and power, written by a respected Brussels journalist.

76 "It is a habit": Klaus Brinkbaumer et al., "Deadly for Europe: Interview with Juncker and Schulz," *Der Spiegel,* July 8, 2016.

78 After more than two decades: Florian Eder, "Martin Schulz Chooses Berlin over Brussels," *Politico Europe*, November 24, 2016.

79 Tusk is strongly backed: Agata Gostyńska-Jakubowska, "Juncker—Tusk: A Clash of EU Visions," *EU Observer,* September 16, 2016.

79 In their view, a faltering Europe: Interviews at the Federal Chancellory in Berlin, Germany, May-June 2016.

80 Indeed, in the aftermath: Ivan Krastev, "After Brexit, Europe's Dueling Nostalgias," *New York Times,* July 14, 2016.

81 "Never before have I seen": Charlemagne, "State of Disunion," *The Economist*, September 17, 2016.

83 If they push too hard: Anne-Sylvaine Chassany et al., "Anti-Brussels Rhetoric Goes Mainstream Across Europe," *Financial Times*, September 16, 2016.

83 Yet when pressed: Guy Verhofstadt (vice president of the European Parliament), "Europe's Leadership Crisis," *Project Syndicate*, September 22, 2016.

86 But Juncker and other EU leaders: James Kanter and Stephen Castle, "EU Leaders Talk Tough on Brexit and Warn That Time Is Short," *New York Times*, December 7, 2016.

89 "Sometimes it seems": Sam Jones and Henry Foy, "NATO and EU Put on Show of Unity After Brexit Vote," *Financial Times*, July 9, 2016.

90 It also expands: Judy Dempsey, "NATO and the EU Agree to End Their Rivalry," *Carnegie Europe,* July 8, 2016.

92 Indeed, climate change experts: See "The Brussels Wall: Tearing Down the EU—NATO Barrier," about future threats to the West caused by war, drought, and climate change, by William Drozdiak in *Foreign Affairs*, May-June 2010.

92 During his time as Norway's prime minister: Interview with NATO secretary-general Jens Stoltenberg, during his visit to Washington, D.C., on April 6, 2016.

CHAPTER FIVE: MADRID

94 Spain's Great Recession: Miguel Anxo-Murado, "Spain's Anger Management," *New York Times*, December 25, 2015.

94 The eruption of separatist sentiment: David Gardner, "Separatism Threatens the Future of Spain," *Financial Times*, September 6, 2012.

94 During the ten months: Ishaan Tharoor, "Catalonia Sees Itself as the Nation-State of the Future," *Washington Post*, September 20, 2016.

97 In the absence of any compromise: Raphael Minder, "With Spain in 97 Deadlock, Catalans Renew Calls for Independence," *New York Times*, September 11, 2016.

101 Led by the charismatic: Juan Cristobal Nagel, "Is Spain About to Embrace Chavismo?" *Foreign Policy*, November 19, 2014.

105 "We must not be more": Florian Eder, "Wolfgang Schäuble Bails Out Spain, Portugal," *Politico*, July 27, 2016.

106 In the process: Tobias Buck, "Spanish Socialists and the European Left's Malaise," *Financial Times*, October 4, 2016.

107 But he acknowledged: Camino Mortera-Martinez, "Spain's Groundhog Day: Why Madrid Needs a Government," *Centre for European Reform*, September 12, 2016.

107 "Having a government": Jeannette Neumann, "Rajoy Re-Elected Prime Minister of Spain," *Wall Street Journal*, October 29, 2016.

108 "The institutions of the Spanish state": Tobias Buck, "Catalan Independence Movement Dealt Fresh Blow," *Financial Times*, December 14, 2016.

108 Other EU governments: "Breaking Up Is Hard to Do: Elections in Cat-

alonia May Launch a Secession Battle Europe Is Not Ready For," *The Economist*, September 26, 2015.

110 "We are sitting at the table": Interview with Raül Romeva, Catalonia's Foreign Minister, in a conversation held in Washington, D.C., September 14, 2016.

110 Upon taking the oath of office: Stephen Brown and Hans von der Burchard, "A Catalan Exit Plan," *Politico*, May 9, 2016.

CHAPTER SIX: ROME

114 More than one hundred: Gaia Pianigiani, "Romans Put Little Faith in Mayor as Their Ancient City Degrades," *New York Times*, July 22, 2015.

114 His main associate: Nick Squires, "Mafia Capitale: Rome Hit by Mobster Scandal," *Daily Telegraph*, December 3, 2014.

115 "Do you have any": Elisabetta Povoledo, "Italy Gasps as Inquiry Reveals Mob's Long Reach," *New York Times*, December 11, 2014.

117 "This was an opportunity": Interview with Mario Monti in his Palazzo Giustiniani office in Rome, March 18, 2016.

118 "Italians have always been": Interview with Giuliano Amato at his office at Rome's Constitutional Court, March 22, 2016.

121 "I realized that Italy": Interview with Prime Minister Matteo Renzi in New York City during his United Nations visit, September 20, 2016.

130 That prompted a spate: Patrick Browne, "Italy's Five Stars Hit Potholes in Rome," *Politico Europe*, October 12, 2016.

CHAPTER SEVEN: WARSAW

134 They tried to prove: Joanna Berendt, "Poland Exhumes Ex-President's Body in Inquiry of 2010 Plane Crash," *New York Times*, November 14, 2016.

135 In no other Western democracy: Henry Foy, "Poland's Kingmaker," *Financial Times*, February 26, 2016.

135 In Kaczyński's view: Leonid Bershidsky, "A Nationalist Eastern Europe Could Reshape the EU," *Bloomberg Views*, September 7, 2016.

136 His ruling party: Laurence Norman, "Poland Poses Latest Challenge to the European Union," *Wall Street Journal*, May 26, 2016.

140 The court ruled that: Jan Cienski, "Poland's Constitution Crisis Deepens After Court Verdict," *Politico*, August 11, 2016.

141 "As your friend and ally": Rick Lyman and Joanna Berendt, "Obama

Rebukes Poland's Right-Wing Government," *New York Times*, July 8, 2016.

142 Meantime, Culture Minister Piotr Gliński: Alison Smale and Joanna Berendt, "Poland's Conservative Government Puts Curbs on State TV News," *New York Times*, July 3, 2016.

143 Polish bishops have rejected: Rick Lyman, "Pope Francis Encounters Socially Conservative Church in Poland," *New York Times*, July 26, 2016.

144 In building razor-wire fences: Jan Culik, "Fencing Off the East: How the Refugee Crisis Is Dividing the European Union," *The Conversation*, September 16, 2015.

144 Since then, in defiance: Henry Foy and Andres Byrne, "Orban Lashes Out at Western Elites Running EU," *Financial Times*, June 8, 2016.

147 Nearly 40 million Polish: Ivan Krastevin, "Why Poland Is Turning Away from the West," *New York Times*, December 12, 2015.

CHAPTER EIGHT: COPEHNAGEN

153 "Hygge is an experience": Edwin Heathcote, "Hygge: The Danish Key to Happiness or Pseudo-Wisdom?" *Financial Times*, December 16, 2016.

154 Denmark spends proportionately: Eduardo Porter, "Job Training Works, So Why Not Do More," *New York Times*, July 5, 2016.

154 "I guarantee the welfare": Mike Alberti, "The High Road to High Wages: Denmark's Answer to the U.S. Model," *Remapping Debate,* September 14, 2011.

156 Bent Melchior: Adam Taylor, "A Danish Politician Explains Why It's OK to Take Valuables from Refugees," *Washington Post*, January 27, 2016.

158 "There is a strong temptation": Interview with Bo Lidegaard in Copenhagen, May 12, 2016.

159 "The cornerstones of Europe": Richard Milne and Peter Spiegel, "Brexit: Fraying Union," *Financial Times,* February 25, 2016.

160 He was forced to resign: Harry Cooper, "Danish Anti-Fraud Politician Accused of Misusing EU Funds," *Politico Europe,* October 19, 2016.

160 What Stoejberg fears most: Hugh Eakin, "Liberal, Harsh Denmark," *New York Review of Books*, March 10, 2016.

161 Applicants must also pass: Dan Bilefsky, "Denmark's Tougher Citizenship Test Stumps Even Its Natives," *New York Times*, July 7, 2016.

162 René Redzepi: Mark Bittman, "Prince of Denmark," *New York Times*, November 3, 2011.

163 Twelve artists accepted the challenge: Simon Cottee, "Did the Terrorists Win in Denmark?" *Foreign Policy*, October 28, 2016.

164 "It's an extremely expensive model": Interview with Rector Lykke Friis, at her office at the University of Copenhagen, May 12, 2016.

164 "Money is not as important": "Happiest in the World," Official Website of Denmark, 2016.

165 Following the ensuing uproar: Suzanne Daley, "Danes Rethink a Welfare State Ample to a Fault," *New York Times*, April 20, 2013.

169 "Around the world": Interviews at the Lord Mayor's Office in Copenhagen's Town Hall, May 13, 2016.

CHAPTER NINE: RIGA

172 "It's very complicated": Interview with Mayor Nils Ušakovs at Riga's Municipal Hall, April 15, 2016.

173 That has not stopped: Paul D. Miller, "How World War II Could Begin in Latvia," *Foreign Policy*, November 16, 2016.

173 Shirreff was NATO's second-ranking officer: General Sir Richard Shirreff, *2017: War with Russia: An Urgent Warning from Senior Military Command* (London: Coronet, May 2016).

177 The country's interior minister: Carol J. Williams, "Latvia Worries About Putin's Goals," *Los Angeles Times*, May 2, 2015.

178 "These are not just innocent": Interview with Latvia's foreign minister Edgars Rinkēvićs during his visit to Washington, D.C., on February 25, 2016.

179 "We lost our independence": Charlotte McDonald-Gibson, "Latvia Wary of Ethnic Russians," *Time*, October 3, 2014.

181 "He's the first presidential": Richard Milne, "Baltics Fear for Any US Policy Changes to NATO," *Financial Times*, November 12, 2016.

182 A Rand Corporation study: David A. Shlapak and Michael Johnson, "Reinforcing Deterrence on NATO's Eastern Flank: Wargaming the Defense of the Baltics," *RAND Corporation*, 2016.

183 This area, known as: Julian E. Barnes, "Closing the Gap: NATO Moves to Protect Weak Link in Defenses Against Russia," *Wall Street Journal*, June 17, 2016.

183 The nightmare scenario: Gordon Lubold, "Russian Fighter Buzzes U.S. Air Force Plane over Baltic Sea," *Wall Street Journal*, April 17, 2016.

185 Yet those early days: David E. Hoffman, "In 1983 War Scare, Soviet Leadership Feared Surprise Attack by U.S.," *Washington Post*, October 24, 2015.

186 "You cannot ignore the fact": Interview with Ušakovs, Riga Town Hall, April 15, 2016.

186 "terrorist state that must": Rayyan Sabet-Parry, "Lithuanian President Calls Russia a Terrorist State," *Baltic Times,* November 20, 2014.

186 While Lithuania offered: "No Arms to Ukraine, Vows PM," Latvian Public Broadcasting, November 25, 2014.

CHAPTER TEN: ATHENS

191 "Sorry, but there is": Firsthand accounts provided through interviews in Brussels with EU leaders and ministers who participated in the European summit on July 11, 2015.

193 After one of the: Stefan Wagstyl and Anne-Sylvaine Chassany, "German Brinkmanship Tests Eurozone Cohesion," *Financial Times*, July 13, 2015.

193 "the odd principle of": Yanis Varoufakis (Greece's former finance minister), "Greece, Still Paying for Europe's Spite," *New York Times*, May 31, 2016.

195 As a result, Greece: Tony Barber, "The Drawn-out Drama of Greek Debt Has No End in Sight," *Financial Times*, December 19, 2016.

196 The country was shut out: See *Game Over: The Inside Story of the Greek Crisis*, by former Greek finance minister George Papaconstantinou, for a first-person account of the country's debt and financial crisis. Athens: Papadopoulos Publishing, 2016.

196 In 2010, as it became: Interview with Jean-Claude Trichet in *Der Spiegel*, May 15, 2010.

197 The money loaned to Greece: Joseph Stiglitz, "How I Would Vote in the Greek Referendum," *The Guardian*, June 29, 2015. See also Joseph Stiglitz, *The Euro: How a Common Currency Threatens the Future of Europe* (New York: W. W. Norton, 2016).

198 "We will get every": Merkel speech to the Bundestag about European debt crisis, September 7, 2011.

200 While the European Union: Reporting from five-day visit of U.N. Refugee Agency sites in Idomeni, Lesbos, and Athens, April 15–20, 2016.

201 After praising his compatriots: Tsipras speech to Greek parliament about refugee crisis, February 24, 2016.

202 "I wake up every": Interview with Minister Mouzalas in his Athens office, April 19, 2016.

206 "It was a personal nightmare": Interview with George Papaconstantinou during his visit to Washington, D.C., October 13, 2016.

206 Golden Dawn hailed Trump's election: Liz Alderman and Niki Kitsantonis, "Greece, Seeking a Dose of Stability, Is Rattled by Trump's Win," *New York Times*, November 14, 2016.

208 "The fight with our creditors": Interview with Kyriakos Mitsotakis at his party headquarters in downtown Athens, April 19, 2016.

208 Nikos Pappas: Nektaria Stamouli, "Greece Raises $275 Million from TV License Auction," *Wall Street Journal,* September 2, 2016.

209 After two difficult years: Kerin Hope, "Highest Greek Court Blocks Syriza Media Law," *Financial Times,* October 26, 2016.

CHAPTER ELEVEN: MOSCOW, ANKARA, TUNIS

211 As Richard Holbrooke: In several conversations before his untimely death in 2010, Holbrooke explained to me his strategic vision that the United States can best preserve its basic foreign policy interests and cope with new challenges like the rise of China by deepening its collaboration with Europe and other liberal democracies. For a full account of Holbrooke's peacemaking efforts in the Balkans, see his memoir *To End a War* (Random House, 1998).

212 In the words of: Interviews with Carl Bildt in Washington, D.C., April 29, 2015, and Brussels, Belgium, November 30, 2016.

212 A decade ago: See Robert Cooper, *The Breaking of Nations: Order and Chaos in the 20th Century* (Atlantic Monthly Press, 2004). Cooper, a former British diplomat, served as chief diplomatic strategist for Javier Solana, the EU's first high representative for common foreign and security policy. Solana and Cooper sought to wield Europe's broad array of soft-power instruments to expand its global influence but encountered resistance from France, Germany, and Britain, which were reluctant to cede national sovereignty over foreign policy to the European Union.

214 "Europe has never been": "A Secure Europe in a Better World," *EU Security Strategy,* December 12, 2003.

215 "In international relations": Dmitry Medvedev, "Why I Had to Recognize Georgia's Breakaway Regions," op-ed, *Financial Times,* August 26, 2008.

215 As Solana recalled: Interviews conducted with Javier Solana in Brussels, Belgium, March 19, 2016, and Washington, D.C., October 20, 2016.

218 In an interview with BBC: Marine Le Pen interview on *The Andrew Marr Show,* BBC News, November 13, 2016.

218 With European voters: Max Fisher, "French Election Hints at Slide Toward Russia," *New York Times,* December 1, 2016.

220 Obama consulted Erdoğan: Interview with White House National Security Council officials, October 2016.

221 When Chancellor Merkel asked: Interviews at Federal Chancellery, Berlin, Germany, May and June 2016.

223 By that time, Erdoğan's dreams: Henri J. Barkey, "Erdogan's Foreign Policy Is in Ruins," in *Foreign Policy*, February 4, 2016.

225 "What do we expect": Mehul Srivastava, "Erdoğan Moves in on Executive Presidency," *Financial Times*, November 8, 2016.

225 Once seen as the crucial player: "Two Cheers for Hypocrisy: Turkey's Bid to Join the EU Is a Bad Joke, but Don't Kill It," *The Economist*, October 15, 2016.

229 That failure, in turn: Marwan Muasher, "An Economic Ultimatum for the Arab World," *Project Syndicate*, November 16, 2016. Muasher is a former deputy prime minister of Jordan who is now vice president for studies at the Carnegie Endowment for International Peace.

230 The huge barriers to jobs: *Arab Human Development Report* (United Nations Development Program, November 29, 2016).

230 As many as 160 million: Brian Walsh, "Migration: We Ain't Seen Nothing Yet," *Politico*, November 14, 2016.

230 After learning that more: Statistics published by the International Organization for Migration, November 11, 2016.

231 "We have to invest": "Germany Says Time for African Marshall Plan," Reuters, November 11, 2016.

CHAPTER TWELVE: WASHINGTON, D.C.

234 "America First will be": Transcript of Trump foreign policy speech at Mayflower Hotel, Washington, D.C., in *New York Times*, April 27, 2016.

235 He indicated that under: Robert Kagan, "Trump Marks the End of America as World's Indispensable Nation," *Financial Times*, November 19, 2016.

235 "If you listen to": Carl Bildt, "It's the End of the West as We Know It," *Washington Post*, November 15, 2016.

236 "We should not harbor": Joschka Fischer, "Goodbye to the West," *Project Syndicate*, December 5, 2016.

237 Marine Le Pen: Angelique Chrisafis, "Marine Le Pen Says Trump Victory Marks Great Movement Across World," *The Guardian*, November 9, 2016.

237 "I told him that": by Linda Kinstler, "What Trump Means for Central and Eastern Europe," *The Atlantic*, November 28, 2016.

240 A 2014 WIN/Gallup International survey: Ivan Krastev and Mark Leonard, "Europe's Shattered Dream of Order: How Putin Is Disrupting the Atlantic Alliance," *Foreign Affairs*, May-June 2015.

241 Many Republicans: John McCain, "Donald Trump Retreats from Trade Deals at His Peril," *Financial Times*, December 6, 2016.

242 American automobile, computer, and pharmaceutical companies: See Edward Alden, *Failure to Adjust: How Americans Got Left Behind in the Global Economy* (Rowman & Littlefield, 2016).

243 At a time when: Francis Fukuyama, "US Against the World? Trump's America and the New Global Order," *Financial Times*, November 11, 2016.

245 During the 1936 election: Bill Keller, "Our New Isolationism," *New York Times*, September 8, 2013.

247 It also foreshadowed the transformation: See Dean Acheson, *Present at the Creation: My Years in the State Department* (New York: W. W. Norton, 1969), for a definitive account of building the postwar order. Also see Walter Isaacson and Evan Thomas, *The Wise Men: Six Friends and the World They Made* (New York: Simon & Schuster, 1986).

250 A 2013 survey found: Max Fisher, "American Isolationism Hits 50-Year High," *Washington Post*, December 4, 2013.

250 A striking 70 percent: Ibid.

250 But today, the United States: Robin Niblett, "Liberalism in Retreat: Demise of a Dream," *Foreign Affairs*, December 12, 2016.

251 "It provides us with stability": J. William Fulbright, *The Arrogance of Power* (New York: Random House, 1966).

EPILOGUE

258 "The times in which we could totally rely": "Donald Trump Makes It Hard for Europeans to Keep Their Cool," *The Economist*, June 1, 2017.

259 "but an arena where nations": H. R. McMaster and Gary D. Cohn, "America First Doesn't Mean America Alone," *Wall Street Journal*, May 30, 2017.

263 a survey by the Infratest Dimap polling group: "Germans Losing Trust in the United States," *Die Welt*, February 2, 2017.

263 A Pew survey in 2016: Bruce Stokes, Richard Wike and Jacob Poushter, "Europeans Face the World Divided," Pew Research Center, Global Attitudes & Trends, June 13, 2016.

264 "We Germans need to prepare": "Steinmeier says Germans must be ready for turbulent times under Trump," Reuters, January 22, 2017.

266 "Nationalism means war!": "Francois Mitterrand: Le nationalisme, c'est la guerre!" YouTube, https://www.youtube.com/watch?v=ILtIBVMerW8.

INDEX